The World's Most Beautiful Chef, Divina Noxema Vasilina, Presents
Gourmet Confessions of a Supermodel

Art and photos: Jean Philippe Laplagne
Editing: Jean Philippe Laplagne
Illustrations: Rae Crosson

Book cover and contents design: Dodger Design Studio
Art Director: Jean Philippe Laplagne

iUniverse books may be ordered through booksellers or by contacting:

iUniverse
1663 Liberty Drive
Bloomington, IN 47403
www.iuniverse.com
1-800-Authors (1-800-288-4677)

ISBN: 978-1-5320-4635-3 (sc)
ISBN: 978-1-5320-4637-7 (hc)
ISBN: 978-1-5320-4636-0 (e)

Library of Congress Control Number: 2018906261

Print information available on the last page.

iUniverse rev. date: 08/03/2018

The World's Most Beautiful Chef, Divina Noxema Vasilina, presents

GOURMET
Confessions
of a Supermodel

by Jean Philippe Laplagne
Layout and design by Jean Philippe Laplagne,
with illustrations by Rae Crosson

She's serving up some mighty fine deliciousness inside these pages!

To my delicious mama

I'd like to dedicate this cookbook to the one woman who is even more beautiful than Miss Divina—my late mother, Yvonne. She gets first billing. Not one to crave fame, she probably would have been hiding at the back of the room and the paparazzi would have racked her nerves. It is hard having a supermodel in the family! Well, I'm not really a supermodel.

From an early age, my mother supported my creative side and encouraged me to be what I wanted to be. She was there for me in my times of need and gave support throughout my life. She inspired me to be a better person. Who I am today is because of her. She was my rock and moral guide in life. I hope I can be even half the wonderful person she was. She was a tangible reason Mother's Day exists. She always gave me her unconditional love and I am eternally grateful for her. I am blessed that she was my mother. I and my family will always miss her.

Contents

*The right menu
is as important as the
right perfume.*

Contents

Preface

My mother inspired my love of cooking at an early age. She is an incredible cook, and her meals are always made with love. Whether fancy or not, there was always a large variety of items on the menu during my childhood, including many family recipes handed down from my grandmother. I enjoyed helping out in the kitchen, and I was always ready to taste-test the batter! All the while I was under my mother's feet in the kitchen, she was, unbeknownst to her, teaching me a valuable skill and talent that would blossom over the coming years.

The original 1991 cookbook

I was a shy kid but learned at an early age the joy of making people laugh. I was known throughout elementary and high school as a funny guy, always with a smile on my face. That love for making people laugh helped influence my direction in life and helped form the basis of this book. My first introduction to cooking instructions outside the home was in elementary school in the class Bachelor Survival. I still get a kick out of the name of that class. But hey, you got to start somewhere!

My first attempts at cooking for others formally started once I moved out of the family house and into my first apartment while in college, where I was majoring in graphic design. Money was tight, so I learned how to be creative with my menus and ingredients. You can do a lot with potatoes!

Gradually, after many failed attempts and a few successes, I became a better cook. I discovered that I wasn't so bad in the kitchen. A few years later, after some successful dinners, friends and family were asking for my recipes. After much prompting (by dear ole mama), I started to write down my recipes. As a result, I accumulated many recipes, stashed away in binders and cookbooks.

I have lived in Portland, Oregon; New York; Washington, DC; and San Diego. Living in these great cities helped me develop and fine-tune my approach to life and my recipes. I'm always inspired by the places I've called home and the creative people surrounding me.

Some years ago, at the request of a friend, I started a small catering business. It was just me cooking, setting up, and serving at my catered engagements. I was fortunate to cater events for a few Fortune 500 companies and small private clients. I always offered a wide variety of recipes and foods on my catering menu, often inspired by the delicious foods I grew up with.

I started this cookbook back in November 1991 as a holiday stocking stuffer gift. The computer was a new design tool for me. My first attempt at this book was a very simple spiral-bound book with sparse design elements and only thirty-one recipes (modeled after Baskin-Robbins's "31 flavors"). Each recipe section opened with a 1950s vintage photo of a woman with my cross-eyed and goofy face placed over the woman's face. I have always believed that a good laugh is the best gift! The book was an immediate hit with friends and family. The images brought a lot of laughs, but the recipes were tried and true. I was encouraged to do more with the book. At that time, the Miss Divina character had not yet been created. With time and money being two strong forces in the world, the idea for a more elaborate book sat on the shelf for a number of years while I focused on other matters in my life. I always hoped to create something I would be pleased with and proud of, though, and my thoughts about this book were never too far back in my mind. My love for all things retro helped me in designing this book as well. It took time and a lot of tinkering to get this book to the bookshelves, but like a good simmering soup, it couldn't be rushed.

You're probably wondering about Miss Divina. She was inspired with the help of a special friend, Robert Greenblatt. Rob and I share the same sense of humor and same love of crazy voices. The characters of Miss Divina Noxema Vasilina and Blanche Itche are the result of our humorous back-and-forth bantering together. One day, while joking around, we created voices for two old aristocratic ladies that were always over-the-top polite to each other. From there the phrase "You are so divine!" was uttered, and the seed for Miss Divina's character was planted. From *divine* grew *Divina*. Eventually, that led to the *Noxema Vasilina* portion of her name. To me, the two character names sound like the names of an Italian drag queen and an old hag. Without Rob's jokes and laughter, Miss Divina Noxema Vasilina might never have come to fruition.

Most likely, you have a few good cookbooks in your kitchen already. This cookbook is a collection of my own original recipes with a few recipes from my family and friends sprinkled in here and there. Included are some recipes I grew up with that have fond memories attached to them of family dinners and holiday parties. We all have those favorite foods that take us back to our childhoods. Got that fuzzy feeling when you recall those foods? Within these pages, you'll find recipes for delicious, simple home cooking and many tempting comfort foods we all love. I have created these recipes to be simple, easy to make, and unpretentious. You don't always need a hundred steps or a hundred spices to make soup! These recipes are streamlined as much as possible to help the beginner and experienced chef glide through the preparation process. Easy-to-follow steps and helpful hints will help you cook successfully and confidentially. And there is more! Miss Divina and Blanche Itche have whipped up some delicious hints to help you along the way—some serious, some humorous. I hope after reading some of the "Supermodel Hints," you'll have a few laughs!

Like many people, I've had many successes along the way and a few failures in my attempts at cooking. I still have some failed attempts with new recipes, and I still have to use a timer for boiling eggs in case I forget they are on the stove! Don't give up! A delicious menu is right around the corner!

Whether you purchased this book or it was a gift, I hope you will find it a welcome addition to your cookbook collection, an enjoyable experience, and a resource you will use often. Enjoy the helpful and sometimes-humorous "Supermodel Hints" and, as I like to say, let your taste buds do the walking!

Acknowledgments

Many special people have given me love, support, and encouragement in my life—too many to be all listed here. But I feel a few special callouts are necessary.

A special mention to my friend Robert Greenblatt. He has always been a great supporter of the crazy, creative side of my brain. I am indebted to him for his role in the creation of Miss Divina, more than I can ever fully thank him for. His encouragement throughout our friendship helped me get this book to where it is today.

The design of this book would be nothing if it wasn't for the spectacular illustrations of Rae Crosson. His illustrations helped take this book to the next level. His steady contributions, built on my ideas and sketches, brought the two characters of Divina and Blanche to life. He was ever so patient with my tweaks to his work.

I am deeply indebted to my editors and agents at iUniverse Publishing, Michelle Horn, Kelsey Adams, Victoria Goodwin, and Dianne Stuart for their contributions and expertise in their fields who gave advice, provided information, corrected text that I had written, and helped me clarify my recipes. Without their valuable input, this book would be incomplete.

My family, though probably not always understanding of my creative side of life, has been great. Special thanks for their love, support, and attention. In addition (and in no special order) thanks must go to Beatriz Ruiz, Alfonso Arteche, Arnold Ashley, Dan Arrayan, Barbara Levine, Beny Lopez, Hans Johnson, Pam Morrell, Katrina Helzer, Dylan Mazy Ennis-Helzer, Jeffery Houston, Gayle Ennis, Kiki Greka, Lori Olson, Michael Dees, Nevin Forbes, Randall Reade, Shannon Ennis, Steven Zachary Ennis, Mark Branning, Maya Kalabic, and, last but not least, my late friend Lennox Hood. God rest his beautiful soul. They have all given me love and support and helped make this book become reality. They believed in me when I questioned my ability to complete this book.

Best wishes,
Jean Philippe Laplagne

Introducing Miss Divina

Always be ready to make an entrance.

The first ingredient you need for
successful entertaining is love—
love for family and friends,
love for food, and love for cooking.

I'm a Diva like No Other!

You know my name, Divina Noxema Vasilina: supermodel. To so many people in the civilized world, my name and title have come to symbolize many beautiful and fanciful things.

Many consider me the most beautiful supermodel in the world today. Being a humble girl, I question whether the title has been justifiably awarded. But recently, those in the know have begun tossing a new title at me: *chef*. Some someones have been poking their noses around in my oven, and they've been leaving impressed. I recently received my first Firestone Star award! To be recognized worldwide as a fabulous chef is a huge responsibility—almost as daunting as my extraordinary supermodel beauty. I am a looker and a cooker! It's a big label to live up to. If only Julia Child had looked half as appetizing as her dishes, the old girl might have given me a run for my money. But she didn't, and—ashes to ashes—she never will. Bless her big, sweet soul.

A candid shot as I wrote this book

While Julia and I are both heavily influenced by a European aesthetic, unlike Julia, I was born into it. I was born in the countryside of Tuscany and raised across the continent. I speak fluent "continental." Though my childhood memories are largely set in Italian, French, and Spanish locales, I'm no stranger to things American. As a matter of fact, it was in the Big Apple where food and my good looks first proved a winning combination. If you're to pull off a complete Miss Divina dinner, I hope that you possess at least a hint of the flair that runs through the women in my family. As a supermodel, prodigy, world traveler, temptress, and confidante of the jet set, I often find myself dining at society's best tables. Sadly, it all falls short of the meals I had growing up at home. Perhaps I'm spoiled when it comes to food, but it's no surprise. I was blessed to have grown up with a mama and a nana who really knew their way around a saucepan.

I come from a long line of exotic, beautiful men and women. Together, my nana (Jeanne), Miss Petit Escargot, and mama (Yvonne), Miss Tinned Meat, have turned nearly as many heads as I have. But while I've had to spend most of my time dodging paparazzi and slinking about in high fashion, Mama and Nana grew up in a different time. They were expected to hang their heels and raise families. Despite the conventional limitations put on their short careers, neither woman ever turned out a bitter batter. If they harbored any

Nana, Miss Petit Escargot

Mama, Miss Tinned Meat

spite, they kept it locked in the liquor cabinet.

The upside to their mandated duties to family and kitchen is that they taught me how to cook. You might say they were drafted to the cause, even if they weren't conscious of the fact. That is not to say they were unconscious. These grande dames always kept both heels on the linoleum, even though the wine flowed steadily in our home. In the kitchen, they were naturals. I should note that while not exactly my equals in terms of beauty, Mama and Nana certainly knew their way around men as much as their kitchens. My dear old nana, God bless her soul, was always popping something into the oven. When I wasn't strutting my wares down a catwalk, I loved to watch her cook. I was always Nana's willing guinea pig. It was at Nana's elbow in the kitchen that I picked up some of my "supermodel secrets" that my friends are always pestering me to share. If she had a choice in the matter, I'm sure Nana would still be whipping up bountiful feasts peppered with pearls of wisdom. Unfortunately, open flames and knives are strict no-nos for the sweet residents of Sunset Acres. And Nana's medicine dosages seem to have taken a toll on her pearls of wisdom as well. Not to worry—you still have me!

My Papa, Guglielmo Giacomo Ennio Noxema Vaselina,
my international man of mystery!

Dear Little Blanche

What can one say about delightful yet misunderstood Blanche L. Itche? (She won't tell me what the L stands for, but I suspect it stands for "Lush.") Blanche has been my devoted friend, assistant, and confidante for many years. Through the good and the bad, she has been by my side, doing whatever it takes to keep this diva happy and comfortable. No small feat, I'll have you know! But Blanche knows hard work. Before I met Blanche, she was a notoriously controversial high school cafeteria cook somewhere in the Midwest. Just one glance from her and no one dared to ask what the daily special was. It only takes one hepatitis outbreak to kill a career, though. After her career in food service went sour, she took up burlesque. Her skirts were a little too short, her heels a little too high, her body flat where it should have been curved, and her hair a little too … much. Granted, it was a brief career move.

Some may have turned their backs on poor Blanche, but who has as much fun as whores? She swears the navy officially classified her as a friendly port. She teases that her nickname was "Sleaze with Ease"

Dear, dear Blanche Itche—or should it be "poor, poor Blanche"?

Itche. You might think she's unrefined, and to the eye, she is. And yes, she sometimes has a habit of scratching at the most inappropriate places and times. But kinder souls feel that it is just part of her "earthy" charm. However, beneath her vodka-soaked crust is a truly delightful woman. But don't get me wrong. Blanche doesn't drink every day, only those that end in a *y*. It was Blanche who suggested I name some of my recipes after some dear friends and family. I know you will appreciate her as much as I do. You'll get to hear a bit more from my dear friend Blanche Itche on the following pages. I've offered her a few pages of her own, on the condition that she write about me. See what she has to say at the beginning of the recipe sections and near the end of the book, in a section entitled "All about the Girl." She managed to squeeze her way onto some recipes pages as well, the pushy bitch. Blanche offers informative tips and tattles some particularly juicy gossip—"Supermodel Hints"—at the bottom of many of my recipes. That naughty girl! What will I do with her?

I may have my little helpers, and I may not have six children to feed, but still I cook. During free moments, I can always hear the call of the kitchen. The sound of the flame lighting on the gas stove fires my imagination. Buttering a pan feeds so many of my senses. I find Zen-like peace on the cutting board. This calling has received many compliments courtesy of my adventurous friends, who have allowed me to stick any number of things in their mouths for review. Luckily, most of my experiments have turned out to be winners, so the worst any of my friends have suffered is a few extra pounds. That always leaves me looking thinner. Win-win! And to the delight of my male fans, I always look stunning while in the kitchen. How does one describe the look of sheer ecstasy displayed on their faces? For a full testimonial, you'll have to ask them. I am much too modest to tell you. Go to my dearest friend Blanche; she'll spill the beans. Go ahead—ask her! She'd love the attention, and a bottle of fine vodka. She'll tell you that there are three things that models are good at: achieving the perfect pouty face, teasing our hair (and men), and knowing how to eat. Some even take extra measures to stay slim after eating up a storm, but that's another story altogether!

Fifteen Suitcases and Four Miles High, a Reflection

In my unique life, the world has offered me so much, and I am grateful. It's so important that I take time to reflect upon that. I never lose sight of the fact that everyone must envy me, so as I lead the life that so many others wish they had, I'm mindful to take advantage of my privileges. In that sense, I'm only doing it for them. By sharing a glimpse of my fortunate life with others, I feel I have done my part in making this troubled world a little brighter. It's a gift I made myself. Isn't that the most thoughtful sort of gift? I like to think I have a big heart.

That big heart allows me to love people. Especially my fans. Especially the men! Some of my peers, other supermodels and the like, sometimes dart around public spaces in disguise. I, however, abhor a mask, save for my eye mask. I think disguise is ridiculous. If you've earned a following, as I have, be proud of it. Don't hide from it! I want to be recognized. The people adore stumbling upon a chance sighting of me in the streets almost as much as I enjoy giving it to them. I dread the day when I walk down Park Avenue and no one recognizes me, though chances of that are slim, thankfully. I just can't imagine it, and I wouldn't want to! When I hear people scream, "There's Miss Divina!" it makes my day. I always give them a little something back. "Bonjour! Yes, it's me! Lucky you! Aren't I fabulous?" My fans and I have such an intimate rapport. I love to sign their autograph books. With their little sparrow rib cages, not all supermodels can be as bighearted. That's what makes it so serendipitous that I'm at the top of the hierarchy. Can you imagine the depths of despair if the people were waiting for some nameless, clumsy blonde Swedish supermodel to brighten their dreary days? If she's so great, why is she doing a second-rate cable TV show? So don't let that Swedish ice queen's ear-to-ear smiles and blathering about motherhood fool you. My recipe for life is to be a giver, not a taker. You can't be a giver if you are bitter. So smile, baby!

Success is a beautiful thing, and I love it. I don't mind that from success follows demands on me. I try to strike a balance with demands of my own. The demands I put on people are big. I expect perfection. At rare moments, I get it. In my world, second best is not an option. Though I am often told that I have achieved perfection, I feel I haven't done anything professionally with which I am completely satisfied. Though I guess, as a stunning vixen, I must have. I am always striving for ever-greater heights. I have worked like a demon to be a great supermodel, actress, chef, and role model. I grew up believing I could be a fine actress or anything I put my mind to. And I just can't wait for the next great script to come my way. I'm hard on myself and those around me, but I do have feelings. I'm an actress—I have all of them!

A scene from my smash-hit cable movie,
Satan and Fallen Angels

Here I am arriving at another red-carpet event with my faithful, if not unusual, sidekick, Blanche Itche, not far behind.

I'm convinced that the more I travel, the more I can bring to all my roles. A fashion shoot in Morocco, for example, introduced me to a fabulously innovative new recipe for couscous. I'm like a shark who will suffocate if she stops moving. I will choke on the mundane and sink straight to the bottom.

As I write this, my agent, Michele Dees-Moss, and I put the final details together for upcoming engagements in the next six weeks in as many countries. There's a film offer on my desk. I'll read the script tonight, and if I like it, I'll plan on two months in London to film. A good television show comes along? Yes, I can get out to LA the third week of November for my cameo. There are panel shows and talk shows that need a yes or no. One week might have me on a Bangkok catwalk, the next at an opening in Cannes. It's all in a day's work for this Cannes-do girl!

Every job has its dangers. Even supermodel-actress-chefs have to keep an eye out for occupational hazards. A recent trip to Rio de Janeiro springs to mind. As the plane taxied in, I noticed thousands of people crowding the airport. "Who on earth are they waiting for?" I wondered aloud. It's a lucky thing Blanche was along to clear things up for me, even if I must apologize that her demand for endless free cocktails on our international flights is likely a leading cause of the airlines' current economic troubles. Anyway, she put down her precious little bottle of vodka long enough to answer, "They want you, darling!"

Well, you know, it's true I love a motorcycle escort. But the welcome to Rio de Janeiro was a bit much. On the way from the airport to my hotel on Avenida Atlântica, hordes of people lined the street, pressing their curious little faces against the limousine windows. It was frightening, exciting, and very flattering, all at once. It was an awful lot like my "*first time*," but with a bigger crowd. Thank God for those hunky Brazilian motorcycle officers. They got us to the hotel safely and as fast as possible without running over a single devoted fan. (Though I think the driver may have clipped a nun in a crosswalk. I said two Hail Marys, just to be safe.)

Upon my arrival in Rio de Janeiro for one of my numerous public appearances around the world. Too warm for a fur, but a girl must make a spectacular entrance!

One day, during another trip, in a department store to promote my new perfume, Divina, Nº 10, so many people pressed forward to shake my hand that they pushed my entourage and me against the glass counters. Panic caught me in my twenty-four-inch waist! Well, we immediately excused ourselves to the powder room and never went back to the showrooms. We were whisked out the door, into my awaiting limo, and headed for the airport. Poor, dear Blanche still shudders when she thinks of how close we came to going through the plate glass counters.

Even if the friendliest crowds can sometimes be terrifying, so can the testiest film directors. The perils of my profession come flying at me from both the bottom up and the top down. No matter how you slice him, the acclaimed film director Jean-Michael Es Doté is the top! Despite his reputation for being "very challenging," I agreed to work with him during my last film, *Satan and Fallen Angels*. It didn't take long at all to see that he deserved every bit of that reputation and then some. At our first rehearsal, he took one look at me and snarled, "You and your damned padded breasts!" He called out in fury and demanded I remove the pads. I quickly tried to extract the thin pads I had on—for support only!— but in my rush, my girls accidentally tumbled out of my dress for all to see. Before you could yell, "Wardrobe malfunction on the set!" I burst into tears. At least I'd proven that my goods were the real thing! Monsieur Es Doté scampered off, rightfully embarrassed. To make amends, he poured on the star treatment for the rest of the filming, and I naturally became his raven-haired girl. We got along just swell after that! A man endowed with … so many graces—such a sexy, desirable man—can really make a woman feel vital and alive. The thought of him still excites me. I can't tell you how many frocks I've ripped through in my dressing room just trying to recreate that moment. Oh! Now who's embarrassed?

Though my outfits themselves aren't always excessive, my wardrobe needs may still be considered a tad excessive by some. But it's all part of the job. Unfortunately, traveling with an ample collection can be daunting today. The golden age of travel is just a memory. Now there are maximum baggage allowances and fees. I suppose it's all the same, as my rooms in Paris don't have the closet space. My Beverly Hills spread—now those are some closets! And my Manhattan penthouse I call Casa Goldilocks—just right! It's even seen a bear or two. In my line of work, I must travel a lot, but I love it. To be fair, my big heart always takes a moment away from the in-flight champagne and canapés to pity those people back in coach with their plasticware and deep vein thrombosis. I wonder whether the good people at Coach are aware of how the airlines are sullying their good name. Say "coach" on any plane, and I can guarantee that not many will immediately entertain thoughts of the most adorable $3,000 leather wallet. The front of the airplane is a different world, though. I simply adore being thirty thousand feet up. And for all that talk you hear about the airlines' clubs in airports, don't you believe 'em. They keep the best stuff a mile high.

In the upcoming pages I'll share some of my secrets to entertaining. You'll be thankful for my helpful hints!

The Best Is Yet to Come

In the coming pages, I will offer many delicious recipes for making your affairs more rewarding for you and more impressive to your guests. With my help, people will leave your table awed. You will have won them over, and not just because you're gorgeous or a bit trampy. It will be because you're an expert host. For you, I have written this book devoted to entertaining, cooking, and having a sensationally sinful time.

I have included a section titled "The Purr-fect Evening" that details designing the most deliciously sensuous evening for a taste of life in the Miss Divina lane. Careful—curves ahead! I will guide you in how to set a gorgeous table, whom you should (and should not) invite, how to create the right atmosphere, and how to choose the right music. Of course I'll also guide you through a menu guaranteed to stimulate a purr-fectly seductive evening.

Peppered throughout these pages, you'll find a few hints that I swear by. I hope they make the culinary process more enjoyable for you and your guests. I live by these simple rules. If you know what's best for you, you will too. Your life will be so much more rewarding after reading, and living by, my recipes for success. These simple, helpful hints for a successful life will help you to impress even the most skeptical rival without even chipping a nail in the process!

For those of you with supermodel aspirations of your own, I have included a section on being the bellissima you. Are you in need of a makeover? Is your love life a bit drab these days? Well, I will help you with that too. I'll help you make the most of what God gave you. Where he fell short with you, I will help you pick up the slack.

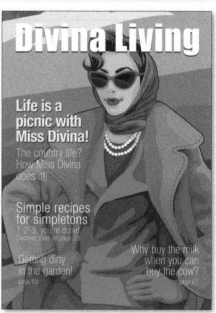

Here's just a sample of the countless magazines featuring me on the cover and extolling my beauty, talents, and extraordinary humanitarian endeavors. Many of these may be on your coffee table right now! I'm fortunate to have the world-famous photographer Ashley Arnold do most of my photo shoots. He does the most beautiful work in the business.

Because my family and fans have been begging me for ages to share my recipes, you now have this lovely cookbook to add to your collection of cookbooks by infamous people. I have such a weakness for people begging me. Again, that damn big heart of mine! I hope you will enjoy these recipes as much as I have enjoyed cooking them. Follow my simple instructions and advice, and I guarantee that your life will be much more stimulating. You'll have everyone eating out of your hands, or at least off your plates. If you're as good as me, you may have to enter a domestic-goddess witness-protection program.

I hope that you will glean some knowledge from these pages and that they will inspire you to make your life more beautiful, rewarding, and certainly tastier! In closing, I would like to thank all the little people. Honestly, compared to my fame as Miss Divina, you are little. Buon appetito!

Faithfully yours, *Divina Noxema Vasilina*

The Perfetta Evening

It Starts at the Door

At Chez Divina, a guest's perfect evening starts at the door. Just like Dorothy opening that Kansas shack's door onto a Technicolor Oz, my door opens onto an exotic new paradise.

A lovely home means two things to me. First, it's a place to welcome friends and make them feel comfortable. Second, it is the palette on which you'll serve a gorgeous feast. Feeding who you care about—or the people you have to entertain—is just one of the most satisfying things I know how to do. Good food is one of my passions, and it's easy for me to dream up dinner menus. But nothing can sour a guest's taste buds like an untidy home. And what about the decor? If it's shabby—and I don't mean shabby chic—then redecorate!

Accordingly, I make sure my house is always in perfect order. Cleanliness is next to godliness! Though I have large staffs to help keep my penthouses and the family villa in order, I feel deep, intense satisfaction when I

Take time to relax prior to your party. If you follow my advice, it will undoubtedly be a spectacular party.

get down on all fours. How else can I guarantee my floors have been scrubbed spotless? Scrubbing is the greatest exercise in the world. It gives me rosy cheeks, in more ways than one, and I have a ball. A lovely home says so much about you to your guests. It says you've arrived, that you're in control, and that you're thoughtful enough to care about their comfort. If you find you've been caring just a tawdry bit too much about others' comfort, your home is also a sanctuary you can wrap around yourself after a scandalous session of naughtiness.

My Magical Touch

Millions of words have been written about how to look lovely, entertain gracefully, and make people feel welcome in your home. There is, however, another element that no amount of studying, reading, or mirror gazing can give you: charm. Charm is not only being soft-spoken, relaxed, and at ease. It is also being generous. I hope the ideas and suggestions I give you will help you give an impressive and successful evening.

Whether you are planning a party for fifty or just a cozy dinner for two, you can always make it a memorable event that your guests will recall fondly for ages. Remember that you are a lady or a gentleman. You deserve the best, and you must give your best. Charm is grace—graciousness. Charm is a touch of magic. Try to make it part of your way of life. That is my magic. I trust you to emulate me and pour it on, honey!

With your home clean, it's time to get your act together, sweetie! Plan out the entire evening—the decor, the guests, and, of course, the menu. Assemble all your ingredients and utensils before preparing any delicious dishes. For you ladies, keep your lipstick and compact with you at all times. And for heaven's sake, that martini should never be more then an arm's length away! For me, my choice cocktail is the Bikini Martini. See the recipe on p. 32 in the "Cool Cocktails" section of this book. There isn't much to it, but it hits all the right spots! A relaxed and happy host is one of the few things we have left from a more leisurely era. And everyone needs an outlet for stress. Mine has fifty-three stores and a personal shopper.

It doesn't necessarily take money (but that doesn't hurt!) to have successful parties, large or small. If you do your job right, guests will assume you must be hiding all sorts of staff in your kitchen. I, however, do have all sorts of staff in my homes. When I am not doing the cooking, I have Juanita in the kitchen. Juanita is such a gem. You might think it a bit demanding that I've never given her a day off, but don't be too harsh, because I have given her help in the kitchen. There are always two butlers and four housemaids, all doing their assigned jobs efficiently and quietly, or else! The difference between Juanita and myself is that when I'm in the kitchen, I do the job for love. Juanita and I determine the menu a few days prior to the event and do what can be prepared beforehand to help streamline the party preparations. And to spare your hired help, set limited hours for your party, and be firm with your guests when it's time to end the party!

The In Crowd—Inviting the Right Guests

A certain Hollywood celebrity columnist once said, "Miss Divina not only gives a party; she gives great … well, she *is* the party!" I love throwing vast parties on the spur of the moment and having hordes of fans around. That's one secret to a good party: it should look spontaneous. All the arrangements should seem effortless, as if they floated down from a nearby cloud, and you should look as if you have nothing to do but enjoy yourself. Nobody wants to see you running around with a sweaty brow and your hair in a bun, weeping because the fish is overcooked. They want to celebrate you, not pity you!

Another important secret is knowing how to mix people. Even the simple realization that people should be mixed and that some thought must go into deciding whom to throw together will put you head and shoulders above most of today's mediocre hosts. Mix your guests carefully. Throwing a dinner for a mixture of burly bachelors can be the greatest thing since kiss-proof lipstick, but not if you seat a cattle rancher next to a vegetarian novelist. Choose men who have a little something in common—besides you—and tell them to fasten their seat belts and loosen their ties, because it's going to be a sensuous night! One of my guests asked me once whether that was a little forward. My response to that was "I'm a forward kind of gal." From a man's viewpoint, dinner with me is truly a splendorous thing. I make them believe they are kings for a short hour or two before letting them know who is really in charge. I often wonder whether men realize the power we women have over them. Nothing like a little Miss Divina to bring out the animal in a man! A trained animal, that is.

Of course, the animals needn't be exactly alike. Do try to sprinkle just a hint of anarchy when writing your guest list. The best parties are a crazy mix. Invite a famous trial lawyer, a few easy actresses, a couple of HGTV interior designers, a professional jockey, a painter, your young visiting friends from Rome, a successful dress designer, a politician (progressive, of course), a gay hairdresser, a few corporation presidents, and

I ask you, who can top living in a Paris penthouse overlooking the little people below? And at Miss Divina's expense!

a university professor. Mix them all together, and then try to pry them apart long enough to eat! If you put any thought into it, rather than just calling whomever you think might be available, you're ahead of most people. Choosing guests who complement one another—perhaps a pilot who will impress an athlete and vice versa—will certainly give your parties the best word-of-mouth advertising.

It is especially important to have all age groups represented. I've never noticed any generation gap. My parties include the old and crusty to the sinfully young and naive. Usually the old have the money, and the young are just gorgeous. All young people are bright and attractive and have something to say. All age groups love to listen to my fabulous life. And in that regard, they make wonderful guests.

One thing I learned at my sorority, I Felta Thi, is a carefully planned dinner should never be ruined by rudeness, which is not at all the same as being forward. Being forward is asking a guest seated next to you to butter your muffin. Rudeness, on the other hand, is being late or discourteous. Be sure your guests know that tardiness and discourtesy will not be permitted. And that I like my muffin with extra butter.

I never regale my guests with an account of the neighborhood gossip, unless it's a particularly juicy bit! After that kind of party, people will say, "I had the most wonderful evening. Let me tell you who I met. And, oh, you must hear what Dr. So-and-So said about …" They'll look forward to the next dinner party you invite them to, if they're so lucky!

Setting the Right Atmosphere

You have decided on the menu and mixture and number of guests; now you need to choose the right music for the evening. When I get everything together and gather my friends for a party, I am always thoughtful about choosing the music. I expect you to be as well. What kind of gathering are you having?

Set the perfect table for your romantic candlelight supper.

Is it a formal or casual event? What sort of guests are you entertaining? How about something sexy if your guests are members of the opposite sex or something sophisticated for mixed company? Steamy jazz, like Billie Holiday or Eartha Kitt, is perfect for getting a man in the right mood for Miss Divina. If the party is a mixed group, try some light classical or a sultry soundtrack to one of my movies, such as *Double-Breasted Indemnity*.

When planning a dinner or cocktail party, I go into hostess mode, getting out the handmade cloth napkins, the good china, and Nana's silver. I think handmade napkins add a personal touch to a table setting. Needless to say, the porcelain and crystal need to sparkle, and the silver must shine until your gorgeous face reflects in it. I've collected some lovely tablecloths and cloth napkins; some fabrics for my table come from all corners of the world. Set the table with some darling candles. Candles should always light your table, and if you have them, make use of some soft wall sconces. I love candles throughout the house. Always remember: everyone looks gorgeous in candlelight. For a bit of whimsy, I mix up my table settings. I'll choose the serving plates, cups and saucers, glasses, and silver from my many sets to create a bohemian or eclectic look. I love to show off all the beautiful table china and glassware I have collected over the years on my many global adventures. Besides yourself, always have an attractive centerpiece. Go to the florist and order the most beautiful arrangements possible. I keep my flower arrangements low so that the gorgeous guests at my table don't have to crane their necks to see and be seen by whomever is opposite.

In my Beverly Hills home, just beyond the dining area is the swimming pool. To set a mood, I float gardenias and candles. I love to have the doors to the terrace open on warm evenings. If there is a light breeze, all the better. I love the sight of sheer curtains flowing in a gentle wind. How delicious it is to sit in the candlelight, almost holding our breath, talking about the delightful ambience and my dinner presentations. On evenings like that, my home is like a fairyland. Not like Michael Jackson's Neverland, but a mystical experience with candles reflecting in the pool, soft breezes, the slightest hint of floral scents, and soft, indirect lighting on the trees and shrubbery. I love it as much as my guests do.

Even with a buffet, people must sit down to eat. I would never ask guests to stand around balancing plates, cutlery, napkins, and beverages, all while trying to find a fifth hand to offer me a photo to autograph for them. It's important that everyone is comfortable, and that means chairs. Drape yummy velvets of every color in the rainbow over the dining chairs. Sitting in one of my velvet-covered thrones is like a taste of heaven.

Going All the Way

Go the extra mile for your guests. Show them you thought of them. There are a few things you can do in this regard the day before your dinner. For instance, take dozens of gorgeous calla lilies or your favorite flowers and arrange them in beautiful vases all around the house. Fluff up the throw pillows in the living room. Next, if your budget allows, complete the buffet table, if that is how you are serving your menu, with an eight-foot ice sculpture (carved by you with a chain saw no less if you are so talented). I just wish I always had time to do something more elaborate for my guests. Naturally, I am joking. But I do put a lot of effort into my guests.

Let the Party Begin

When guests come to your home, be prepared. You must be cool, collected, and captivating at six o'clock. The housekeeping must be finished, and any rug rats—ahhh, I mean, darling children—securely tucked away. As host, you should also emerge "finished," with all your beauty treatments complete. Greet your guests groomed, fragrant, and prepared to dazzle your favorite beau, or at least the one at hand.

If you have a spare moment, sit down, close your eyes, and just relax. Sitting for ten to fifteen minutes prior to your guests' arrival will help you compose yourself for the evening. I usually think of myself, and it does wonders for my blood pressure. I think the Bikini Martini in my hand doesn't hurt either. If you can't imagine being successful at all this, then hire someone to cater the event and take all the credit.

Be Interesting!

Do you have a hobby? Gardening, painting, attending charity meetings, or just looking through magazines—whatever your interest, be interesting. Be sure you'll have something to talk about with your guests. And pretend you're interested in what they have to say. If you smile and nod while letting a man talk about his interests at length, he will think you offered witty repartee. Such is the vanity of men. The appearance of being interested in your guests and what they have to say makes them feel they are somewhat worthy of your presence, even when they aren't. One must learn to be a great actress when throwing a party. Follow these steps, and you will always be interesting.

Laughter is always a great path to a successful gathering. Does anyone play the piano? Live music during the cocktail hour will enliven the atmosphere and will certainly give your guests something to talk about! Do you like playful games? Consider putting mind-provoking challenges to your guests while still in the cocktail hour or after dinner before dessert. Pull out that old game of Twister! That might create some compromising situations for your guests and something to laugh about in the future. But make sure your entertainment is lighthearted and fun. No Gloomy Guses allowed!

Being a guest involves some responsibility too. As a guest, you must dress like a movie star, the ones that dress like human beings. It is an insult to the host to arrive looking like you just finished the gardening, much less the gardener! Clean up and doll yourself up. Show your host you care.

Also try to help your host. I always go up and introduce myself to strangers, especially the men. After all, the host can't be everywhere at once. I usually say, "Hello! I'm Divina Noxema Vasilina." They gasp and say, "You must be kidding! We'd never know it!" Droll, aren't they?

Recipes for a Successful You

A Script for a Complete Woman

Being me has its perks. But not all of you are so lucky. I am used to being served by handsome male servants. When I travel, I prefer to walk to my plane along a sleek velvet carpet in pink or chartreuse. Once on board, I am immediately eased into relaxation by handsome, tight-shirted male attendants. They start by removing my expensive shoes and putting on my Cinderella slippers. Soon after, surrounded by a cloud of fresh orchids or long-stemmed roses, I am offered French champagne and Russian caviar. All the while, these men's hands are attending to my gorgeous, gorgeous body—fluffing my pillow and such. Follow my advice, boys and girls, and you may be lucky enough to experience Miss Divina's life! If you want to try to approach the life I live, keep reading.

The Bellissima You!

You may have been Miss America 1970, but do you still look like 1970? Are you today's with-it person—elegant, poised, groomed, and glowing with health? Or are you a plump copy of Miss 1970? Are you sleek and smooth? Or, rather, bumpy in the wrong places? Does your hair look like something out of *There's Something about Mary*? How about your posture? Do you stand gracefully? Or are you a modern

Your jewelry box doesn't overflow with diamond and pearls? Make *yourself* the purr-fect evening accessory.

equivalent of the hunchback of Notre Dame? Do you look better from the back or the front? Do you look like you are wearing a potato sack? Do you even care?

Okay, so let's create your own program for a glowing face and lovely hair. Be desirable. Every morning before breakfast, start with these few simple routines. Even if it is six o'clock in the morning, arise, shower, apply just the right amount of makeup, comb your hair, and splash on a dash of eau de cologne. Please put on lipstick and earrings! It's feminine and provocative. If you're going out, a hat adds still more. It frames the face. A well-dressed woman without a fabulous hat is like a Rembrandt without a frame. Choosing the right clothes and jewelry to wear does wonders for your morale, as well as men's! Wear your highest heels and tightest-fitting clothes to create a sensuous dish—you! Make a grand entrance in all your glory. Stun them with your beauty when you walk into the

It's amazing what you can do with leftovers!

breakfast room. June Cleaver had it together when she wore her pearls to breakfast. Now that is a lost America I long for!

And to the gentlemen in the crowd: Are you groomed like a sexy, masculine man should be? Is your hair styled well, beard nicely trimmed? I expect a certain level of personal hygiene from my men. If you have long hair or a beard, please trim it nicely and shave all that unruly hair on your neck. Save the unruly for the bedroom! I feel closer to a man who is well groomed and appealing rather than the farmhand oozing scents from the barnyard! A pretty or handsome host seated across the table is much more appetizing to the senses when nicely groomed.

Stand erect, chest out, head back. Good posture shows breeding. It will impress the men in your life and make all other women wish they were you. Of course my triple-D bosom helps matters. Get yourself a beautiful mirror. The bigger, the better. Look into that mirror and say, "Mirror, mirror, on the wall, who's the fairest of them all?" Well, that marvelous mirror will reply, "My dear, you are a living doll!" And make sure your current beau is as radiant as you are. If he looks attractive and relaxed, so will you. And you'll look all the more stunning when beautiful people are surrounding and admiring you.

In Hollywood and other fabulous destinations, such as the French Riviera, the beautiful abound. While in Nice between gigs, my dear girlfriend Lennoxia and I sat having a delicious afternoon when a famous Hollywood actress who shall remain unnamed strolled past. Lennoxia asked me whether I thought the actress had had any work done. My response was "Honey, she's a quilt!"

Don't let your girlfriends talk that way about you! Take care of yourself. Avoid the knife! Somehow you should squeeze in the time for your regular beauty routines, visits to the hairstylist, and shopping trips to replenish your wardrobe. Your man expects you to look better than ever, doesn't he? Have you become the most uninteresting and unsightly woman in the world? That poor man! You must make time to freshen yourself and ensure that everything looks relaxed and inviting. Your man chose a woman who was sexy, gorgeous, gracious, and interesting. The same thing goes for lovely clothes. A woman should have them,

Ask yourself this: For whom do you dress? Be beautiful even when photobombed.

if she can wear them right. When she's young, graceful, and slim, she can show them off like an angel. A girl must always take care of her hands and feet too. You never know when you might need to wrap them around a man. And don't forget to wear gloves when out and about!

When it comes to sunning myself, I must admit I truly enjoy catching Rays—and Robertos and Alfonsos and Daniels and Michaels! I can live without the necessities of life—as long as I have the luxuries! But not too much sun. You know the saying, "Rays today, raisins tomorrow!"

Moisturize, moisturize, moisturize! Need I say it again? Take good care of your skin. Be soft and supple to the touch. If only we would all make a habit of using moisturizer regularly. But not at bedtime, when it only gets smeared over the pillowcases and your man's pajamas instead of staying on your face where it will do some good. Do as I do, and make your own face cream. See my recipe Is That a Sour Cream and Cucumber Salad in Your Pocket? I especially enjoy having this salad / face cream around the lunch hour. Have a yes face. It comes in handy late at night too. No man wants to hold hands with a woman whose skin is rough and calloused. I know a woman who once said, "I've worked all my life to afford to buy myself diamonds, and now my hands are too old." This woman was only forty-two or so, but she had work hands, ugly hands that were no fit background for the beautiful big diamonds she had just bought.

Your hair and skin should have an expensive, well-cared-for look. When you take good care of your body, you'll glow with health. If, like me, you can't spend your life in curlers, get a stunning hat to hide that bad-hair-day hair!

Being the woman your man most enjoys going to bed with isn't quite enough—or won't be for long, unless you're me. Sex is beautiful, very personal, and magnificent. But like all marvelous things, you should come in a lovely wrapping. Have you ever opened a Christmas present that was hastily wrapped with old brown paper and messy tape? Not even wrapped as a gift? You think, *Good grief, they must have stepped or sat on this before sending it!* Packaging is very important. How can any woman present herself in a careless package?

18

When alone with my current lover, I touch up my makeup until my face is perfect, then slip into something simple and comfortable. My preference is a fur-lined teddy with matching high-heeled slippers. What an exciting change for the evening! And my beau, he adores my bedtime look. Often, he takes one look at me, takes my face in his hands, kisses me all over, and squeals, "You're the most beautiful thing I've ever seen in my life!" How could I not believe him?

For Whom Do You Dress?

Choose the stunning gown you'll wear. As a superb hostess who's experienced in giving great parties, I play the role I know by heart. My first suggestion? Rehearse your dinner! I don't mean rehearse stirring the martinis; I mean rehearse yourself! Whether you're having only six for dinner or fifty for cocktails, wear a lovely gown. As hostess, you have earned the right to look special, even if your skin looks like an old suitcase. If you've got it, flaunt it. If you don't, fake it. When all the other "ladies" wear short skirts, you can look smashing in a long evening gown or in hostess pajamas. You can sparkle, glitter, and greet the guests in a riot of color. It's your special privilege. It's also how you move that counts. Slink into the room like Mata Hari drenched in musky perfume. We all want big wardrobes, lots of dresses, and matching shoes. My rule is don't buy a dress until you can afford all the right accessories, or until your current sugar daddy can afford to buy them for you. Not every dress is right for you. Wear stunning clothes with good labels. I think a long slit on an evening gown gives the body such a lovely kind of movement. It suggests sex but not overtly. Get yourself lovely skirts for dancing and lush, solidly beaded dresses, as well as chiffons—simple, elegant, feminine chiffons. No woman should be without one for a romantic evening.

My delicate rib cage is a challenge to any dress designer. I'm lucky to be able to have my clothes made according to my own sketches. Sometimes I envy women who can walk into a store, pick something off the rack, and say, "I'll take it!" I've never been able to do that, due to my measurements: forty-eight-inch bust, twenty-four-inch waist, and thirty-six-inch hips. My frame has special needs. Only top designers do it for me. My favorite designer/seamstress, Busty Ross, suits me perfectly. I am just a simple girl, but I realize too well that we all have our crosses to bear.

Two words: plan and accessorize. People are always debating whether we women dress for men, for other women, or for ourselves. On occasion, I dress for all three. Femininity for men, color for women, and something very crazy for myself. Jewelry is an essential accessory. I would feel undressed without my jewels. One of my handsome admirers, a Texan, always presented me with the loveliest jewels! But I had to grin and bear it every time he called me "mamsielle"!

The Divina Diet

Now, ladies, you know the world expects us to be slim and trim. That's a tall order for some of you girls. Naturally, everyone needs to be careful not to overdo it when it comes to eating the wrong things. Too much of a good thing can be just too much. Your tiny little figure is going to rebel if you don't listen to me! My motto is simple: "When in doubt, less chocolate cake and more rice cakes."

I recently admired this sweet, young model wannabe. I asked her, "What's your secret?" Her reply was "I starve. I'm the hungriest girl in New York." I'm often asked if I diet. (I wish interviewers would come up with more interesting and original questions.) I reply, "No, I just stop eating when I'm content." I eat most of the things I like, but sparingly and slowly. I simply cannot gulp down a meal. Have you ever noticed that people who eat quickly have no interest in food and invariably have potbellies? Sometimes I get up at five in the morning and have a piece of my delicious King Alfonso Cinnamon Apple Pie and a skim cappuccino. An apple a day! At six thirty, I eat my scrumptious Divine Quiche Divina and a few thin slices of my Hunnie Fay Baker Ham with Grand Marnier Glaze. Fish is a wonderful beauty food, and I try to eat it every other day. My favorite fish recipe is my Hollie Butte (a Hell-of-a-Butt) Grilled Halibut. I have a kitchen in my dressing room, and I usually share breakfast with my makeup girl, "Missy" Randi Reade, and my talented hairdresser, Lori S. Olson. The S stands for "Shampoo."

My Program for a Sexy Figure

Have you ever noticed how lovely ballet dancers always look? Whether they are walking down the street or across a living room, they not only carry themselves like angels but also have happy expressions, because for years they have worked all day in front of mirrors. They all have at least one thing in common: they all move with the most perfect grace, almost as if they're floating. They look proud—and they damn well should be! There is no excuse for not having a good big mirror, even if you must give up a little luxury in order to buy one. Better still, have a triple mirror, the kind you find in dress-shop fitting rooms. A good mirror lets you see yourself coming and going. That "going" look may give you something to think about. Make a point of glancing at yourself every time you pass a mirror. It'll do wonders for you. It does me!

Now, honey, you don't need me to tell you that men are very strange. When women go wrong, men go right after them. They fall for the first girl with a tight skirt and sensational cleavage, both of which I have. Most of them are leg watchers too. For me, both swimming and dancing strengthen my legs, chest, and back muscles, so that I'm often able to go without a bra, even on camera. But remember, darling: cup size isn't everything. It's what's inside the cup that really matters! I stretch a lot, even when flying to one of my fashion gigs. A beautiful woman also stands beautifully. Stand serenely, and stand tall. I think that heels help. But not too high. You want to walk gracefully! I advise girls to "look to the stars." I don't mean that in a philosophical sense, although that could certainly apply. I mean that a lifted head ensures a lovely neckline and an air of confidence. It also gives the impression that you are better than anyone else. Maybe you are. But if you can't control your cleavage, your perfume, your walk, and your eyelashes, you'd better stay out of the game. So don't just stand there—select a sexy pose and work it!

Massage those tired muscles. I know women who pay a masseur $150 an hour to come in the morning and massage them while they're still half asleep. I love massage. It won't replace sex, but it's a luxurious feeling. In my mind, at $150 an hour, your masseur should be the one only wearing a towel! I know—I'm just so scandalous!

Fragrance Is Feminine

Your final accessory is perfume. I always wear eaux de colognes during the day. I can't get around to perfume before four in the afternoon. Heck, sometimes I don't even get up until four o'clock! I think perfumes can be overpowering to the people you work with and a little too much for daytime. But a whiff of the right cologne—the right one for a woman's particular personality—should be served right up with the bacon and eggs. And in the evening, apply sparingly my own perfume, Divina N° 10. Guaranteed to make your man growl! Oh darn, I plugged my perfume again!

My perfume, Divina N° 10, is guaranteed to drive any man crazy for you!

Put Some Color into Your Spirits

All my friends say, "Treasure yourself." I follow that advice by doing extraordinary amounts of self-pampering. But no, I don't have a bladder problem! I surround myself with happy colors: yellow, coral, hot pink, lavender, and Mediterranean blues and greens (my favorites). These colors remind me of all the sexy men I have in my life and the beaches I have had them on. But remember: some colors are not for everyone. You should choose colors that work with your skin tone. A lot of women I know are afraid to wear hot pink because it takes a magnificent complexion like mine to pull it off. That's one shade that may show you for what you really are: a brazen hussy. I like lavender too. Lavender looks effortlessly chic and is stunning with a good suntan. It's a perfect shade for linen. I *love* lightweight linen—I practically live in it.

Moving In for the Kill

Do people consider you a dominating bitch? Good, clean fun is overrated! This calls for the most beautiful feminine tact. Every woman wants to make her man happy, and a big part of that is letting him think that he's the boss. Women are born flirts, but once girls get themselves married, they forget the romance. That's exactly when the flirting should really begin. You should never cease to tease your man. It makes him want you all the more. The more he wants you, the longer you will keep him. It is not unusual to find myself wearing a stunning new diamond necklace or bracelet after a particularly juicy flirting session the night before. Women often ask me how they can live up to my example. They whine, "I'm just a housewife," or "I'm a mother, and the kids are growing up," or "You're Miss Divina, but I'm not!" Oh, how true, how true. Those poor women. How can they ever accomplish all I have? And I never even try—I am that good! But in a pinch, any woman can be a delicious dynamo. I tell them to just read my book and it will all fall into place.

Even these days, after liberation and marches for women's rights, a lot of women are still coming fresh into the business world who were brought up to believe that their purpose in life was to please a man, run a home, and raise children. Leave it to me to set them straight! Men are here to please us. But men, as I've already noted, are funny. Some men may be bored with their wives, but the idea of their wives working, having careers of their own, and, heaven forbid, making more money than them sends them straight up a wall. Maybe if we reversed the roles, with the woman coming home from work ready for sex, then the man would be the one "too tired" that night. Maybe you'll take the upper hand with the man in your life! After all, deep down, men really love to be dominated by women far more than they will admit.

I have a dear friend who once worked at the White House. In one private but tremendously important meeting, one that could have decided the fate of the world, she was the only woman present. She wore her diamonds and a sexy but simple red dress. She sure did turn some heads! In my opinion, without her, we might now be part of some Eastern bloc country. Yes, I know the Eastern bloc doesn't exist anymore—proof of how successful she was! She's "covered" three American presidents, flown in Air Force One countless times, and been photographed with most of the crowned heads still left in the world. She fits perfectly into any setting, from a party for a famous rock star to an embassy banquet, and she's always suitably dressed for the occasion, whatever it may be. Too bad she took herself off the market politically. We sure could use her to fix the mess in Washington, DC, these days. Her motto is simple: "Conduct yourself like a lady, and you'll always be treated like one." She's never "one of the boys."

Finally, Applause, a Bow ... and Solitude

You were the star of the evening, and they gave you a standing ovation. It's two in the morning, and you have thrown the last guest out the door. The help is cleaning up. You did your best to make everything perfect and everyone feel welcomed. Now it's time to sit back and enjoy the evening's memories. For just this moment, bask in the glory of what you've accomplished, because tomorrow those nasty guests may be talking to the tabloids! Don't worry; if you did your job well, you'll always come out smelling like a rose. Time to get some sleep. A good night's sleep does wonders for the complexion and keeps that glow in your eyes that people will notice. The press certainly will notice it tomorrow! Put on some soft music and lie down on some cushy pillows and warm blankets, which are essential for feeling comfortable and relaxed. Time to relax to the quiet early-morning sounds in your bedroom or that wonderfully delicious bathtub. Don't forget the bath oils. Soaking alone in the tub is the best way to unwind and meditate. Always keep in mind that no matter how popular you are, you need time for solitude. Take it from

Some compare my moves on the runway to the world's most graceful ballerinas.

me, supermodel extraordinaire. Would I steer you wrong?

Well, there you have it. I hope these suggestions and helpful hints will make all the difference at your next soiree. When you do it right, everyone wins. You'll come out looking like a star and adding to the image you wish to create of yourself. You may not be Divina Noxema Vasilina, but you can buy my book and emulate me. Add hosting to the list of all the wonderful things you do and do well. Remember: look pretty, stand straight, and give 'em hell! Your guests will certainly be impressed at how well everything came out and

Relaxing in your favorite café or restaurant is just the treat you need to indulge in every once in a while! Yes, you can have your parfait and eat it too!

Invite a few friends over and enjoy a relaxing day by the pool. Don't have a pool? Oh, for shame!

A stroll in the park with my two basenji pups, Stoli and Abby, is great exercise for them and me.

how stunning you looked while doing it. They may be envious, but that's just more icing on the cake, n'est-ce pas?

I adore hearing about how my life has changed someone else's. What are your thoughts about all the wonderful things I have imparted? I do want to hear about how I've helped you, but that does not mean I want to hear all about the bitter, empty parts of your life. My philosophy? If it doesn't happen to me, does it really matter?

Thank you again for letting me enhance your life, making it less than humdrum. The following pages will provide you with some delicious recipes to make your dining experience more enjoyable and rewarding. I know that all the wonderful things you'll glean from my cookbook are going to change your drab, dreary life. The world can always be more beautiful. Let's do our part. So sit back, relax, and enjoy a few chocolates. Not too many, though! A plump girl is a lonely girl! … So they tell me.

Cool Cocktails

Too many libations may lead to diminished inhibitions!

Afternoon Delight (p. 29)

You have a big night ahead of you. Once you've decided on the guests, table atmosphere, music, and menu, you can get down to the delicious job of how to start the evening festivities. That usually means drinks.

Throughout, your evening must be accompanied by wonderful cocktails, wines, and aperitifs. Everyone knows that I am partial to the cocktail hour. I love a good martini, like a Coco Chanel Martini or a French Martini, and there are times when I need a strong whiskey. When I am in that mood, I like to drink a simple Americano Highball. If I'm in a fruity mood, I must have a delicious Sex on the Beach cocktail.

If you have a large group of wine connoisseurs, choose the appropriate wines according to your menu. The wrong wine — or, God forbid, a cheap one — can ruin all your hard work. I never pull out a boxed wine, thank you very much! If you need help, just let your wine merchant know what you're serving. Your wine merchant is an expert, and you should get to know him or her. If you become chummy enough, your wine merchant may soon count as a frequent dinner guest who will always bring you the perfect bottle of wine.

If you have a few extra dollars, there should be a bartender for the first part of your party. No host can enjoy himself or herself if glued to the bar mixing drinks for a dozen people. Of course, I am used to being served by handsome male servants. Sometimes a close male friend will clamor to serve me by tending bar, but a paid bartender, perhaps a hot, young, muscled college boy, is a better investment. Afterward, you may pay him the going rate. For my money, I always go for the college boys. They are always so eager and keen to please.

But don't encourage your guests to drink too much. An hour for predinner cocktails is plenty. More than that, and people will become sodden and not very amusing. Too much drink in them, and it's all downhill from there! A tipsy guest can be a treat, but a drunk one may cause a scene and can't appreciate or even taste the food, making a mockery of your hard work.

The right servers can make
or break the perfect party.

Blanche Itche, the gift that keeps on giving!

Also, a cocktail hour that's more than an hour leaves nondrinkers starving and bored. Plus, too much drink can ruin a perfectly good figure! But in moderation, the upcoming cocktail recipes are sure to impress.

Cocktail Glass Guide

champagne flute

highball glass

champagne glass

champagne tulip

brandy snifter

martini glass

old-fashioned /
lowball glass

collins glass

margarita glass

beer mug

cocktail glass

shot glass

pint glass

coupe glass

mason Jar

hurricane glass

poco grande glass

goblet

Irish coffee glass

wineglass

Afternoon Delight

Makeup:

3 ounces rum
3 ounces peach liqueur
16 ounces cranberry juice
16 ounces Gatorade energy drink
2 ounces ginger ale

Garnish:
orange or lime slice

Glass:
cocktail glass

Application:

- Add all ingredients except ginger ale to a cocktail shaker or pitcher.
- Add ice, cover, and shake.
- Add ginger ale and stir.
- Chill and serve over ice in a cocktail glass.
- Garnish with an orange or lime slice.

Americano Highball

Makeup:

2 ounces blended whiskey
ginger ale

Garnish:
lemon twist

Glass:
highball glass

Application:

- Pour the whiskey into a chilled highball glass over ice.
- Add ginger ale to fill.
- Garnish with a lemon twist.

Angel's Kiss

Makeup:

1 1/2 ounces crème de cacao
1 1/2 ounces heavy cream
1 1/2 ounces brandy

Garnish:
maraschino cherry

Glass:
champagne glass

Application:

- Pour the crème de cacao into a 5-ounce champagne glass.
- Using the convex side of a bar spoon, slowly pour the cream over the crème de cacao, making sure not to disturb it, to create a layered effect.
- Using the same technique, layer the brandy over the cream.
- Garnish with a maraschino cherry.

Bar Slut

Makeup:

3 ounces vodka
2 ounces cranberry juice
3 ounces Red Bull
2 ounces 7UP

Garnish:
orange slice

Glass:
small mason jar

Application:

- Add vodka to a mason jar filled with ice.
- Add cranberry juice.
- Add Red Bull and splash 7UP on top.
- Stir and garnish with an orange slice.

Between the Sheets

Makeup:

1 ounce cognac
1 ounce triple sec
1 ounce light rum
1/4 ounce freshly squeezed lemon juice

Garnish:
lemon twist

Glass:
cocktail or martini glass

Application:

- Combine all ingredients in a shaker and shake with ice.
- Strain into a chilled cocktail or martini glass.
- Garnish with a lemon twist.

Big Banana Dick-iri

Makeup:

1 ounce light rum
1/2 ounce spiced rum
1/2 ounce crème de banane, preferably Bols Banana
half a banana, roughly chopped
1/2 ounce freshly squeezed lime juice
1/2 ounce rich simple syrup

Garnish:
half a banana, sliced in half vertically

Glass:
margarita glass

Application:

- Add all ingredients plus a cup of ice into a blender, and blend until smooth.
- Pour into a margarita glass.
- Garnish with half a banana, sliced in half vertically.

Supermodel Hint

Simple syrup is one part sugar to one part water—a staple in any beverage maker's repertoire.

Bikini Martini

Makeup:

2 ounces gin
3/4 ounce blue curaçao
1/4 ounce peach schnapps
1/4 ounce freshly squeezed lemon juice

Garnish:
orange twist

Glass:
martini glass

Application:

- Place all ingredients in a cocktail shaker with ice.
- Shake and chill.
- Strain into a chilled martini glass.
- Garnish with an orange twist.

Bloody Mary

Makeup:

1 pinch celery salt (for glass rim)
1 lemon or lime wedge (for glass rim and the drink)
2 ounces premium vodka
4 ounces tomato juice
2 dashes hot sauce, preferably Tabasco
2 teaspoons prepared horseradish
2 dashes worcestershire sauce
1 pinch ground black pepper

1 pinch smoked paprika

Garnish:
celery stalk, lime wedge, and slice of bacon (optional)

Glass:
pint glass or goblet

Application:

- Pour some celery salt onto a small plate.
- Rub the juicy side of the lemon or lime wedge along the lip of a pint glass or goblet.
- Roll the outer edge of the glass in celery salt until fully coated.
- Fill with ice and set aside.
- Squeeze the lemon or lime wedge into a shaker, and drop it in.
- Add the remaining ingredients and fill with ice.
- Shake gently and strain into the prepared glass.
- Garnish with a celery stalk, a lime wedge, and a slice of crisp, thick bacon.

Breakfast Martini

Makeup:

1 1/2 ounces gin
2 teaspoons orange marmalade
3/4 ounce freshly squeezed lemon juice
1/2 ounce simple syrup

Garnish:
lemon twist

Glass:
cocktail glass

Application:

- Add all ingredients to a cocktail shaker and fill with ice.
- Shake and strain into a cocktail glass.
- Garnish with a lemon twist.

Champagne Cocktail

Makeup:

1 sugar cube
Angostura bitters
champagne

Garnish:
lemon or orange twist

Glass:
champagne flute

Application:

- Place a few drops of Angostura bitters on the sugar cube and drop into a champagne flute.
- Top with a luxury champagne or a sparkling wine.
- Garnish with a lemon or orange twist.

Coco Chanel Martini

Coco Chanel Martini

Makeup:

3 ounces coconut vodka
1 ounce elderflower liqueur, such as St-Germain

Glass:
martini glass

Application:

- Add all ingredients to a shaker and fill with ice.
- Shake and strain into a martini glass.

Cupid Cocktail

Makeup:

16 ounces champagne
1 ounce cherry liqueur
1 ounce peach schnapps
4 ounces freshly squeezed orange juice
2 strawberries

Garnish:
strawberry slice, orange slice, and maraschino cherry

Glass:
highball or champagne glass

Application:

- Add all ingredients to a shaker.
- Shake and strain into a chilled glass.
- Garnish with a strawberry slice, orange slice, and maraschino cherry.

Dirty Sicilian

Makeup:

1 pinch celery salt (for glass rim)
1 pinch pepper (for glass rim)
1 lemon or lime wedge (for glass rim)
2 ounces vodka
1/2 ounce limoncello
1 ounce Sicilian green olive juice

Garnish:
rosemary sprig

Glass:
martini glass

Application:

- Pour some celery salt and pepper onto a small plate.
- Rub the juicy side of the lemon or lime wedge along the lip of a martini glass.
- Roll the outer edge of the glass in the salt-and-pepper mixture until fully coated.
- Fill a cocktail shaker with ice and add the vodka, limoncello, and olive juice.
- Shake well and pour the drink mixture into the prepared martini glass.
- Garnish with a floating rosemary sprig.

Devil's Tail

Makeup:

1 1/2 ounces rum
1 ounce vodka
1 tablespoon lime juice
2 teaspoons grenadine syrup
2 teaspoons apricot brandy

Garnish:
maraschino cherry

Glass:
champagne flute or martini glass

Application:

- Crush half a cup of ice cubes. Place in a blender.
- Pour all ingredients into the blender with the crushed ice.
- Blend until smooth.
- Pour into a champagne flute or 6-ounce martini glass.
- Garnish with a maraschino cherry and serve.

Earthquake Cocktail

Makeup:

3 ounces cognac
1/2 ounce absinthe

Garnish:
lemon twist

Glass:
cocktail glass

Application:

- Add all ingredients to a shaker and fill with ice.
- Shake and strain into a cocktail glass.
- Garnish with a lemon twist.

French Martini

Makeup:

1 1/2 ounces vodka
1/4 ounce Chambord raspberry liqueur
1/4 ounce freshly squeezed pineapple juice

Garnish:
lemon twist

Glass:
cocktail or martini glass

Application:

- Pour all ingredients into a cocktail shaker.
- Shake with ice and pour into a cocktail or martini glass.
- Garnish with a lemon twist.

Harvey Wallbanger

Makeup:

1 1/2 ounces vodka
4 ounces orange juice
1/2 ounce Galliano

Garnish:
orange slice

Glass:
highball glass

Application:

- In a highball glass almost filled with ice cubes, combine the vodka and orange juice.
- Stir well.
- Float the Galliano on top and garnish with an orange slice.

Italian Stallion

Makeup:

1 1/2 ounces bourbon whiskey
1/2 ounce sweet vermouth
1/2 ounce Campari
1 dash bitters

Garnish:
lime slice

Glass:
cocktail glass

Application:

- Stir all ingredients with ice in a pitcher.
- Mix well.
- Strain into cocktail glass.
- Squeeze lime slice over drink and drop into glass.

London Buck

Makeup:

2 ounces dry gin
ginger ale

Garnish:
lemon wedge

Glass:
highball glass

Application:

- Fill highball glass halfway with ice.
- Add gin.
- Top with ginger ale.
- Give two gentle stirs.
- Garnish with a lemon wedge.

Maiden's Blush

Makeup:

1 1/2 ounces gin
1/2 ounce triple sec
1 teaspoon cherry brandy
1 ounce lemon juice

Garnish:
maraschino cherry

Glass:
cocktail glass

Application:

- Combine all ingredients in a shaker half filled with ice cubes.
- Shake and strain into a cocktail glass.
- Garnish with a maraschino cherry.

Mimosa

Manhattan

Makeup:
2 ounces whiskey
1 ounce sweet vermouth
1–2 dashes bitters
orange peel

Garnish:
maraschino cherry

Glass:
cocktail glass

Application:
- Place ice in a cocktail shaker.
- Add the whiskey, vermouth, and bitters and shake.
- Rub the orange peel around the rim of the cocktail glass.
- Strain the drink into the glass.
- Add a maraschino cherry for garnish.

Mimosa

Makeup:
2 ounces orange juice
1 tablespoon Grand Marnier
1 dash orange bitters
4 ounces brut champagne

Garnish:
orange twist or slice

Glass:
champagne flute

Application:
- Fill champagne flute two-thirds full of freshly squeezed orange juice.
- Add the Grand Marnier and a dash of orange bitters.
- Top with brut champagne.
- Garnish with an orange twist or slice.

Napoleon Cocktail

Makeup:

1 sugar cube
2 dashes bitters
1 teaspoon cognac
1 tablespoon Grand Marnier
champagne, preferably extra dry

Garnish:
orange twist

Glass:
champagne flute

Application:

- Sprinkle a sugar cube with 2 dashes of bitters.
- Place the sugar cube in a champagne flute.
- Pour the cognac over the sugar cube.
- Add the Grand Marnier.
- Fill the glass with champagne.
- Garnish with an orange twist.

New Orleans Buck

Makeup:

2 ounces aged rum
1 ounce freshly squeezed orange juice
3/4 ounce ginger syrup
1/2 ounce lime
1 dash bitters
soda water

Garnish:
candied ginger and orange wedge

Glass:
collins or highball glass

Application:

- Combine all ingredients except soda water in a shaker and whip (shake with a small amount of ice for a few moments).
- Strain into a chilled collins or highball glass.
- Top with soda water.
- Garnish with candied ginger and an orange wedge.

New York Cocktail

Makeup:

2 ounces blended whiskey
1 ounce lemon juice
1 teaspoon granulated sugar
1 teaspoon grenadine

Garnish:
lemon twist

Glass:
cocktail glass

Application:

- Pour all ingredients into a cocktail shaker with ice cubes.
- Shake well.
- Strain into a chilled cocktail glass with ice.
- Garnish with a lemon twist.

Nympho

Makeup:

1 ounce Malibu rum
1 ounce peach schnapps
1 ounce spiced rum

Garnish:
fresh peach slice and lime slice

Glass:
lowball glass

Application:

- Add all ingredients to a cocktail shaker with ice.
- Shake well and strain into a lowball glass with ice.
- Garnish with a fresh peach slice and lime slice.

Opera Cocktail

Makeup:

1 1/2 ounces gin
1/2 ounce Dubonnet
1/4 ounce maraschino liqueur
1 dash orange bitters

Garnish:
orange or lemon twist

Glass:
martini glass

Application:

- Place all ingredients in a mixing glass that is half filled with ice.
- Stir vigorously until the ingredients are well chilled—about 20–30 seconds.
- Strain the mixture into a martini glass.
- Garnish with a twist of orange or lemon.

Orgasm

Makeup:

1 ounce coffee liqueur
1 ounce amaretto
1 ounce Irish cream
heavy cream

Garnish:
maraschino cherry

Glass:
old-fashioned or cocktail glass

Application:

- Pour the coffee liqueur, amaretto, and Irish cream into a cocktail shaker filled with ice.
- Shake well.
- Strain into an old-fashioned or cocktail glass filled with ice.
- Fill with heavy cream.
- Garnish with a maraschino cherry.

Parisian Cocktail

Makeup:

2 ounces dry vermouth
1 1/2 ounces gin
1/2 ounce crème de cassis

Garnish:
blackberries

Glass:
coupe glass

Application:

- Add all ingredients to a mixing glass with ice.
- Stir well.
- Strain into a coupe glass.
- Garnish with blackberries.

Pink Panty Dropper

Makeup:

1/2 can of beer
1 ounce vodka
1 ounce tequila
pink lemonade

Garnish:
lemon slice

Glass:
highball glass

Application:

- Add beer to a highball glass that is half filled with ice.
- Add vodka and tequila.
- Add the pink lemonade to top off glass.
- Mix well.
- Garnish with lemon slice.

Pink Pussycat Cocktail

Pink Pussycat Cocktail

Makeup:

1/2 ounce gin
1/2 ounce Chambord raspberry liqueur
3/4 ounce freshly squeezed grapefruit juice
1/2 ounce pineapple juice
1 splash grenadine

Garnish:
lime slices and lemon slices

Glass:
highball glass

Application:

- Fill a highball glass with ice.
- Add gin and raspberry liqueur. Then add grapefruit and pineapple juices.
- Add grenadine and stir well.
- Garnish with lime slices and lemon slices.

Queens Cocktail

Makeup:

1 ounce gin
1 ounce dry vermouth
1 ounce sweet vermouth
1 ounce pineapple juice

Garnish:
lemon twist

Glass:
cocktail glass

Application:

- Combine all ingredients in a shaker.
- Shake with ice and strain into a chilled cocktail glass.
- Garnish with a lemon twist.

Satan's Whiskers

Makeup:

1/2 ounce gin
1/2 ounce Grand Marnier
1/2 ounce sweet vermouth
1/2 ounce dry vermouth
1/2 ounce orange juice
1 dash orange bitters

Garnish:
orange slice, mint leaves, and black olive

Glass:
cocktail glass

Application:

- Add all ingredients to a shaker and fill with ice.
- Shake and strain into a cocktail glass filled with ice.
- Garnish with an orange slice, mint leaves, and a black olive.

Sex on the Beach

Makeup:

1 1/2 ounces vodka
1/2 ounce peach schnapps
1 1/2 ounces orange or pineapple juice
1 1/2 ounces cranberry juice
1/2 ounces Chambord raspberry liqueur or crème de cassis

Garnish:
orange slice

Glass:
highball glass

Application:

- Add all ingredients to a shaker and fill with ice.
- Shake and strain into a highball glass filled with fresh ice.
- Garnish with an orange slice.

Sex on the Snowbank

Makeup:

finely grated coconut (for glass rim)
1 lemon or lime wedge (for glass rim)
1 1/2 ounces Malibu rum
3 tablespoons coconut cream

Garnish:
finely grated, fresh coconut

Glass:
martini glass

Application:

- Pour some finely grated coconut onto a small plate.
- Rub the juicy side of a lemon or lime wedge along the lip of a martini glass.
- Roll the outer edge of the glass in the finely grated coconut until fully coated.
- Set glass aside.
- In a blender, add one cup of ice cubes, the rum, and the coconut cream, and blend until smooth.
- Carefully pour into the martini glass.
- Sprinkle a pinch of grated coconut in the center of the drink.

Slippery Nipple

Makeup:

1/4 ounce grenadine
1/2 ounce sambuca
1/2 ounce Irish cream

Glass:
shot glass

Application:

- Create the "nipple" of the cocktail by pouring the grenadine into a shot glass.
- Carefully add the sambuca to create the next layer.
- Then carefully pour the Irish cream.
- The combo is meant to be consumed as a shot, so the layered flavors combine in your mouth.

49

Sloe Comfortable Screw

Makeup:

1/2 ounce Southern Comfort
1/2 ounce sloe gin
1/2 ounce vodka
orange juice

Garnish:
orange wedge

Glass:
highball glass

Application:

- Combine the Southern Comfort, sloe gin, and vodka in a cocktail shaker with ice.
- Shake well.
- Strain into glass with fresh ice.
- Top off with orange juice.
- Garnish with an orange wedge.

Snow Bunny

Makeup:

1 1/2 ounces Anchor Christmas Spirit
1/2 ounce ginger liqueur
1/2 ounce lemon juice
1/2 ounce honey syrup
1/2 ounce egg white
2 ounces Anchor Christmas Ale
3 dashes bitters

Garnish:
shaved or grated nutmeg and three drops of bitters

Glass:
beer mug or highball glass

Application:

- Add all ingredients except for the ale and bitters to a cocktail shaker.
- Dry-shake. Then add ice and shake again.
- Double-strain into a beer mug or highball glass and top with ale.
- Garnish with nutmeg and three drops of bitters.

Wedding Bells Cocktail

Makeup:

1 ounce cherry brandy
1 ounce vermouth
1 ounce gin
1 ounce orange juice

Garnish:
maraschino cherry

Glass:
martini or coupe glass

Application:

- Mix all ingredients over ice cubes in a cocktail shaker.
- Shake well and strain into a chilled glass.
- Garnish with a maraschino cherry.

Widow's Dream

Makeup:

2 ounces Bénédictine
1 ounce cream
1 egg

Glass:
martini glass

Application:

- Fill a shaker with ice cubes.
- Add all ingredients.
- Shake vigorously and strain into a chilled martini glass.

Zaza Cocktail

Wintery Candy Cane Martini

Makeup:

1 candy cane, crushed (for glass rim)
1 lemon or lime wedge (for glass rim)
2 ounces strawberry vodka
4 dashes white crème de menthe
2 1/2 ounces cranberry juice

Garnish:
small peppermint candy cane, whole

Glass:
martini glass

Application:

- Place crushed candy canes on a small plate or saucer.
- Rub the juicy side of the lemon or lime wedge along the lip of a martini glass.
- Holding the glass by the stem, rotate the rim to coat with candy cane.
- In a cocktail shaker, combine the vodka, crème de menthe, and cranberry juice with ice. Shake until well combined.
- Strain into the prepared glass.
- Garnish with a whole small candy cane; serve immediately.

Zaza Cocktail

Makeup:

1 1/2 ounces gin
1 1/2 ounces red Dubonnet
1 dash bitters

Garnish:
lemon twist

Glass:
cocktail glass

Application:

- Shake all ingredients with ice.
- Strain into a chilled cocktail glass.
- Garnish with a lemon twist.

The AntiOX (blackberry/sage)
- Mix in a pitcher 10 cups of water; 1 cup of blackberries, very slightly crushed; and 3–4 sage leaves.
- Leave in refrigerator overnight before serving.

Note: Sage leaves have the highest antioxidant content of any herb.

The Classical (lemon/cucumber)
- Mix in a pitcher 10 cups of water; 1 cucumber and 1 lemon, thinly sliced; 1/4 cup fresh basil leaves, finely chopped, and 12 fresh mint leaves, finely chopped.
- Leave in the refrigerator overnight before serving.

The Digestive (fennel/citrus)
- First, infuse 1–3 grams of dried and crushed fennel in 150 milliliters of boiling water for 5–10 minutes. Allow to cool.
- Mix in a pitcher 10 cups of water; the juice of 1 lemon (put the leftover lemon in the mix as well); 1 small orange, thinly sliced; 12 fresh mint leaves, finely chopped; and the infusion of fennel seeds.
- Leave in refrigerator overnight before serving.

The Exotic (pineapple/mint)
- Mix in a pitcher 10 cups of water; 1 cup of cubed pineapple; and 12 fresh mint leaves, finely chopped.
- Leave in the refrigerator overnight before serving.

The Granite (strawberry/lime or raspberry/lime)
- Mix in a pitcher 10 cups of water; 6 strawberries or raspberries; 1 lime, thinly sliced; and 12 fresh mint leaves, finely chopped.
- Leave in the refrigerator overnight before serving.

The Traditional (apple/cinnamon)
- Mix in a pitcher 10 cups of water, 1 cup of cubed apple, 2 cinnamon sticks, and 2 teaspoons of ground cinnamon.
- Leave in the refrigerator overnight before serving.

The Watermelon (watermelon/rosemary)
- Mix in a pitcher 10 cups of water, 1 cup of cubed watermelon, and 2 rosemary stems.
- Leave in refrigerator overnight before serving.

The Zingibir (ginger/tea)
- In advance, heat 1 teaspoon of ginger in 2 cups of tea. Let it cool down.
- Mix in a pitcher 10 cups of water, the 2 cups of ginger tea, and 4–5 pieces of fresh ginger, cut into cubes.
- Leave in the refrigerator overnight before serving.

The Lady and the Ladle

Serving the Purr-fect Menu

By Blanche Itche

As with any good European family worth its pedigree, a Vasilina family function is worthless without course after course of the best bounty the earth has to offer. Generations of extended family come together to feast and gossip. Whether a huge holiday meal or a modest everyday supper, everything is always delicious and hearty. Naturally, everyone's attention is always on Miss Divina, and the conversation, which offers a much-welcomed diversion from the hairy mole on Uncle Giuseppe's nose, is, well, almost always about Miss Divina. When the family isn't talking about Miss Divina or considerately discussing how to best help one of the young, pregnant, unmarried

A typical everyday meal for Miss Divina's friends and family. She doesn't do anything small, and there must be champagne!

cousins or how to punish one of the young male cousins who'd gotten a girl pregnant, the conversation always turns to food. There is an abundant amount of food to salivate over. Despite the praise heaped upon Miss Divina at the table, she has always thought that there is no better way to express a sort of familial love than cooking a wonderful meal for family and friends! A meal filled with love need not be fancy. All it needs is to come from the heart. Cooking to please other people is at the top of the list of things Miss Divina loves the most. Well, maybe second on that list!

In a household of six children, dinner was always an undertaking for Miss Divina's mama, Yvonne. This is not to say they were in the funeral business. All the children learned the value of a euro by putting in time as kitchen assistants. Miss Divina's father, Guglielmo Giacomo Ennio Noxema Vasilina, was an international banking tycoon, and his job helped them live well, even if his calling wasn't supermodel glamorous. Though the Vasilina household could certainly afford the grocery bill, it's still a marvel that Miss Divina's mother could craft exciting meals daily. Add to that the fact that, at any given time, at least four of her sisters were on bulimia diets, always screaming for food. Never mind the toll those diets took on the plumbing! I often ask myself how she managed. As for myself, I don't need to mimic her mama's resourcefulness. At home, when Miss Divina doesn't have free time to whip up a stunning meal, she has a staff and entourage that follow her every whim.

Good help is not hard to find, especially in countries with ruined economies! Just ask me, Blanche Itche, her devoted personal assistant and dearest friend and confidante.

Miss Divina believes in the old Japanese adage that if you give a hungry man a fish, you feed him for a day, but if you teach him how to fish, you feed him for a lifetime. The same goes for cooking that fish! Miss Divina and I will try to teach you how to prepare wonderful meals and may suggest recipes to accompany other recipes. But she can't always hold your hand, and you'll need to teach yourself some things in food preparation. She's got better fish to fry!

We know it can be hard sometimes to make important decisions when, in this case, your whole evening depends on everyone enjoying and judging you on the food you put before them. Honey, let's face it— they're gonna judge ya, so do your best, and the heck with those naysayers! May I make a suggestion now? Wear sharp shoes so you can "accidentally" shin those naysayers under the table every now and then. But that's just me.

Tasty Hors d'Oeuvres

To be a success, nothing should jiggle!

Barbie Q. Oysters with Lemon Brine (p. 62)

Whetting Their Appetites

Whether you're planning a cocktail party, barbecue, clambake, picnic, or cast party, Miss Divina has so very many exciting culinary ideas for you, right here in these pages. She always offers her guests a wide range of choices. Of course, she is always the main course. But she is the exception to the rule. She demands a good host not fall back on some comfortable recipe over and over and over. Some people tend to serve the same food each time they entertain because they've found a few foolproof recipes. Guests arrive knowing they're going to get sliced ham or a stroganoff or whatever the house specialty may be. Not so at Chez Divina. At her home, the only thing guests may predict is that they'll be splendidly surprised. No one ever knows what Miss Divina will serve or wear!

Signorina Canta Elopé's Prosciutto and Melon

As I stated before, good food is one of Miss Divina's passions, and it's easy for her to dream up dinner menus. If you don't share that same level of passion for food, you can still create wonderful menus. Just be methodical, aware of seasonal availability, cooking times, and so on. When you dress yourself, consider color, texture, taste, and balance. Do the same with your menu! You must start the party with some hors d'oeuvres and finger foods to whet your guests' appetites. Indulge them with a wide variety of hors d'oeuvres, such as paper-thin slices of Signorina Canta Elopé's Prosciutto and Melon, Elvira's Escargots, or She-Deviled Eggs des Pyrénées. Maybe you should consider recipes that can be made the day before, like Catherine the Great's Chilled Crab Dip, Pâté Supermodel Laplagne, One Cheesy Cheese Ball, Spicy Mexican Pool-Boy Dip, or The Grapes, That's a Wrap. Preparing some of the dishes ahead of time may give you extra time at the salon to look your best at the head of the table.

The Queen's Tea Sand-Wishes

Some cranky naysayers may balk at Miss Divina's menus, whining that they cannot afford trainloads of caviar or a large staff. Well, you poor dears! Let's say, for example, you are throwing a birthday bash for the man in your life. If it's his birthday and he loves caviar, skip the cappuccinos at your favorite café for a couple of days. Give up that hat that you don't need. Wear a turban for God's sake! What your man gives you may be more precious than any hat, which may look horrible on you anyway. Look at some of the best-bred royal families—hats don't help them in the least!

Fashionista Smoked Salmon Pâté (p. 67)

Alta Moda Bruschetta with Olive Tapenade and Shrimp

Makes 24 bruschettas.

Makeup:

1 fresh french baguette
1 (12-ounce) can anchovy fillets
1/2 cup kalamata olives, pitted
1/4 cup extra-virgin olive oil
2 teaspoons aged wine vinegar
2 teaspoons capers
2 teaspoons minced garlic
2 teaspoons fresh tarragon
1 teaspoon fresh basil
1 teaspoon salt
1 teaspoon freshly ground black pepper
1/2 cup butter, room temperature
48 large shrimp, cooked and shelled
1/2 cup grated romano cheese
fresh, small basil leaves, for garnish

- Preheat oven to broil (500 degrees F).
- Thinly slice baguette diagonally into 24 pieces; set aside.
- In a food processor, mix anchovies, olives, olive oil, vinegar, capers, garlic, tarragon, basil, salt, and pepper.
- Mix until all ingredients form a paste-like mixture.
- Transfer olive mixture to a small side bowl; then set aside.
- Lightly butter one side of each slice of bread.
- Place each slice on one or two large cookie sheets and lightly broil in oven for 2–3 minutes.
- Remove and cool for 1 minute.
- Spread a light layer of olive mixture evenly on each bread slice.
- Place two shrimp on each slice and sprinkle romano cheese on each slice.
- Return to oven and broil for 1 minute, or until cheese melts.
- Remove and transfer to serving platter.
- Garnish with fresh basil leaves.

Supermodel Hint
If you can, grill the bread. Grilling the bread is less about the grill marks and more about the smoky flavor you'll achieve.

Barbie Q. Oysters with Lemon Brine

Makes 24 oysters.

Makeup:
Brine
1 1/2 cups butter, melted
1/4 cup worcestershire sauce
3 tablespoons lemon juice
2 tablespoons sugar
1 1/2 tablespoons chopped parsley
1 tablespoon hot sauce, such as Tabasco
1 tablespoon dill weed (optional)
1 teaspoon black pepper

Oysters
24 fresh oysters in shells
1/2 cup grated parmesan cheese
1/2 cup green onions, finely chopped

Application:
Brine
- Mix all ingredients for brine in a large, nonmetallic container.
- Stir brine really well until salt and sugars dissolve.
- Set aside covered for 1–2 hours.

Oysters
- Wash off the outside of the oysters.
- Place oysters on a preheated grill and cook until they start to open.
- Wearing oven mitts, pry open oysters with a sharp knife.
- Scoop out each oyster and place into the deeper side of the two shell sides.
- Place back on the grill and brush on brine mixture.
- Sprinkle on grated parmesan cheese.
- Cook each oyster for another 3–5 minutes.
- Sprinkle finely chopped green onions on each oyster.
- Serve hot off the grill.

Supermodel Hint
Whether you have a fabulous villa like Miss Divina or just a humble trailer down by the river, this is a wonderful dish to make outside on a warm summer evening. And after these, it'll get a whole lot hotter inside!

Catherine The Great's Chilled Crab Dip

Serves 10-20 people.

Makeup:

1 (8-ounce) package cream cheese, room temperature
1 (10.5-ounce) can cream of mushroom soup
1 envelope unflavored gelatin
2 (6-ounce) cans lump crab, drained
1/4 cup mayonnaise
1 medium red onion, finely diced
1 cup finely diced celery
2 tablespoons fresh, finely chopped parsley
2 tablespoons freshly ground pepper
2 tablespoons salt
2 teaspoons garlic powder

Application:

- In a medium saucepan, over medium-low heat, melt cream cheese with the cream of mushroom soup.
- When cheese is completely melted and mixed with soup, remove to a medium mixing bowl and set aside.
- Mix gelatin with 3 tablespoons of water.
- Add to cream cheese / soup mixture and stir in completely.
- Add crab, mayonnaise, onion, celery, parsley, pepper, salt, and garlic powder.
- Stir completely.
- When mixture is thoroughly mixed, pour into a greased plastic mold. Do not use a metal mold.
- Let stand refrigerated for at least 4 hours or more in order to chill and set.

Serving note: Serve with fresh slices of celery and carrots, sliced and toasted french bread, or crackers. For a large gathering, double this recipe.

Not divulging any names, but a model Miss Divina once worked with loved this crab dip so much that she would do anything if it meant getting more. That slut!

Catwalk Coconut–Turkey Meatballs in Mushroom Sauce

Makes about 25–30 meatballs.

Makeup:
Meatballs:
1 1/2 pounds ground turkey
1/2 cup bread crumbs
1 egg
1/4 cup shredded coconut
2 tablespoons Italian seasoning
1 teaspoon garlic powder
1/2 teaspoon salt
2 tablespoons extra-virgin olive oil

Mushroom Sauce:
2 tablespoons coconut oil
1/3 of a medium onion, thinly sliced
1 1/2 pounds mushrooms, chopped
1 (15-ounce) can coconut milk
1 teaspoon garlic powder
salt and pepper to taste

Application:
Meatballs:
- In a medium bowl, mix ground turkey with bread crumbs, egg, coconut, Italian seasoning, garlic powder, and salt.
- Using a tablespoon, scoop the turkey mixture and form into small meatballs.
- In a large skillet, heat olive oil at medium temperature.
- Add meatballs to heated olive oil and brown, stirring occasionally to brown each side.
- Remove meatballs to a dish and set aside.

Mushroom Sauce:
- Heat coconut oil in a large pot over medium heat.
- Add onion and sauté for about 3 minutes.
- Add mushrooms and sauté until soft.
- Add coconut milk, garlic powder, pepper, and salt.
- Bring to a simmer, stirring occasionally.
- Add meatballs.
- Cover and simmer for about 15 minutes, stirring occasionally.
- Serve warm in a serving bowl with decorative picks for your guests to use.

Supermodel Hint
Miss Divina often doubles this recipe, since it is always a huge crowd-pleaser. Polite guests would never admit it, but they love to fondle these meatballs at the buffet table!

Critic's Choice Chicken Wings

Makes 4 servings.

Makeup:

20 chicken wings/drumsticks
1/4 cup extra-virgin olive oil
1/4 cup soy sauce
3 cloves garlic, finely chopped
4 teaspoons chili powder
2 teaspoons garlic powder
salt and ground black pepper to taste

Application:

- Preheat oven to 375 degrees F.
- Wash and dry the chicken wings.
- In a large, resealable plastic bag, combine olive oil, soy sauce, garlic, chili powder, garlic powder, salt, and pepper.
- Seal and shake to combine.
- Add chicken wings, reseal, and shake to coat.
- Line a baking sheet with aluminum foil.
- Arrange chicken wings evenly on baking sheet.
- Cook wings for 25 minutes, or until crisp and cooked thoroughly.

Serving note: Serve with Chunky, Plus-Size-Girl Blue Cheese Salad Dressing (see p. 230), No-No Nanette's La Tomate et Bleu Dip (see p. 74), or your favorite dipping sauce.

Supermodel Hint

We've shared our classic Chunky Plus-Size-Girl Blue Cheese Salad Dressing, but you can serve these wings with your choice of dips on the side. A few dips that Miss Divina likes to serve wings with are honey-garlic sauce, honey-mustard sauce, and ranch dipping sauce.

Makes 12 servings.

Makeup:

1 cup unsalted butter
1/4 cup shallots, finely chopped
1 cup spinach, finely chopped
2 tablespoons finely chopped garlic
1/3 cup fresh basil, finely chopped
1 teaspoon finely grated lemon zest
1 phyllo dough sheet (a.k.a. filo dough), thawed
3 strips of bacon, cooked and crumbled
12 escargots (often found at gourmet food shops)
1 teaspoon freshly ground black pepper

Application:

- Preheat oven to 375 degrees F.
- Lightly grease a small baking sheet with butter.
- In a small saucepan, melt butter over low heat.
- Add shallots, spinach, and garlic to butter.
- Sauté for about 3 minutes.
- Remove from heat; add basil and lemon zest.
- Mix thoroughly and set aside.
- Cut phyllo dough into 12 squares, but keep together; don't separate squares yet.
- Brush phyllo squares with butter mixture.
- Evenly distribute a small amount of butter mixture and bacon bits over the phyllo squares.
- Place 1 escargot on each square.
- Season with freshly ground pepper.
- Brush more butter mixture over each escargot.
- Bring edges of phyllo dough up and around the escargot and twist slightly at top where the pastry gathers. (For a more decorative look, tie a small piece of clean baking string around the top of each pastry.)
- Place finished escargots on the prepared baking sheet.
- Brush escargots with remaining butter.
- Bake for 20 minutes, or until the crusts are golden brown.
- Place pastries on a bed of mixed greens and edible flowers.
- Serve immediately.

Supermodel Hint

Most of Miss Divina's friends are sophisticated enough to eat snails. My Miss Divina usually has plenty of fresh snails around, even if they are sometimes from her garden.

Fashionista Smoked Salmon Pâté

Makeup:

16 ounces cooked salmon, grilled or broiled,
 skins and bones removed
1 (8-ounce) package cream cheese, room temperature
1 tablespoon freshly squeezed lemon juice
2 teaspoons freshly grated sweet red onion
1 teaspoon prepared horseradish
1/4 teaspoon salt
1/4 teaspoon liquid smoke
3/4 cup chopped pecans
3 tablespoons chopped fresh parsley
french bread, thinly sliced, for serving

Application:

- In a food processor or blender, mix together salmon, cream cheese, lemon juice, onion, horseradish, salt, and liquid smoke.
- When mixed thoroughly, turn into serving dish, spreading evenly.
- Refrigerate until set.
- Sprinkle with chopped pecans and parsley.
- Serve with sliced french bread.

Supermodel Hint

If you want to make this mousse a bit more decorative, pipe it onto bread or crackers using a pastry bag and a decorating tip (use the tip with the largest opening). Also try this served as a dip for vegetables.

Makes 12 servings.

Makeup:

8 ounces fresh tuna steak
2 tablespoons raspberry jam
6 hard-boiled eggs, cooled
3 tablespoons mayonnaise (or plain yogurt)
1 tablespoon finely chopped green olives
1/4 cup Havarti cheese, finely grated
1/2 teaspoon lemon pepper
1/2 teaspoon salt
1/2 teaspoon garlic powder
1/2 teaspoon oregano
1/2 teaspoon paprika
1/2 teaspoon crushed red pepper
1 teaspoon wasabi paste
paprika, for garnish
green olives, sliced, for garnish

Application:

- Prepare outdoor grill according to your specific grill instructions or preheat broiler to 500 degrees F.
- Using a pastry brush, glaze tuna with raspberry jam.
- Grill or broil tuna until cooked thoroughly.
- Set tuna aside to cool.
- When tuna is thoroughly cooled, crumble and set aside.
- Slice hard-boiled eggs in halves.
- Carefully remove yolks as not to break the egg whites.
- Add yolks to a mixing bowl.
- Carefully rinse egg whites in warm water and drain upside down on a paper towel.
- Crush yolks with a fork and add tuna and all remaining ingredients except paprika and egg whites.
- Mix until well blended and somewhat smooth.
- With a small teaspoon, stuff each egg white with mixture and sprinkle with paprika.
- Garnish each egg with a slice of green olive.

Note: To make egg salad for sandwiches, chop the egg whites, mix in with all ingredients, and serve on pita or your favorite bread.

Supermodel Hint

Before slicing the eggs, run the knife under warm water. This helps the knife slice more easily through the egg whites, preventing tearing.

Makes 12 servings.

Makeup:

For Glaze
1/2 cup butter
2 tablespoons brown sugar
1 tablespoon worcestershire sauce
1 tablespoon dijon mustard
1 tablespoon poppy seeds

For Rolls
cooking spray
1 can refrigerated pizza crust
3/4 pound deli ham, thinly sliced but not shaved
6 slices swiss cheese, thinly sliced
6 slices gouda cheese, thinly sliced

Application:

For Glaze
• Combine butter, brown sugar, worcestershire sauce, mustard, and poppy seeds in a saucepan over medium heat.
• Whisk until butter is melted and glaze is smooth and combined.
• Cover and refrigerate for up to 24 hours.

For Rolls
• Preheat oven to 350 degrees F.
• Coat a 9 x 13–inch baking dish with cooking spray.
• Unroll pizza dough onto a cutting board and press into approximately a 13 x 18–inch rectangle.
• Top with ham and cheese slices, alternating between swiss and gouda cheese slices.
• Starting on the longer side of the rectangle, roll up the edge tightly.
• When you reach the end, pinch the seam together and flip the roll so that the seam is facedown.
• Cut into 12 slices, approximately 1 inch thick.
• Arrange in prepared baking dish.
• Bake for 15–20 minutes, or until crust is slightly golden.
• Remove from oven and brush glaze evenly over the rolls.
• Bake for additional 5 minutes, or until crust is golden.
• Serve warm.

Supermodel Hint
*These mouthwatering party rolls make a great appetizer.
Save this recipe for the holidays; your family
will love you for it!*

Jenn Durr's Lobster-Stuffed Eggs

Serves 2–3 people (makes 8 servings).

Makeup:

4 hard-boiled eggs
1/4 pound cooked lobster (about 1/2 cup), finely
    chopped
2 radishes, finely chopped
2 tablespoons finely chopped scallions
2 tablespoons finely chopped celery
2 tablespoons mayonnaise (or plain yogurt)
2 teaspoons lemon juice
1/8 teaspoon hot sauce, such as Tabasco
2 teaspoons salt
2 teaspoons lemon pepper
1/2 cup finely shredded green cabbage, for garnish
1/2 cup finely shredded red cabbage, for garnish

Application:

- Halve the eggs crosswise and remove yolks.
- Carefully rinse egg whites in warm water and drain upside down on a paper towel.
- In a small bowl, mash egg yolks.
- In a medium bowl, combine lobster, egg yolks, radishes, scallions, celery, mayonnaise (or yogurt), lemon juice, and hot sauce.
- Add salt and lemon pepper.
- Stir all ingredients together thoroughly.
- Divide cabbage evenly onto plates, forming nest on each.
- Fill each egg white with lobster mixture and arrange eggs in the nest.

Supermodel Hint

You would think the fresher the egg, the better, right? Not quite. Super-fresh eggs can be impossible to peel, leaving you with pockmarked, sad eggs. Of course, you don't want to let them get too old!

Ladybug Mozzarella and Tomato

Makes 24 servings.

Makeup:

2 large, fresh mozzarella cheese balls (approximately
 8 ounces each, but size may vary by packaging)
1 teaspoon paprika, for garnish
24 cherry or grape tomatoes
24 fresh small basil leaves
12 whole black olives
2 tablespoons balsamic vinegar
1/2 teaspoon cornstarch

Application:

- Slice mozzarella carefully and evenly into 24 slices of equal size.
- Place mozzarella slices on a cold platter.
- Sprinkle a small amount of paprika on the mozzarella slices.
- Place one small basil leaf on each slice.
- Slice the cherry or grape tomatoes in half lengthwise.
- With a small knife, carefully make a small 1/4-inch slice at one end of each tomato slice.
- Place one tomato half on each mozzarella slice, on top of the basil.
- Carefully tuck each side of the sliced tomato in slightly, to simulate wings.
- Slice off the closed ends of the black olives and place in front of the tomato slices.
- Mix 1/2 teaspoon of cornstarch with just enough balsamic vinegar to thicken the balsamic vinegar to a paste.
- Place two small drops on the "back" of each tomato slice. If you have one, an eyedropper is helpful for this step.
- Place in refrigerator and serve chilled. Do not cover, or you will ruin the dots on the tomatoes.

Supermodel Hint

Use the photo above to help guide you in the assembly of this fanciful dish. Miss Divina's sweet little nephew and nieces, Jeffrey, Dylan, and Brooklyn, love to help her assemble these! But they love to devour them even more!

Miss Kitty Hawke's Stuffed Clams

Serves 4–6 people (makes 24 clams).

Makeup:

24 small cherrystone clams (any variety clams can be
   substituted if needed)
1/2 cup water
1/4 cup white wine
2 tablespoons extra-virgin olive oil
2 teaspoons finely minced garlic
1 small white onion, finely chopped
1 small red onion, finely chopped
1/4 cup bread crumbs
2 tablespoons finely chopped capers
2 tablespoons clam broth (leftover after steaming crabs)
1 tablespoon hot sauce, such as Tabasco
4 strips of bacon, fried and crumbled
1/4 cup finely grated parmesan cheese

Application:

- Clean clams and place in a large covered pot containing water and wine.
- Steam clams until they open.
- Set aside and let cool in the broth.
- While clams cool, heat sauté pan over low heat.
- Add olive oil, garlic, and onions and sauté for 5 minutes, or until onions are golden brown.
- Remove from heat and add bread crumbs, capers, 2 tablespoons of the clam broth, and hot sauce.
- Combine well and set aside.
- Remove clams from their shells and finely chop the clam meat.
- Add clams and bacon to bread crumbs mixture and mix well.
- Preheat oven to broil.
- Rinse off clam shells and dry with paper towel.
- Stuff each shell with bread crumbs mixture, mounding slightly.
- Gently compress mixture into shell.
- Place stuffed shells on a baking sheet and sprinkle with parmesan cheese.
- Broil for 1 minute, or until cheese is melted, but do not overbroil.
- Serve immediately.

Supermodel Hint

It was a cold, windswept day on the North Carolina coast when Miss Divina first sampled this recipe of her dear friend and fellow supermodel Miss Kitty. Her name may imply cuddly and soft, but she is genuine alley cat!

My-Film-Has-Been-Panned Pizza Dip

Serves 8–10 people.

Makeup:

1 (8-ounce) package cream cheese, room temperature
1/2 cup milk
1 cup mozzarella cheese, divided
1/2 cup grated parmesan cheese
1/2 teaspoon garlic powder
1 cup tomato pasta sauce, or My Italian Cousin René's
   Sauce di Pomodoro (see p. 207)
2 tablespoons dried Italian seasoning, divided
1/2 cup black olives, sliced
salt and freshly ground pepper to taste
fresh french bread, sliced

Application:

- Preheat oven to 400 degrees F.
- In a small saucepan, combine cream cheese and milk over medium heat. Whisk together until smooth.
- Mix in 1/2 cup mozzarella, parmesan cheese, and garlic powder.
- Stir until melted.
- Cook for 5 minutes, or until thickened.
- Pour mixture into an ovenproof dish and use a rubber spatula or spoon to smooth out.
- Pour pasta sauce on top of cheese mixture and smooth out evenly.
- Season with 1 tablespoon Italian seasoning.
- Sprinkle remaining 1/2 cup mozzarella over the top.
- Top with remaining 1 tablespoon Italian seasoning and sliced olives.
- Place baking dish in oven and bake for 8–10 minutes, or until bubbly.
- Remove from oven and serve immediately with crusty bread slices.

Supermodel Hint

Instead of pizza night, why not pizza-dip night! That campy movie you'll be watching will be just as terrible as if you had pizza!

No—No Nanette's La Tomate et Bleu Dip

Makeup:

1/2 cup crumbled blue cheese
1/2 cup red wine vinegar
2 tablespoons extra-virgin olive oil
1 tablespoon ketchup
1 teaspoon sugar
1/2 teaspoon worcestershire sauce
1/2 teaspoon hot sauce, such as Tabasco
1 cup cottage cheese

Application:

- In a large mixing bowl, add blue cheese, vinegar, olive oil, ketchup, sugar, worcestershire sauce, and hot sauce.
- Stir until all ingredients are mixed thoroughly.
- Add mixture to a blender with cottage cheese.
- Blend at medium speed until smooth.
- Pour into a bowl and chill for about 30 minutes before serving.

Serving note: Serve with chicken wings and fresh vegetables of all colors, such as carrots; red, green, and yellow bell peppers; celery; cauliflower; mushrooms; cherry tomatoes; and broccoli.

Note: To make a dressing instead of a dip, simply omit the cottage cheese and blend all ingredients together. Chill for at least 30 minutes before serving.

Supermodel Hint

I just adore this spicy little dip! It's the perfect accoutrement for Miss Divina's
Critic's Choice Chicken Wings and fresh vegetables.

Old Appian Way Country Pâté

Makeup:

1 pound ground veal round
1 pound ground pork sausage
1/2 pound ground turkey
1/2 pound cooked chicken livers
1 cup port
1/2 cup brandy
1 cup chopped onions
1/2 cup chopped celery
3 tablespoons chopped garlic
1 tablespoon freshly ground black pepper
2 1/2 teaspoons salt
1/2 teaspoon cayenne pepper
1/4 teaspoon dried french thyme
1/4 teaspoon dried oregano
11 bay leaves, divided
2 egg whites
1 cup whole pistachios
1/4 cup finely chopped parsley
24 slices bacon

Application:

- In a mixing bowl, combine veal, pork, turkey, and chicken livers.
- Add port, brandy, onions, celery, garlic, pepper, salt, cayenne, thyme, and oregano.
- Mix well, place 3 bay leaves on top, and cover with plastic wrap.
- Refrigerate for 24 hours.
- After 24 hours, remove meat mixture from the refrigerator and drain, discarding the liquid.
- Remove and discard bay leaves.
- Preheat oven to 350 degrees F.
- Using a food processor, grind the meat until thoroughly mixed.
- Transfer mixture to a large bowl. Add egg whites, pistachios, and parsley. Mix well.
- Line bottom and sides of two earthenware terrines with bacon. Leave enough of the bacon overlapping all sides of the pan so that the bacon will completely cover the top of the mixture when folded over.
- Divide mixture equally between the two pans, pressing down with your fingers.
- Fold overlapping bacon slices over mixture to encase it.
- Top each pâté with 4 bay leaves.
- Set the two pans in a roasting pan large enough to accommodate both and place in oven.
- Bake for 1 hour, or until the internal temperature reaches 200 degrees F.
- Remove from oven and carefully drain off any excess fat, by pouring or by using a baster.
- Cover pans with aluminum foil and refrigerate for at least 8 hours before serving.
- Remove and discard bay leaves.
- Cut pâtés into 1/2-inch slices and serve.

Supermodel Hint

Country pâté is best paired with French dijon mustard spread over warm sliced french bread and delicious gherkins (also known as cornichons) on the side.

Old Roma Goat Cheese and Figs

Makeup:

10 fresh figs
4 ounces goat cheese, room temperature
2 tablespoons maple syrup
2 tablespoons fresh honey, divided
1/2 teaspoon cinnamon, divided
sliced almonds, for garnish
pomegranate seeds, for garnish (optional)

Application:

- Remove the stems of the figs and, without cutting completely through, cut into quarters from the top down to the base of the fig.
- In a small mixing bowl, add goat cheese, maple syrup, 1 tablespoon honey, and 1/4 teaspoon cinnamon, and mix thoroughly.
- Place cheese mixture in a sandwich bag.
- Snip the corner to allow a small hole for piping the cheese.
- Pipe cheese into the center of each fig.
- Garnish with sliced almonds and pomegranate seeds (optional).
- Drizzle remaining 1 tablespoon honey over the figs, sprinkle remaining 1/4 teaspoon cinnamon on top, and serve.

Supermodel Hint

Ripe figs are very delicate and highly perishable. Store them in the refrigerator in a shallow plastic storage container lined with paper towels and loosely covered with plastic wrap for no more than three days.

One Cheesy Cheese Ball

Makeup:

2 (8-ounce) packages cream cheese, room temperature
3 1/2 cups shredded sharp cheddar cheese
1/2 cup grated parmesan cheese
1/2 cup crumbled blue cheese
1/2 cup crumbled bacon
1/4 cup mayonnaise
1/2 teaspoon dried onion flakes
1/2 teaspoon dried oregano
1/2 teaspoon worcestershire sauce
1/2 teaspoon dried chives
1/2 teaspoon garlic powder
1 cup chopped deluxe mixed nuts
1/2 cup chopped pecans

Application:

- In a medium mixing bowl, combine cream cheese, cheddar cheese, parmesan cheese, blue cheese, bacon, mayonnaise, dried onion flakes, oregano, worcestershire sauce, chives, and garlic powder.
- Mix well.
- Shape mixture into a ball.
- Place mixed nuts and pecans in a large plastic bag, and crush with a rolling pin.
- Pour crushed nuts on a large plate.
- Roll cheese ball over crushed nuts.
- Refrigerate for at least 2 hours before serving
- Remove from refrigerator about 30 minutes before you are ready to serve.

Serving note: Serve with assorted crackers and Granny Smith apple wedges.

Supermodel Hint

*I insisted Miss Divina include my favorite cheese ball in this book.
I often sit up late at night and eat in bed while watching late-night
reality shows! There's nothing better than cheese
and crackers in bed, unless it's a man!*

Pâté Supermodel Laplagne

Makeup:

8 ounces chicken livers
1/2 cup chicken broth (or 3 bouillon cubes with 2 cups
    boiling water)
1 medium onion, chopped
1/4 cup butter
4 slices bacon, cooked and chopped
1/4 cup dijon mustard
1 teaspoon fennel seeds
1/4 teaspoon dried french thyme
garlic powder and freshly ground black pepper to taste
1/4 cup Grand Marnier or sherry
1 small red onion, very thinly sliced; 1 jar gherkins
    (also known as cornichons); and french bread,
    thinly sliced, for serving

Application:

- Mix chicken livers, chicken broth, onion, butter, bacon, mustard, fennel seeds, thyme, garlic powder, and pepper in saucepan.
- Heat to boiling, stirring occasionally.
- Turn heat down to low and simmer uncovered until livers are cooked thoroughly, about 10–15 minutes.
- Drain and reserve liquid for later.
- Put mixture and Grand Marnier or sherry into a blender and blend until smooth.
- Add reserved liquid only when needed if the pâté is too dry; too much liquid will result in the pâté not solidifying.
- Spoon into a serving dish or jar and chill for 3 hours.
- Serve with red onions, gherkins, and your favorite fresh, warm, thinly sliced french bread, all placed on side dishes.
- Place onion ring on bread, spread pâté on bread, and top with one sliced gherkin if desired or eat gherkins separately.

Supermodel Hint

*Kings, princes, presidents, and a few paupers throughout the centuries have been seduced with this family recipe.
I should know! I keep all the scandalous diaries under lock and key!*

Provence-Girl Prawn and Scallop Fondue

Serves 4 people.

Makeup:

24 large sea scallops, cooked
24 large prawns, cooked
2 tablespoons extra-virgin olive oil
1 small red onion, finely chopped
1 clove garlic, finely chopped
1 (4-ounce) can tomato paste
4 cups sharp white cheddar cheese, grated
2 tablespoons white wine
2 teaspoons *herbes de provence*
1 teaspoon salt
1 teaspoon freshly ground black pepper
3 cups chicken or fish stock

Application:

- Divide scallops and prawns among four plates.
- Cover and chill until needed.
- Heat olive oil in a medium saucepan over medium heat.
- Add onion, garlic, and tomato paste and sauté for 10 minutes.
- Add cheese, wine, *herbes de provence*, salt, and pepper.
- Stir for 2–3 minutes.
- Transfer mixture to a blender and puree until smooth.
- Transfer mixture to a fondue pot.
- Add chicken or fish stock into fondue pot.
- Heat until simmering.
- Transfer fondue pot to table and adjust flame so stock continues to simmer.
- Dip the scallops and prawns in the fondue with fondue forks and enjoy.

Note: If you have seafood lovers and want to add to the seafood count, do so!

Supermodel Hint

Prawns must be washed and deveined. If the seafood is jumbo sized, it is best to slice it in half or cut it into bite-size pieces so it is not too dense to cook thoroughly.

She–Deviled Eggs des Pyrénées

Makes 12 servings.

Makeup:

6 hard-boiled eggs
2 tablespoons dijon mustard
2 tablespoons hot dog relish
2 tablespoons mayonnaise
2 tablespoons minced onion
1 teaspoon garlic powder
1 teaspoon dill seed
1 teaspoon salt
1 teaspoon pepper
1 teaspoon paprika, for garnish
sliced black olives, for garnish
1 carrot, peeled and shaved, for garnish

Application:

- Slice boiled eggs in halves.
- Carefully remove yolks as not to break egg whites.
- Add yolks to a medium mixing bowl.
- Carefully rinse egg whites in warm water and drain upside down on a paper towel.
- Crush yolks with a fork and add mustard, relish, mayonnaise, onion, garlic powder, dill seed, salt, and pepper.
- Mix until well blended and somewhat smooth.
- With a small teaspoon, stuff egg whites with mixture. Alternatively, if you have a frosting piping bag, use that to create a more decorative filling.
- Sprinkle with paprika, and garnish each egg half with two small peels of carrot in an X pattern and one slice of olive.

Note: To make egg salad for sandwiches, omit the carrot, chop the egg whites and black olives and mix in with all ingredients, and serve on pita or your favorite bread.

Supermodel Hint

In the Vasilina household, these eggs are a must at every family or holiday gathering.
But make lots of them, for they go fast and leave a trail of wide smiles whenever they touch the lips of anyone lucky enough to be at Miss Divina's festivities.

Makeup:

1 large, ripe honeydew melon
1 large, ripe cantaloupe
1/2 pound prosciutto, thinly sliced
fresh seedless grapes, red and green
fresh mint leaves, for garnish

Application:

- Cut each melon into quarters. Then cut those quarters into halves.
- Cut peel off of each melon slice with a sharp knife.
- Cut each melon slice into 1/2-inch-thick slices.
- If the prosciutto is packaged, carefully separate the slices from each other. The slices tear very easily, so take your time to carefully separate.
- Wrap prosciutto diagonally around each melon slice and place on serving platter.
- Alternating melon variety, surround platter with prosciutto-wrapped melon.
- Place grapes with stems in the center of the melon on the plate and garnish with mint leaves.
- Cover and chill before serving.

Note: Guests may eat the mint if desired.

Supermodel Hint

To get your man hot and bothered, eat this seductively as you would eat a juicy strawberry. A hot summer evening will help entice him to remove a few garments as well.

Silky Satin Cheese Fondue

Makeup:

1 1/2 cups dry white wine
1 tablespoon cornstarch
1 tablespoon finely ground black pepper
1 garlic clove, finely minced
1/2 pound emmental cheese, coarsely grated
   (approximately 2 cups)
1/2 pound gruyère cheese, coarsely grated
   (approximately 2 cups)

Application:

- Add wine to a medium saucepan and bring to a simmer over moderate heat.
- Stir together cornstarch, pepper, and garlic in a cup.
- Gradually add cheese to pot, stirring constantly in a zigzag pattern (not a circular motion) to prevent cheese from balling up.
- Cook until cheese is melted and creamy; do not let boil.
- Stir cornstarch mixture again and stir into fondue. Bring fondue to a simmer and cook, stirring, until thickened, 5–8 minutes.
- Transfer to fondue pot set over a flame.

Suggestions on what to dip:

cubes of french bread
cubes of apple and pear
roasted potatoes
julienned raw red bell pepper
blanched broccoli florets
any fresh vegetables, such as cauliflower, tomatoes, and so on

Supermodel Hint

Emmental and gruyère are the most commonly used cheeses in a classic fondue, but you can try other low-moisture cheeses. Not every fondue recipe calls for cornstarch, but I find it keeps the cheese and wine from separating.

Spicy Mexican Pool-boy Bean Dip

Makeup:

1 (16-ounce) can chili con carne with beans
1 (8-ounce) package cream cheese, room temperature
8 ounces extra-sharp cheddar cheese
1 tablespoon hot sauce, such as Tabasco
1 tablespoon taco sauce
chili peppers to taste
corn chips (blue, yellow, and/or white), for serving

Application:

- Mix all ingredients in a large saucepan.
- Heat over medium heat, stirring constantly until cheese is melted.
- Serve hot in a fondue pot or serving bowl.
- Serve with all varieties of corn chips.

Supermodel Hint

Beware! This dish is more addictive than a boatload of steamy gossip! And just spicy enough that you may need to jump into the pool with the pool boy to cool off!

Steal His Art–ichoke Dip

Makeup:

1 (12-ounce) jar artichoke hearts, well drained
1 cup mayonnaise (or plain yogurt)
1 cup grated parmesan cheese
1 clove garlic, minced or crushed
1 tablespoon dijon mustard
1 teaspoon lemon juice
1/8 teaspoon salt
french bread, thinly sliced, for serving

Application:

- Preheat oven to 350 degrees F.
- Place artichokes, mayonnaise (or yogurt), parmesan cheese, garlic, and mustard in a blender.
- Process until chopped, not pureed.
- Add lemon juice and salt.
- Put into a lightly greased, shallow baking dish.
- Bake for 20–25 minutes, or until lightly brown on top.
- Blot off any excess oil with a paper towel.
- Transfer to a serving dish and serve hot with thinly sliced and toasted french bread.

Supermodel Hint

This dip can be made ahead up to 24 hours, refrigerated, and reheated. Sprinkle with parmesan cheese and bake in the oven just before serving to give the dip a bit of a crispy crust everyone loves.

Makeup:

1/3 pound ground Italian sausage
1 pound large cremini mushrooms (approximately 36 mushrooms about 2 inches in diameter)
1 small red onion, finely chopped
1 small green bell pepper, finely chopped
4 tablespoons butter, divided
1/2 cup bread crumbs
1/2 teaspoon salt
1/2 teaspoon pepper
1/2 teaspoon ground french thyme
1/2 teaspoon ground turmeric
1/4 cup finely shredded parmesan cheese

Application:

- Preheat oven to 350 degrees F.
- Clean mushrooms and cut off stems.
- Cook sausage in a skillet and set aside to cool.
- Finely chop mushroom stems to measure out to 1/3 cup.
- Cook and stir 1/3 cup chopped mushroom stems, onion, and green bell pepper in 3 tablespoons butter until tender, about 5 minutes.
- Remove from heat.
- Stir in sausage, bread crumbs, salt, pepper, thyme, and turmeric.
- Heat remaining 1 tablespoon butter in a baking dish until melted.
- Fill mushroom caps with the stuffing mixture.
- Place mushrooms filled sides up in baking dish.
- Sprinkle parmesan cheese on tops and bake for 15 minutes.
- Reset oven control to broil (500 degrees F).
- Broil for 2 minutes. Serve hot.

Supermodel Hint

You'll eat these up just like juicy rumors about your best girlfriend's sex life! And if she doesn't have one, make up something! Be clever enough to keep them glued to your saucy rumors!

Makes 8 sandwiches.

Makeup:

1 small loaf French- or Italian-style country bread
   (enough for 16 slices of sandwich bread)
horseradish sauce, to taste
1/2 pound paper-thin, air-dried imported
   French-style ham
1/2 pound gruyère cheese, thinly sliced
1/2 cup butter, room temperature (enough to butter
   the bread)
1/4 pound extra-aged white cheddar cheese, grated

Application:

- If needed, cut bread into 16 (3/8-inch) slices.
- Spread small amount of horseradish sauce on 8 bread slices.
- Place ham and gruyère cheese on top.
- Top sandwiches with remaining bread slices.
- Heat a heavy skillet over medium heat.
- Preheat broiler.
- Butter one outer side of sandwich.
- Place sandwich, butter side down, in skillet, weighed down with heavy plate.
- When sandwiches are golden brown on bottom, butter faceup side and flip.
- Brown other side.
- Remove and place on broiling sheet.
- Sprinkle on white cheddar cheese.
- Heat under broiler until cheese melts and browns.
- Serve warm.

Supermodel Hint

If you cannot find French-style ham in your local gourmet store, you may substitute Italian prosciutto or Spanish jamón in its place.

Sweet-and-Dour Meatballs

Makeup:

1 pound lean ground turkey or lean ground beef
1 1/2 cups bread crumbs
2 eggs
1 tablespoon salt
1 tablespoon freshly ground black pepper
1 (24-ounce) jar mixed fruit jelly or jam
1 (8-ounce) jar dijon mustard

Application:

- Mix ground turkey, bread crumbs, eggs, salt, and pepper.
- When completely mixed, create cocktail-size meatballs, about 1-inch in diameter.
- Brown meatballs in a skillet.
- Drain any grease that may be left after meatballs are half cooked.
- In a medium saucepan, mix jelly and mustard.
- Simmer until sauce is smooth.
- Place browned meatballs in a large saucepan and add mustard-and-jelly sauce.
- Heat on low for 60 minutes.
- Serve hot in a covered dish with sufficient sauce to cover meatballs.

Note: You may serve with toothpicks or cocktail forks, or you may also use a slotted spoon if you will be serving this dish as a course or in a buffet.

Supermodel Hint

This recipe is shared by one of Miss Divina's bitter playwright friends. "She" had a gender-identity crisis and changed her name to Jarrina, but Miss Divina still calls her Bill.

Makes 20 servings.

Makeup:

1 cup couscous
1 chicken breast
1/4 cup toasted pine nuts
2 tablespoons extra-virgin olive oil, plus additional
  for drizzle garnish
1 teaspoon orange zest, grated
2 tablespoons freshly squeezed orange juice
2 tablespoons finely chopped fresh basil, divided
2 teaspoons dried mint, crumbled, divided
1 teaspoon salt, divided
1 teaspoon freshly ground black pepper, divided
20 grape leaves
2 tablespoons freshly squeezed lemon juice
1/2 cup chicken broth

Application:

- Prepare outdoor grill according to your specific grill instructions or preheat broiler to 500 degrees F.
- In a small bowl, soak couscous in cold water for 1–2 hours prior to preparing grape leaves.
- Drain couscous and set aside on a paper towel to dry. Cover with second paper towel.
- When dry, place couscous in a small bowl and set aside.
- Grill or broil chicken breast for 10 minutes, or until cooked on both sides.
- Set chicken aside to cool.
- Return to couscous and add pine nuts, olive oil, orange zest, orange juice, 1 tablespoon basil, 1 teaspoon mint, 1/2 teaspoon salt, and 1/2 teaspoon pepper. Mix well.
- Shred chicken into very small pieces.
- Add chicken to pine nut mixture and mix well.
- Place clean sheet of waxed paper on work surface.
- Lay out one grape leaf at a time on waxed paper.
- Place approximately 2 tablespoons of mixture lengthwise on each grape leaf. Adjust the amount of mixture according to the leaf size.
- Gently roll up each grape leaf tightly and place seam down in a large sauté pan with lid.
- Pack leaves together closely and sprinkle on lemon juice and remaining 1 tablespoon basil, 1 teaspoon mint, 1/2 teaspoon salt, and 1/2 teaspoon pepper.
- Pour chicken broth over leaves.
- Cover with lid slightly ajar.
- Simmer for 10–15 minutes.
- Place cooked leaves on plate and chill.
- Serve cold with drizzled olive oil over tops.

Supermodel Hint

*In Italy, grape leaves are available in every city or corner market. But in America,
they are usually sold in jars in specialty and gourmet food stores.*

The Queen's Tea Sand-Wishes

Makes 24 tea sandwiches.

Makeup:

12 slices white sandwich bread
1/2 cup salted butter, room temperature (enough to butter the bread)
8–10 ounces thinly sliced roast beef or chicken breast or 1 cucumber, peeled, sliced, and seeded

Application:

- Butter slices of bread on one side.
- Lay roast beef, chicken, or cucumbers evenly on the buttered side of half of the bread slices, one variety per sandwich.
- Top sandwiches with remaining bread slices, buttered side down.
- Cut off crusts and cut sandwiches diagonally in quarters to create triangles.
- Arrange on serving plate.

Serving note: Serve with fresh, hot loose-leaf tea.

Supermodel Hint

Every man wishes he could be alone with Miss Divina to sample her sandwiches. It makes for quite a delicious afternoon. She entices them with all three varieties of sandwiches.

Sinful Soups

What the people want is glamour

Il Postino and the Farmer's Daughter's Gazpacho (p. 105)

The kitchen is the heart of your home. Do you love to eat well? To entertain? To sit with your admiring friends around the kitchen table? Even if this doesn't sound like you, read on. This section will still help you to make yourself exciting, breathtaking, and desirable—not only as a host, but also as a sex kitten in the kitchen. Men will grovel at your feet!

Okay, it's time to pull out the pots and pans and get the first courses going. Soup is a good start after the hors d'oeuvres you plan to serve. Soups are always a crowd-pleaser, and no matter what season of the year, Miss Divina has you covered.

Be careful not to turn the heat up too high in the kitchen! You might not make it to the dining table!

Soups should most always be made the day before or the morning of your dinner parties. Most soups are so easy, even I, "88 Thumbs" Blanche, can make them with ease. Look over the delicious recipe options Miss Divina has given you in this book and choose the one that suits the type of menu you will be serving and the season of the year. Creamy Spinach and Green Pea Soup à la Von Stieger and Ginger-Man Irish Potato and Italian Sausage Soup are just two superb recipes for hearty soups perfect for a cold and dreary winter day. They'll warm up your bones and maybe even make you want to cuddle with your significant other.

If it's a hot and steamy summer day, you'll probably want a light and cold soup, like Cool-as-a-Creamy-Cucumber Soup or Il Postino and the Farmer's Daughter Gazpacho, or a lovely summery fruit soup, such as Make-My-Mouth-Water-melon Gazpacho. Oh! My mouth is watering right now!

Preparing the perfect meal, like choosing the perfect accessories to go with the perfect dress, can be draining. But don't succumb to stress. Tomayto, tomahto! However you say it, get your ingredients together and get chopping!

Haute Couture Creamy and Silky Asparagus Soup

Pumpkin Soup He'll Fall For

The Great Wall of Chinese Pork Noodle Soup (p. 113)

Makes 10–12 servings, varying depending on serving size.

Makeup:

1 (3-pound) beef chuck roast
1 cup beef stock or broth
1/2 cup barley
1 bay leaf
2 tablespoons vegetable oil
3 carrots, chopped
3 celery stalks, chopped
1 onion, chopped
1 (16-ounce) package frozen mixed vegetables
6 cups water plus more as needed
6 beef bouillon cubes
1 (28-ounce) can chopped stewed tomatoes
1/4 teaspoon ground black pepper
salt and pepper to taste

Application:

- In a slow cooker, add beef chuck roast and beef stock or broth.
- Cook chuck roast until very tender (approximately 4 hours on high), adding barley and bay leaf during last hour of cooking.
- Remove meat, and chop into bite-size pieces.
- Discard bay leaf and set beef, broth, and barley aside (you will add these back into the final soup).
- Heat oil in a large stockpot over medium-high heat.
- Sauté carrots, celery, onion, and frozen mixed vegetables until tender.
- Add water, beef bouillon cubes, chopped stewed tomatoes, 1/4 teaspoon pepper, and beef/barley mixture.
- Bring to a boil, reduce heat, and simmer for 1 1/2 hours.
- Add more water if needed.
- Season with additional salt and pepper to taste.

Supermodel Hint

To enhance the flavor of this soup, use beef stock in place of water. It will make a richer flavor that is guaranteed to please even the most finicky person at your table.

Makes 10–12 servings, varying depending on serving size.

Makeup:

3 chicken breasts, deboned
1/4 cup bacon drippings
1 tablespoon salted butter
1 onion, diced
2 celery stalks, diced
1/3 cup diced green bell pepper
6 cups chicken broth
1/3 cup long-grain rice, uncooked
1 (16-ounce) can stewed tomatoes, undrained
1 tablespoon worcestershire sauce
1 bay leaf
2 teaspoons salt, or to taste
2 teaspoons ground black pepper, or to taste
2 teaspoons garlic powder, or to taste
1 (14-ounce) can okra
2 tablespoons parsley, chopped
4 green onions, chopped, for garnish

Application:

- Brown chicken breast with bacon drippings on skillet.
- Remove chicken and let cool.
- Cut chicken into small pieces.
- In a large skillet, melt butter over medium heat.
- Sauté onions, celery, and green bell pepper in butter.
- In a large soup pot, add broth, sautéed vegetables, and chicken.
- Add rice, stewed tomatoes, worcestershire sauce, bay leaf, salt, pepper, and garlic powder.
- Simmer for 3/4–1 hour.
- Add okra and parsley and return to heat.
- Simmer for another 10–15 minutes.
- Remove and discard bay leaf.
- Adjust seasoning to taste, adding additional salt only if necessary. Be careful to avoid too much salt.
- Garnish with chopped fresh green onions just prior to serving.

Makes 10–12 servings, varying depending on serving size

Makeup:

1 tablespoon extra-virgin olive oil
2 cloves garlic, minced
1 small onion, diced
1 tablespoon lemon juice
4 cups peeled, seeded, and thinly sliced cucumbers, divided
1 1/2 cups vegetable broth
1/2 teaspoon salt
1/4 teaspoon freshly ground pepper
1/4 teaspoon cayenne pepper
1 avocado, diced
1/4 cup chopped fresh parsley
1/2 cup low-fat plain yogurt
fresh mint leaves

Application:

- Heat olive oil in a large saucepan over medium-high heat.
- Add garlic and onion and cook, stirring occasionally, until tender, 1–4 minutes.
- Add lemon juice and cook for 1 minute.
- Add 3 1/2 cups cucumbers, broth, salt, pepper, and cayenne; bring to a boil.
- Reduce heat and cook at gentle simmer until cucumbers are soft, 6–8 minutes.
- Transfer soup to a blender.
- Add avocado and parsley; blend on low speed until smooth.
- Refrigerate for 4 hours before serving.
- Remove chilled soup from refrigerator and stir in yogurt until mixed thoroughly.
- Pour soup into serving bowls.
- Just before serving, garnish with remaining cucumbers and mint leaves.

Supermodel Hint

*If it's a hot summer evening and the man across the table from you is equally as hot,
I recommend this soup to cool things down before they get too hot to handle!*

Makes 10–12 servings, varying depending on serving size.

Makeup:

1/4 cup butter
2 cups chicken broth, divided
1 (8–12-ounce) package frozen spinach
1 (8–12-ounce) package frozen green peas
1/2 cup flour, plus additional as needed
4 cups warm water
1 teaspoon oregano, or to taste
1 teaspoon salt, or to taste
1 teaspoon pepper, or to taste
1 teaspoon sage, or to taste
1 teaspoon tarragon, or to taste
1 teaspoon garlic powder, or to taste
1 cup milk or half-and-half
1/2 cup sour cream, for garnish
paprika, for garnish

Application:

- In a large pot, melt butter and 2 tablespoons of broth over medium heat.
- Sauté spinach and peas in butter/broth.
- Remove from heat and add flour.
- Add water and remaining chicken broth to pot.
- Add seasonings and transfer to a blender or food processor. Puree until smooth.
- Transfer pureed vegetables/broth back to pot and simmer over low heat for about 1 hour.
- Add milk or half-and-half.
- Sift in more flour to thicken if desired.
- Simmer another 1 hour or so.
- Adjust seasonings if needed.
- Serve with a dab of sour cream in center and paprika sprinkled on top.

Supermodel Hint

You can definitely add cream to your soup. Whether you use a few tablespoons or a few cups, cream gives soup a silky, rich flavor and a mouthful of deliciousness.

Crème de la Crème Chestnut Soup

Makes 10–12 servings, varying depending on serving size.

Makeup:

4 slices bacon
2 tablespoons unsalted butter
2 large shallots, roughly chopped
1 medium carrot, roughly chopped
1 celery stalk, roughly chopped
10 cups chicken stock
2 1/2 pounds fresh chestnuts, roasted and peeled,
  or 2 (15-ounce) jars whole roasted chestnuts, drained
1 tablespoon french thyme
1 tablespoon dijon mustard
1 bay leaf
1/2 cup heavy cream
1 teaspoon freshly grated nutmeg
salt and freshly ground black pepper to taste

Application:

- Fry bacon in a medium saucepan over medium-high heat until crisp. Chop when cool and set aside.
- Add butter, shallots, carrot, and celery to saucepan; cook, stirring occasionally, until vegetables are soft, 5–7 minutes.
- Add stock, bacon, chestnuts, thyme, mustard, and bay leaf; bring to a boil.
- Reduce heat to medium; cook, slightly covered, until chestnuts are very tender, about 25 minutes.
- Remove from heat and let cool slightly.
- Discard bay leaf.
- Working in batches, puree soup in a blender until smooth.
- Return soup to saucepan and place over medium heat.
- Stir in cream, nutmeg, salt, and pepper; cook until soup is slightly thick, about 5 minutes more.

Supermodel Hint

This fabulous soup is just right for a holiday menu. If you are planning an intimate dinner just for two, serve your man this soup before you roast his chestnuts by the fire!

Dizzy Dazie's Delicious, Hearty Bean Soup

Makes 10–12 servings, varying depending on serving size.

Makeup:

16 ounces dried bean soup mix
4 quarts water, plus additional as needed
1 1/2 cups chicken stock
1/4 cup butter
2 medium garlic cloves, minced, or 2 tablespoons preprepared minced garlic
2 tablespoons ground black pepper
2 tablespoons salt
1 teaspoon dried french thyme
1 teaspoon parsley
1 teaspoon oregano
1 bay leaf
2 carrots, peeled and thinly sliced
1 cup freshly grated romano cheese, for garnish
1/2 cup sour cream, for garnish (optional)
1/2 cup finely chopped green onions, for garnish

Application:

- Soak beans in cold water overnight.
- Skim and discard any float.
- Drain beans and combine with water in a soup pot.
- Bring to a boil over high heat, skimming float from surface.
- Add chicken stock, butter, garlic, pepper, salt, thyme, parsley, oregano, and bay leaf.
- Stir and reduce heat to a simmer.
- Simmer until beans are tender, about 3 1/2–4 hours.
- Skim foam from surface occasionally.
- After beans are cooked thoroughly, add carrots.
- Add additional water if soup is too thick for your individual taste.
- Simmer for additional 2 hours.
- When ready to serve, sprinkle romano cheese over individual servings, place 1 teaspoon of sour cream in center (optional), and sprinkle green onions on top.

Supermodel Hint

Float is the foam on the top of the soup or water. It is also Miss Divina's preferred method of transport during parades, above even a sedan chair.

Don't-Leek-This-Out Soup à la Madame Yvonne

Makes 10–12 servings, varying depending on serving size.

Makeup:

1 bunch of leeks, chopped
1/4 cup extra-virgin olive oil or butter
2 or 3 ham hocks (or 1 cup crumbled bacon)
2 large onions, chopped
2 quarts water
2 cups chicken stock
4–5 large potatoes, peeled and whole
2 tablespoons black pepper, or to taste
1 teaspoon garlic salt, or to taste
2 medium carrots, peeled and whole
1 garlic clove, peeled (optional)

Application:

- Soak leeks for at least 1 hour in cold water. (Leek stalks often have lots of dirt inside them.)
- Rinse the leeks thoroughly after soaking. Set aside.
- In a medium skillet, heat olive oil (or butter) over medium heat.
- Sauté ham hocks and onions for 7–10 minutes.
- Heat water and chicken stock in a large pot over medium heat.
- Add leeks, potatoes, ham hocks, and onions.
- Season with pepper and garlic salt.
- Add carrots and, if desired, garlic clove.
- Simmer 2 hours.
- After 2 hours, remove ham hocks and set aside to cool.
- With a potato masher, in the soup pot, lightly mash potatoes and carrots into chunks; this will thicken the soup.
- Once ham hocks are cool, remove meat from bones and add meat to the soup. Discard the bones, skin, and fat.
- Adjust seasonings as desired; it usually needs more salt, but don't overdo it!

Serving note: Serve hot with fresh sliced french bread.

Supermodel Hint

Leeks are a member of the onion family. Classical Romans and Greeks were very fond of leeks. Roman emperor Nero was nicknamed Porrophagus, or "leek eater." But please, don't burn the house down when making this soup!

Makes 10–12 servings, varying depending on serving size.

Makeup:

2 tablespoons butter
1 large yellow onion, chopped
4 cups chicken stock or broth
4 medium white potatoes, chopped
4 kale stalks, chopped
3 medium carrots, chopped
1 tablespoon black pepper, or to taste
1 tablespoon garlic powder, or to taste
1 tablespoon ginger, or to taste
1 pound ground Italian sausage
6 slices bacon
6 green onions, chopped

Application:

- In a large pot, melt butter over medium heat.
- Add yellow onion and sauté until golden brown.
- Add chicken stock or broth, potatoes, kale, and carrots.
- Season with pepper, garlic powder, and ginger and simmer for 30 minutes.
- While soup simmers, brown and drain sausage and bacon slices.
- Chop bacon into small pieces.
- Add bacon and sausage to soup mixture.
- Simmer for 2 hours.
- Adjust seasonings if necessary.
- Garnish with green onions and serve.

Supermodel Hint

The only Irish famine you'll possibly experience is if you have too many hungry men at your table and they devour all this up! A natural occurrence at Miss Divina's table!

Makes 10–12 servings, varying depending on serving size.

Makeup:

2 tablespoons butter
1 pound thin asparagus, trimmed to remove woody stems and chopped
6 cups chicken stock
1 cup whipping cream
1 cup sour cream or plain yogurt, plus additional for garnish
1 bunch shallots, chopped, divided
1 teaspoon salt
1 teaspoon freshly ground black pepper
freshly grated parmesan cheese to taste, for garnish

Application:

- Heat butter in a skillet over medium heat.
- Add asparagus and sauté for about 2 minutes.
- Add chicken stock and whipping cream and decrease heat to a simmer.
- Simmer until asparagus are tender.
- Add sour cream (or yogurt) and half the chopped shallots.
- Season with salt and pepper.
- Simmer over low heat for at least 1 hour.
- Serve in a large serving bowl or individual bowls.
- When ready to serve, sprinkle parmesan cheese and remaining chopped shallots on top. As desired, also place a dab of sour cream (or yogurt) on the top.

Supermodel Hint

*To swirl sour cream, heat in microwave for 30–45 seconds to warm.
Mix and then use a spoon to create a number of nifty shapes.*

Makes 10–12 servings, varying depending on serving size.

Makeup:

2 1/2 tablespoons butter
1 onion, chopped
1 celery stalk with leaves, chopped
1 1/2 tablespoons chopped fresh basil
2 tablespoons all-purpose flour
1 (16-ounce) can stewed tomatoes
2 1/2 cups water
1 (3-ounce) can tomato paste
1 (28-ounce) can tomato sauce
1 1/2 cups whole milk or half-and-half, for a thicker, creamier soup
2 tablespoons brown sugar
1 teaspoon salt
1 teaspoon freshly ground coarse pepper
round bread loaves, one per guest
sour cream, for garnish
fresh celery leaves, for garnish

Application:

- Melt butter in a medium saucepan over low heat.
- Add onion, celery, and basil.
- Cook, stirring occasionally, until onion is slightly translucent.
- Stir in flour, stewed tomatoes, and water.
- Bring to a boil over medium heat and add tomato paste.
- Reduce heat to a simmer, cover, and simmer for 15 minutes.
- Remove from heat and let cool for 10 minutes.
- Add to a blender and puree until smooth.
- Add back to pot and add tomato sauce, milk (or half-and-half), brown sugar, salt, and pepper.
- Reheat soup.
- Cut tops off bread loaves and set aside.
- Hollow out each loaf, leaving enough side and bottom to keep soup in.
- Place bread bowl on plate and spoon in soup.
- Swirl sour cream on top, garnish with fresh celery leaves, place bread top over the soup, and serve.

Makes 10–12 servings, varying depending on serving size.

Makeup:

1/2 cup crusty french bread cut into 1-inch chunks
2 cucumbers, peeled and chopped
2 pounds tomatoes, coarsely chopped
4 green onions, coarsely chopped
1 red bell pepper, diced
1 red onion, coarsely chopped
1 clove garlic, peeled and chopped
1/4 cup balsamic vinegar
1/4 cup extra-virgin olive oil
1 cup water
1 teaspoon salt, or to taste
1 teaspoon pepper, or to taste
1 cup sour cream (optional)

Application:

- Soak bread for 30 minutes in a small bowl with just enough water to cover.
- After soaking, squeeze out moisture with your hands.
- Save 1/4 cup each of cucumbers, tomatoes, green onions, and red bell pepper for garnish.
- In a blender or food processor, puree bread, cucumbers, tomatoes, green onions, red bell pepper, red onion, garlic, vinegar, olive oil, and water until very smooth.
- Season with salt and pepper.
- Chill for 3–4 hours before serving.
- Garnish with chopped vegetables sprinkled on top, add a spoonful of sour cream in center of each bowl if desired, and serve.

Supermodel Hint

The first secret to a great gazpacho, if we assume your ingredients are ripe and your fridge is cold, is good olive oil, and lots of it.

Makes 10–12 servings, varying depending on serving size.

Makeup:

6 pounds seedless watermelon
2 tablespoons lime juice
2 tablespoons lemon juice
1 whole red chili pepper
1/2 cup sliced red onion
2 garlic cloves
1 zucchini, seeded and diced
1/3 cup minced mint (optional)
sea salt and freshly ground pepper to taste
mint, for garnish

Application:

- Cut watermelon into wedges and peel and seed.
- Put watermelon into a blender, in batches, and puree till smooth.
- Pass puree through colander or sieve to remove any remaining seeds.
- Pour half of the puree into a large bowl and the other half back into blender.
- Add lime and lemon juices, chili pepper, onion, and garlic and puree until smooth.
- Pour seasoned puree into large bowl with reserved puree and stir in zucchini and mint (optional).
- Season to taste with salt and pepper.
- Refrigerate until chilled thoroughly.
- Divide the soup among individual serving bowls, garnish with mint, and serve chilled.

Makes 10–12 servings, varying depending on serving size.

Makeup:

2 tablespoons butter
1/2 cup finely chopped onion
1/2 cup peeled and cubed potato
2 cups vegetable or fish broth
2 (15-ounce) cans creamed corn
1/2 cup finely chopped red bell pepper
1 teaspoon dried french thyme
1 teaspoon freshly ground black pepper
1 teaspoon salt
16 ounces freshly cracked crab (or 2 [6-ounce] cans crab meat)
2 cups half-and-half

Application:

- Melt butter in a medium saucepan over low heat.
- Add onion and potato and sauté.
- In a medium soup pot, stir together broth and corn
- Add onion, potato, red bell pepper, thyme, pepper, and salt.
- Simmer for 15 minutes.
- Add crab meat and half-and-half and simmer on low for 30 minutes. Stir occasionally.
- Serve hot.

Supermodel Hint

*If you want to feel like Miss Divina and fantasize
you are in Newport, Rhode Island, add some shrimp.
It'll be like a holiday by the shore!*

Muscleman Cream of Spinach Soup

Makes 10–12 servings, varying depending on serving size.

Makeup:

1/4 cup sweet butter
2 medium onions, chopped
8–12 ounces spinach (or any vegetable to make any variety of creamed soup)
1/2 cup flour
4 cups warm water
2 cups chicken broth
1 teaspoon nutmeg
1 teaspoon salt
1 teaspoon pepper
1 teaspoon garlic powder
1 cup milk or half-and-half
fresh spinach or parsley, chopped, for garnish
bread, for serving

Application:

- Melt butter in a medium saucepan over low heat.
- Sauté onions in butter.
- Clean and soak spinach.
- Add spinach and steam until slightly reduced in volume.
- Remove from heat, sift in flour, and blend together.
- In a large pot, add warm water, chicken broth, spinach, nutmeg, salt, pepper, and garlic powder.
- Simmer soup for about 1 hour.
- Add milk (or half-and-half).
- Stir and simmer for another 1 hour, stirring periodically.
- Garnish with freshly chopped spinach or parsley just before serving.
- Serve with warm, buttery bread.

Supermodel Hint

Soup is always better the next day, as is Miss Divina. She gets better with age also, even at the tender young age of twenty-three years (a number she's sticking with!).

Makes 10–12 servings, varying depending on serving size.

Makeup:

1/4 cup sweet butter
2 medium onions, chopped
1/2 cup flour
4 cups warm water
2 cups chicken broth
4 large carrots, peeled and chopped
3 medium russet potatoes, chopped
1/2 cup chopped celery
1 teaspoon nutmeg
1 teaspoon salt
1 teaspoon pepper
1 teaspoon garlic powder
1 cup milk or half-and-half
16 ounces clams, cooked and chopped
1 crisp slice of bacon per bowl, for garnish (optional)
bread bowl or gourmet bread, for serving

Application:

- Melt butter in a medium saucepan over low heat.
- Sauté chopped onions in butter.
- Remove from heat, sift in flour, and blend together.
- In a large pot, add warm water, chicken broth, onions, carrots, potatoes, celery, nutmeg, salt, pepper, and garlic powder.
- Simmer until vegetables are cooked, approximately 1 hour.
- Add milk (or half-and-half).
- Add clams and stir.
- Simmer for another 1 hour.
- Garnish with slice of bacon (optional) and serve in a fresh, warm bread bowl or with your favorite buttery gourmet bread on the side.

Supermodel Hint

If it's a blistering Nor'easter, or just a gentle mist outside, this soup is the perfect way to warm up.
The purr-fect accessory to this soup is a roaring hot fire and an equally hot, rugged man!

Makes 10–12 servings, varying depending on serving size.

Makeup:

Soup
1/4 cup butter
3 large yellow onions, thinly sliced
1 large red onion, thinly sliced
6 cups beef stock
1 teaspoon worcestershire sauce
1/2 teaspoon paprika
1 teaspoon salt
1 teaspoon pepper
6 slices gruyère cheese

Croutons
4–6 slices french bread
1/4 cup butter, room temperature (enough to butter the bread)
1/4 cup freshly grated romano cheese

Application:

Soup
• Melt butter in a large saucepan over medium heat.
• Add onions and sauté until golden and slightly translucent.
• Add beef stock, worcestershire sauce, paprika, salt, and pepper.
• Bring soup to a boil.
• Reduce heat and simmer uncovered for 15–20 minutes.

Croutons
• Toast bread on one side under broiler.
• Remove and spread untoasted side with butter.
• Cut bread into small squares.
• Sprinkle with romano cheese.
• Return bread to broiler and toast until lightly toasted.

Assembly
• Ladle soup evenly into ovenproof bowls, if available.
• Place croutons on top and place one slice of gruyère cheese on top of that.
• Return to oven and broil until cheese melts. Serve immediately.

Supermodel Hint
*This is a very inexpensive soup to make, but your guests don't need to know that.
If necessary, throw into the conversation the high cost of gourmet onions.*

Pumpkin Soup He'll Fall For

Makes 10–12 servings, varying depending on serving size.

Makeup:

2 tablespoons butter
2 celery stalks, diced
1 yellow onion, chopped
1 tablespoon all-purpose flour
1 teaspoon salt
1 teaspoon ground ginger
1 teaspoon nutmeg
1 teaspoon cinnamon
3 cups chicken stock
1 (16-ounce) can pumpkin or 1 1/2 pounds diced fresh
   cooking pumpkin
3 medium Granny Smith apples, chopped
4 cups whole milk
1 cup half-and-half
1 cup sour cream, for garnish
1/2 cup chopped green onions or chives, for garnish
1 crisp slice of bacon per bowl, for garnish (optional)

Application:

- Melt butter in a large saucepan over medium heat.
- Add celery and yellow onion and sauté until onion is golden and slightly translucent, about 10 minutes.
- Add in flour, salt, ginger, nutmeg, and cinnamon and cook 3–5 minutes.
- Stir in chicken stock, pumpkin, and apples.
- Simmer mixture for about 30 minutes.
- Pour mixture into a food processor or blender (in batches if necessary).
- Puree until smooth.
- Return to soup pan and stir in milk and half-and-half. Blend well.
- Simmer for another 30 minutes.
- Pour into bowls when ready to serve. Garnish with a dab of sour cream, chopped green onions or chives, and one bacon slice per bowl.

Supermodel Hint

Miss Divina's favorite season is autumn. The turning leaves get her in a cooking mood. This is the perfect autumn soup for after a roll in the hay … ERRR … I mean, a hay ride. Yeah, that's it, a hay ride.

Makes 10–12 servings, varying depending on serving size.

Makeup:

4 cups chicken stock
2 (15-ounce) cans stewed tomatoes
2 (8-ounce) cans tomato sauce
4 medium potatoes, washed and cubed
2 yellow onions, chopped
1 bunch leeks, chopped and cleaned
6 celery stalks, chopped
2 garlic cloves, minced
1 bay leaf
1 tablespoon fennel seeds
1 tablespoon dried french thyme
1 tablespoon dried parsley
1 tablespoon salt
1 tablespoon white pepper
water, sufficient to cover all ingredients in pot
2 1/2 pounds cod, cut into large pieces
1/2 pound cooked small, medium, or large shrimp
  (increase pound amount if large shrimp)
1 pound freshly steamed clams or mussels, in shells, or
1 (6.5-ounce) can chopped clams, undrained
1 pound sea scallops or 2 pounds bay scallops
1/2 pound crab or lobster (optional)
french bread, for serving

Application:

- Combine all ingredients except for seafood in a large soup pot.
- Bring to an easy boil over medium-high heat.
- Reduce heat, cover, and simmer until vegetables are almost tender, about 30 minutes.
- Add seafood except cod and continue simmering for 30 minutes.
- About 20–30 minutes before serving, add cod and simmer until fish flakes easily with a fork.
- Taste the soup and adjust seasonings to taste if needed before serving.
- Serve with fresh french bread.

Supermodel Hint

*Depending on the ingredients you use, such as lobster, this soup can be very expensive, just like Miss Divina.
But, as with fabulous champagne or a night on the town with her, the added cost is worth it!*

The Great Wall of Chinese Pork Noodle Soup

Makes 10–12 servings, varying depending on serving size.

Makeup:

1 tablespoon toasted sesame oil
1 small gingerroot, peeled and finely chopped
2 cloves garlic, minced
2 boneless pork chops, shredded or cubed
4 cups water
4 cups vegetable or beef broth
1/4 cup soy sauce
2 tablespoons teriyaki sauce
1 tablespoon chili powder
salt, pepper, and garlic powder to taste
9 ounces fresh Asian ramen noodles
1 (15-ounce) can corn
1 package (about 8 cups) baby spinach
6 large mushrooms, chopped
1/4 cup frozen peas
1 carrot, grated
4 green onions, chopped
1 egg per guest
2 cups mixed cabbage coleslaw salad mix
toasted sesame seeds, for garnish

Application:

- Heat sesame oil in a large skillet over medium heat.
- Add ginger and garlic and cook, stirring occasionally, for about 2–3 minutes.
- Add pork to ginger/garlic mix and brown meat for approximately 5 minutes.
- In a large pot, add 4 cups water, vegetable or beef broth, soy sauce, and teriyaki sauce.
- Add ginger, garlic, and cubed pork to large pot.
- Add chili powder, salt, pepper, and garlic powder.
- Increase heat to medium high; cover and bring to a low boil.
- Cook for about 10 minutes.
- Reduce heat to low and add noodles and corn. Cook until noodles are just tender, about 5 minutes.
- Add spinach, mushrooms, peas, carrot, and green onions. Simmer for 5 minutes.
- Soft-boil one egg per serving you have planned. (See p. XX for technique.)
- Place a handful of coleslaw mix at the bottom of each soup dish.
- Dish out equal amounts of soup into each bowl.
- Add one soft-boiled egg to each bowl.
- Top with toasted sesame seeds.

Supermodel Hint

Lately, the premier of China has been knocking at Miss Divina's door! With all the new development in Red China these days, I guess he wants to get his hands on Miss Divina's goods! Well, he'll just have to settle for her soup!

Makes 10–12 servings, varying depending on serving size.

Makeup:

5 slices maple-cured bacon
1/4 cup sweet butter
2 medium onions, chopped
1/2 cup flour
4 cups warm water
2 cups chicken broth (or vegetable broth)
4 large carrots, peeled and chopped
3 medium russet potatoes, chopped
1/2 cup chopped celery
1 teaspoon each, nutmeg, salt, pepper and
  garlic powder
1 cup milk or half-and-half
16 ounces oysters, cooked and chopped
bread or oyster crackers, for serving

Application:

- Fry bacon, chop, and set aside for garnish.
- Melt butter in a medium saucepan over medium heat.
- Sauté onion in butter.
- Remove from heat and sift in flour.
- Blend together in a large pot, adding warm water and chicken broth.
- Add carrots, potatoes, celery, nutmeg, salt, pepper, and garlic powder.
- Simmer until vegetables are cooked, about 1 hour or so.
- Add milk (or half-and-half).
- Add oysters.
- Stir and simmer for another 1 hour.
- Garnish with bacon.
- Serve with your favorite gourmet bread or oyster crackers.

Supermodel Hint

We all know Miss Divina has it all, so to speak. Maybe your world is a little less privileged, but you can always make a good soup to make up for the lack of finesse in your drab existence!

Makes 10–12 servings, varying depending on serving size.

Makeup:

1/4 cup salted butter
1 large onion, diced
4 cloves garlic, minced
2 celery stalks, diced
1 large carrot, diced
6 cups chicken broth, plus additional as needed
1 teaspoon dried oregano
3/4 teaspoon salt
pepper and garlic powder to taste
1 (4.5-ounce) can pinto beans
1 (4.5-ounce) can kidney beans
1 (4.5-ounce) can green beans
2 cups seashell pasta (or elbow pasta)
1 (16-ounce) package frozen peas
1 (28-ounce) can diced stewed tomatoes, undrained
1/3 cup finely grated parmesan cheese, for garnish
1/4 cup finely chopped basil, for garnish

Application:

- Melt butter in a large pot over medium-high heat.
- Sauté onion and garlic until translucent, about 5 minutes.
- Add celery and carrot and cook until they begin to soften, about 5 minutes.
- Add broth, dried oregano, salt, pepper, and garlic powder.
- Simmer for 10 minutes.
- Add pinto beans, kidney beans, green beans, and pasta and cook until they are tender, about 10 minutes.
- Add frozen peas and simmer for about 1 hour.
- Add more broth if necessary.
- Add stewed tomatoes and simmer for 20 minutes.
- Serve with finely grated parmesan cheese and chopped basil for garnish.

Supermodel Hint

The acid in tomatoes can keep beans and vegetables crunchy. Don't add the tomatoes until the final 20 minutes when all of the other ingredients are close to tender.

Makes 10–12 servings, varying depending on serving size.

Makeup:

3 tablespoons butter
2 onions, thinly sliced
1 garlic clove, minced
1 tablespoon fennel seeds
2 quarts fish or vegetable stock, plus additional as
   needed
1 (16-ounce) can whole tomatoes, undrained
1 large bunch spinach, chopped
1 bay leaf
1/2 teaspoon dried basil
1/2 teaspoon cayenne pepper
8–10 ounces lobster tails, steamed and chopped
1/2 cup sour cream, for garnish (optional)

Application:

- Melt butter in a large saucepan over medium heat.
- Add onion, garlic, and fennel seeds; cover and cook about 5 minutes.
- Pour in fish or vegetable stock and bring to a boil.
- Stir in tomatoes, spinach, bay leaf, basil, and cayenne.
- Cover and simmer for about 10 minutes.
- Add more broth if thinner consistency is desired.
- Remove and discard bay leaf.
- In batches, puree soup in a blender or food processor.
- Return to pot when all is pureed.
- Simmer for 25–30 minutes.
- Add lobster to the soup and simmer for additional 10 minutes.
- Ladle into bowls and serve with a dab of sour cream in center if you so desire.

Supermodel Hint

*We all want to fit into our favorite clothes, so don't overdo anything. This soup is going to test your self-control!
Everything in moderation, I say! Unless it's a martini. I can't help myself.*

Superb Salads

My life is everyone's fantasy.

Mad Men Iceberg Wedge Salad with Blue Cheese Dressing (p. 127)

I have strict rules about how food is presented. For example, cold food, like Miss Divina's family recipe Nana's Crab Salad, must be on cold plates. There's nothing easier than to stack the dishes in the refrigerator for a couple of hours before serving. I think it's an insult to offer a guest a plate that's come right out of the cupboard. Oh, the uncivilized inhumanity makes me shudder! Another horrid faux pas seen all too often is a messy serving dish. For Miss Divina's sake, wipe the edges of your dishes clean before bringing food to the table. I say sack the server who serves a messy plate to your guests! While Miss Divina's kitchen is vast and completely supplied, you may need to serve your food according to the plates and platters you have available in your home. But please, not chipped or cracked plates. Think of Miss Divina's reputation!

Maserati's Tomato and Mozzarella Salad

Choose your salad menu according to the taste preferences of your guests, and also take the season into account. If it is summer and you have bountiful selections of fresh garden vegetables, then utilize their limited availability to make scrumptious salads that all will marvel at. Try Miss Divina's delicious Maserati's Tomato and Mozzarella Salad or Mandarin-Candidate Chicken Salad—so simple but so impressive.

Are you serving bread with the menu? Hard butter is hard to spread, so it should come room temperature and on a lovely bed of red-leaf lettuce. Only some things should be hard when presented, and butter is not one of them! Keep your bread hot within a cloth napkin or bread warmer.

Signorina Divina's Summery Mint-Watermelon Salad

She's-a-Crazy-Nut-Crusted Tuna with Wild Greens (p. 136)

Cary's North—by—Northwest Chicken Salad

Serves 4 individually or as a platter.

Makeup:

4 boneless, skinless chicken breasts
1 cup mayonnaise or plain greek yogurt,
    plus additional to taste
2 green onions or chives, finely chopped
1 red onion, finely chopped
2 tablespoons dijon mustard
2 tablespoons parsley
1 teaspoon salt
1 teaspoon fresh french thyme
1 teaspoon paprika, plus additional for garnish
1 teaspoon pepper
1/4 cup toasted sliced almonds, divided
1 head of red-leaf lettuce
4 hard-boiled eggs, quartered

Application:

- Prepare outdoor grill according to your specific grill instructions.
- Clean chicken breasts, season, and grill on outdoor grill (I prefer charcoal over gas grilling). Alternatively, you may cook in oven at 350 degrees F if desired.
- Set aside to let chicken cool.
- When chicken is cool, dice into small squares.
- Add chicken to a large mixing bowl with mayonnaise, green onions, red onion, mustard, parsley, salt, thyme, paprika, pepper, and half the almonds.
- Stir, mixing thoroughly.
- Cover and let cool in refrigerator for at least 1 hour.
- Add more mayonnaise to taste.
- Place red-leaf lettuce on plate(s) and spoon chicken mixture in center of lettuce.
- Garnish with eggs, paprika, and remaining almonds.

Supermodel Hint

For any salad that uses mayonnaise, you may need to add more mayonnaise an hour or two later since the mayonnaise tends to be soaked up by the other ingredients.

Cover Girl Grilled Chicken Salad

Makes 4 salads.

Makeup:

4 large boneless, skinless chicken breasts
4 cups mixed salad greens
4 hard-boiled eggs, wedged into quarters
1 medium red onion, sliced
24 sliced black olives
1 cucumber, peeled and sliced
1/2 cup broccoli, chopped
2 tomatoes, wedged into quarters
salad dressing of your choice, for serving

Application:

- Prepare outdoor grill according to your specific grill instructions or preheat oven to 395 degrees F.
- Cook chicken on grill or in oven. Set aside.
- Place 1 cup of mixed salad greens in the center of each salad plate.
- On the edges of each plate, arrange egg quarters, onion, olives, cucumber, and broccoli.
- Place tomato slices on the edges.
- Cut chicken crosswise into slices, maintaining its original form. Place in center of salad.
- Serve with your choice of dressing on the side in ramekins.

Donny and Marie Almond, Apple, and Blue Cheese Salad

Makes 4 salads.

Makeup:
Dressing
1/4 cup lemon juice
2 ounces thinly sliced green onions
1/4 teaspoon salt
1/4 teaspoon pepper
1 cup almond or vegetable oil

Salad
12 cups mixed salad greens
2 Granny Smith apples, cored and sliced
1/4 pound blue cheese, such as Roquefort, crumbled
4 ounces toasted sliced almonds

Application:
Dressing
• Mix together lemon juice, green onions, salt, and pepper.
• Slowly beat in oil; set aside.

Salad
• For each salad, toss 3 cups of salad greens with 1 teaspoon dressing; add to plates.
• Top each salad with sliced apples, blue cheese, and almonds.

Supermodel Hint

Miss Divina slices apples shortly before serving time to prevent air from browning the fruit.

Hail-Caesar Salad with Grilled Chicken

Makes 4-6 servings.

Makeup:

Dressing
1 1/4 cups light extra-virgin olive oil
4 eggs
6 garlic cloves
1/2 cup anchovies
2 tablespoons lemon juice
2 tablespoons sherry vinegar
1 tablespoon dijon mustard
pepper to taste

Salad
2 heads romaine lettuce
1/2 cup croutons (see p. 227 for instructions)
1/2 cup grated parmesan cheese, divided
3 grilled chicken breasts, sliced evenly

Application:

Dressing
- Blend olive oil, eggs, and garlic in a blender; add to a medium mixing bowl.
- Cut anchovies finely; mix in with olive oil, eggs, and garlic.
- Add lemon juice, sherry vinegar, mustard, and pepper; stir thoroughly and set aside.

Salad
- Wash, drain, and dry romaine.
- Tear it into small and medium pieces.
- Add lettuce to a large salad bowl.
- Mix dressing in with lettuce.
- Add croutons and parmesan cheese, saving 2 tablespoons of parmesan cheese for garnish.
- Mix ingredients so dressing is evenly distributed.
- Place sliced chicken on top of salad and serve in a large serving bowl or on individual plates.
- Sprinkle remaining parmesan cheese over salad as garnish.

For shrimp Caesar salad:
For shrimp Caesar salad, substitute grilled shrimp for chicken, 6–10 large pieces per serving.

Supermodel Hint
*Miss Divina admits to being a size queen! I don't mean to contradict when
I declare that she likes her shrimp big. Jumbos are just delightful!*

Makes 2–4 servings.

Makeup:

2 large cucumbers
8 ounces sour cream
4 green onions (or chives), diced
4 teaspoons white wine vinegar
fresh dill weed, chopped, to taste
1 teaspoon garlic salt
1 teaspoon freshly ground black pepper

Application:

- Peel and slice cucumbers into circular disks. Set aside.
- In a small mixing bowl, mix sour cream, green onions (or chives), vinegar, dill weed, garlic salt, and pepper.
- Gently mix with cucumbers.
- Place salad on a large serving plate and chill for at least 30 minutes before serving.

Supermodel Hint

*After dinner, if you have any leftover salad, wear it to bed
as a facial treatment. Your man will thank you in the morning,
and it is great for snacking in the interim if you both work up
an appetite during the night.*

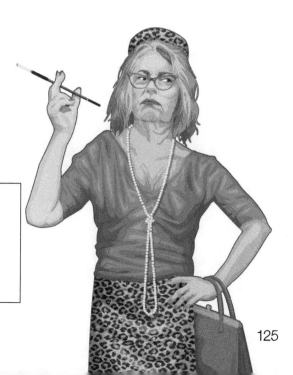

125

Jungle Red Oranges, Beets, and Cucumber Salad

Makes 4 salads.

Makeup:

2 large cucumbers
4 large blood oranges
4 cups mixed salad greens
1/4 cup pine nuts, divided
1 can sliced beets
1/2 cup goat cheese
1/2 cup raspberry vinaigrette
fresh mint, for garnish

Application:

- Clean, peel, and slice cucumbers. Set aside.
- Peel oranges carefully and remove any skin left on. Break orange pieces apart, being carefully not to damage them. Set aside.
- On serving plates, distribute salad greens evenly and sprinkle a few pine nuts on top.
- In an alternating pattern, place cucumber, beets, goat cheese, and orange slices on top of greens.
- Pour a small amount of vinaigrette over salad and top with remaining pine nuts.
- Garnish with fresh mint leaves.

Mad Men Iceberg Wedge Salad with Blue Cheese Dressing

Makes 4 salads.

Makeup:

10 slices bacon
2 heads iceberg lettuce
1 small red onion, chopped
2 medium tomatoes, chopped
freshly ground pepper to taste
blue cheese dressing (see p. 230 for recipe), for serving

Application:

- Fry the bacon and set aside to cool.
- Core and quarter each head of lettuce.
- Clean lettuce and drain any water. Set aside.
- Crumble cooled bacon and set aside.
- Place each lettuce quarter on its own serving plate.
- Sprinkle bacon, onion, and tomatoes evenly over each lettuce wedge.
- Season with pepper.
- Serve with blue cheese dressing over each lettuce wedge.

Supermodel Hint

This old-fashioned salad is back in style with a vengeance! Whether you're an advertising man or a janitor (you poor thing!), you'll feel like you're the latest thing since the push-button phone!

Mandarin–Candidate Chicken Salad

Makes 4 salads.

Makeup:

4 boneless, skinless chicken breasts
1 cup teriyaki sauce
1 large package mixed salad greens
1 cup grated romano cheese
1/2 cup chopped carrots
1 cup glazed pecans
20 cherry tomatoes
1 (11-ounce) can whole peeled mandarin orange
  segments
extra-virgin olive oil and balsamic vinegar to taste

Application:

- Marinate chicken breasts in teriyaki sauce for at least 1 hour.
- Prepare outdoor grill according to your specific grill instructions.
- Grill chicken, cooking fully, and set aside to cool.
- Place mixed greens evenly on four plates.
- Sprinkle cheese over each salad.
- Place carrots and pecans on salads.
- Arrange 5 cherry tomatoes on edge of each plate.
- Place mandarin orange slices evenly on each salad.
- Cut each chicken breast into cubes and place in the center of each salad.
- Pour olive oil and balsamic vinegar over each salad.

Serving note: This dish pairs well with dry white wine.

Supermodel Hint

Miss Divina always loves a good salad. This one is the perfect answer for a warm summer evening.

Maserati's Tomato and Mozzarella Salad

Makes 4–6 servings.

Makeup:

16 ounces large mozzarella cheese
3–5 large, ripe red tomatoes
2 yellow vine-ripened tomatoes (optional, if available)
1/3 cup extra-virgin olive oil
1 teaspoon freshly squeezed lemon juice
2 tablespoons freshly ground black pepper
2 tablespoons salt
pine nuts, for garnish
fresh basil, for garnish

Application:

- If mozzarella is not presliced, slice into 1/4-inch slices; set aside.
- Slice tomatoes into 1/4-inch slices; set aside.
- On a large serving platter, lay out cheese and tomatoes, alternating cheese and tomato slices. If using yellow tomatoes, alternate between red and yellow tomato slices.
- When you have surrounded the plate with cheese and tomatoes, sprinkle olive oil over cheese and tomatoes.
- Sprinkle lemon juice over cheese and tomatoes.
- Evenly distribute salt and pepper over cheese and tomatoes.
- Garnish with basil and pine nuts.

Supermodel Hint

Miss Divina's gardeners love to get their hands on the plump tomatoes in her large garden, and those homegrown tomatoes are perfect for this salad. Miss Divina's mama makes her own mozzarella from a darling recipe handed down from many generations.

Makes 6 servings.

Makeup:

1–1 1/2 pounds ground beef (or ground turkey)
1 cup chopped sweet red pepper
6 tablespoons chopped garlic
1/2 cup chili sauce
1 teaspoon taco seasoning
1/4 teaspoon salt
1/4 teaspoon pepper
1/4 cup canola oil
6 corn tortillas
1 (15-ounce) can refried beans
3 cups shredded lettuce
3 tomatoes, chopped
1 1/2 cups shredded cheddar cheese, plus additional
   to taste
creamy onion or garlic salad dressing to taste
hot sauce (optional)
2 fresh avocados, sliced, for garnish
1/4 cup green onions, chopped, for garnish
1/2 cup sour cream, for garnish

Application:

- In a large skillet, cook beef (or turkey) over medium heat until no longer pink; drain any excess grease.
- Add red pepper and garlic and stir into meat.
- Stir in chili sauce, taco seasoning, salt, and pepper; heat through.
- In a small skillet, heat oil over medium heat.
- Fry tortillas in oil until slightly golden brown and slightly crisp.
- Place tortillas on serving plates, one per plate.
- In a small pan, warm refried beans.
- Layer tortillas with beans and then ground beef.
- Place cheese on top.
- If desired, briefly place tortillas in oven preheated to 200 degree F to melt cheese.
- Add chilled lettuce and tomatoes on top.
- Top with creamy onion or garlic salad dressing, more cheese, and hot sauce if desired.
- Garnish with avocado slices and green onions. Place a dab of sour cream on top to finish.

Supermodel Hint

After a long day sunning yourself on the sandy Mexican Riviera beach, or on your backyard patch of crabgrass, you deserve a little "Riviera dreaming," as I call it.

Nana's Crab Salad

Makes 2–4 servings.

Makeup:

1 head iceberg lettuce
2 pounds freshly cracked crab
2 celery stalks, diced
4 green onions, chopped
salt, pepper, and garlic powder to taste
1 cup mayonnaise (or plain greek yogurt)
2 tablespoons extra-virgin olive oil
2 tablespoons red wine vinegar
1 head red-leaf lettuce
4 hard-boiled eggs, sliced, for garnish
4 tomatoes, sliced, for garnish
3 avocados, sliced, for garnish
black olives, for garnish
marinated asparagus hearts, sliced, for garnish
paprika, for garnish

Application:

- Wash, drain, and chop iceberg lettuce and place in a large bowl.
- Add crab, celery, and green onions.
- Season to taste and toss with mayonnaise (or yogurt) and olive oil to desired consistency.
- Mix in red wine vinegar.
- Refrigerate for at least 2 hours.
- Remove crab salad from refrigerator and add additional mayonnaise if needed.
- Arrange some washed and drained large red-leaf lettuce leaves on a large serving platter.
- Place crab salad on top of red-leaf lettuce leaves and garnish with eggs, tomatoes, avocados, olives, and asparagus hearts. Lightly sprinkle with paprika for color.

Supermodel Hint

*Got a shrimp lover in the house? Prepare this salad the same but substitute shrimp for the crab.
It's sure to please any Bubba you have in your household! And for extra presentation power,
consider serving this salad in half an avocado shell.*

Papa's Delicatessen Meat, Cheese, and Pasta Salad

Makes 10–12 servings.

Makeup:

1 (12-ounce) package *coriandoli* pasta (also known as confetti pasta; garden rotini can be substituted)
1 1/2 cups cubed dry Italian salami
1 1/2 cups cubed ham
1 1/2 cups cubed cheddar cheese
1 1/2 cups cubed swiss cheese
1 (12-ounce) jar artichoke hearts, well drained
1/4 cup green olives, sliced
1/4 cup black olives, sliced
1 (4-ounce) jar pimientos
2 celery stalks, chopped
1/4 cup fresh parsley, divided, plus additional for garnish
salt, pepper, garlic powder, and paprika to taste
vinegar-and-oil dressing to taste
2 hard-boiled eggs, sliced, for garnish

Application:

- Cook pasta as directed on package.
- Drain and rinse pasta in cold water.
- Into a large mixing bowl, add salami, ham, cheddar cheese, swiss cheese, artichoke hearts, green olives, black olives, pimientos, celery, and 2 tablespoons parsley.
- Mix ingredients thoroughly and season to taste with salt, pepper, garlic powder, and paprika.
- Carefully mix in cooked pasta and remaining 2 tablespoons parsley.
- Add vinegar-and-oil dressing to taste. (Reserve extra dressing, as pasta will absorb dressing overnight.)
- Chill salad for at least 2 hours prior to serving
- Spoon chilled pasta salad into a large serving bowl.
- Prior to serving, decorate with sliced hard-boiled eggs.
- Sprinkle with parsley and paprika for color.

Supermodel Hint

You know how all the men just can't wait to get outside and grill? Well, this scrumptious salad of Miss Divina's papa is the perfect complement to any outdoor grilling menu!

Phi Beta Tomato and Cucumber Salad

Makes 4–6 servings.

Makeup:

2 large english cucumbers, peeled and sliced into
   circular disks
3 large tomatoes, sliced
raspberry vinaigrette dressing
4 green onions (or shallots), diced
1 medium red onion, diced
1/4 cup raisins (optional)
1/2 cup crumbled blue cheese
2 tablespoons sesame seeds
garlic powder, salt, and pepper to taste

Application:

- Arrange cucumbers and tomatoes in alternating pattern around large serving dish with sides.
- Pour dressing evenly on top of tomatoes and cucumbers.
- Distribute green and red onions, raisins (optional), blue cheese, sesame seeds, garlic powder, salt, and pepper evenly on top of tomatoes and cucumbers.
- Refrigerate and let marinate for at least 45 minutes prior to serving.
- Serve chilled.

Supermodel Hint

English cucumbers are usually "seedless" and don't have a layer of wax on them. It's been said that they were bred to be easier to digest. Some people think they are sweeter than American cucumbers and have less of a bitter taste.

Sashay! Shantay! Avocado—Blue Cheese Salad

Makes 1 salad.

Makeup:

1 1/2 cups butter lettuce
1 large avocado
1 tablespoon freshly squeezed lemon juice
1/4 cup bacon bits
1/4 cup crumbled blue cheese
5 cherry tomatoes
1/4 cup crushed walnuts
1/2 teaspoon salt
1/2 teaspoon pepper
1/2 teaspoon paprika
1/4 cup Italian-style vinegar dressing

Application:

- Wash and drain lettuce and place a bed for salad.
- Peel and slice avocado into 8 wedges. Place over lettuce.
- Sprinkle dash of lemon juice on each avocado slice.
- Evenly spread bacon bits, blue cheese, tomatoes, and walnuts over salad.
- Season with salt, pepper, and paprika.
- Dribble a little dressing over entire salad.

Supermodel Hint

This recipe was written for one serving. Multiply according to the number of guests you are serving.

Señorita Chica–Dee's Tortilla Seafood Salad

Makes 4 salads.

Makeup:

1/4 cup vegetable oil
8 corn tortillas
1/4 pound cooked lobster or crab meat, finely chopped
1/2 pound large shrimp, freshly steamed or sautéed
1 (11-ounce) can enchilada sauce, mild to hot
1 head iceberg lettuce, chopped
1 (23-ounce) can kidney beans
1 (15-ounce) can whole-kernel corn
1 teaspoon chili powder
1 teaspoon cayenne pepper
1 teaspoon salt
1 teaspoon freshly ground black pepper
1/4 cup finely chopped red onion
2 large, fresh tomatoes, diced
2 tablespoons finely chopped scallions
1 cup salsa, mild to hot, divided
2 cups grated jalapeño Monterey Jack cheese
1 cup sour cream
2 large avocados, sliced

Application:

- Preheat oven to 350 degrees F.
- In a medium skillet, heat oil over medium heat.
- Fry tortillas until slightly golden.
- Lay tortillas flat on paper towels and pat excess oil off with clean paper towel.
- Place two tortillas, slightly overlapping, on each ovenproof plate and set aside.
- Combine seafood and enchilada sauce in a large skillet and cook for 10 minutes over low heat.
- Separate seafood from enchilada sauce and set aside to cool. Save the remaining enchilada sauce, as you'll use it later.
- Place a handful (about 1 cup) of chopped lettuce on top of tortillas.
- Evenly spread kidney beans and then corn on top of lettuce.
- Season top layer with chili powder, cayenne, salt, and pepper.
- Sprinkle red onion, tomatoes, and scallions evenly over each salad.
- Spoon on a quarter of the remaining enchilada sauce and 1/4 cup salsa evenly over each salad.
- Sprinkle cheese on top.
- Evenly place seafood mixture over salads
- Place each plate in oven for 5 minutes to warm and then remove with oven mitts.
- Place spoonful of sour cream in center of each salad, garnish plates with avocado slices, and serve.

Chica-Dee is such a fantastic flamenco dancer. The only problem is that somewhere in the middle of her dance, she turns it into a striptease number. What's that about?

She's—a—Crazy—Nut—Crusted Tuna with Wild Greens

Makes 4 salads.

Makeup:

2 eggs
1/4 cup all-purpose flour
1/2 cup mixed nuts
2 teaspoons salt
2 teaspoons garlic powder
2 teaspoons freshly ground black pepper
4 medium-size, thinly sliced tuna fillets
   (about 1 inch thick)
2 tablespoons salted butter
1/2 cup extra-virgin olive oil, divided
4 cups mixed greens
1/4 cup balsamic vinegar
edible flowers, for garnish (optional)

Application:

- In a medium bowl, beat eggs.
- In a separate bowl, combine flour, nuts, salt, garlic powder, and pepper; mix well.
- Tie tuna fillets together with baking/cooking string.
- Coat tied tuna generously with egg.
- Roll coated tuna in nut mixture; coat generously.
- Melt butter with 2 tablespoons olive oil in a large skillet over medium-high heat.
- Gently place seasoned tuna in skillet and cook to desired doneness, 1 1/2 minutes per side for rare.
- Remove tuna from heat after cooked to desired doneness.
- Let tuna cool for 5 minutes.
- Divide mixed greens onto serving plates.
- Mix remaining olive oil and balsamic vinegar in a small bowl and set aside.
- Cut strings and carefully separate each tuna slice.
- Place equal amounts of tuna on each plate over salad mixture.
- Just before serving, pour light amount of vinaigrette on each salad.
- Garnish with edible flowers (optional).

Supermodel Hint

*Not sure how to tie meat or fish using baking string? Go online and type "tying beef" in the search engine.
It's easy and might come in handy with a beau who gets too friendly at times!*

Signorina Divina's Summery Mint–Watermelon Salad

Makes 4–6 salads.

Makeup:

Minty Syrup
1/4 cup sugar
1/4 water
1/4 cup fresh mint leaves, chopped
1/2 teaspoon ground ginger

Fruit Salad
1 (7–8-pound) seedless watermelon, cubed and chilled
1 pint raspberries
1 pint blackberries
1 pint blueberries
1 pint strawberries, hulled and halved
2 cups seedless green grapes, halved
juice of 3 limes
1 1/2 cups crumbled feta cheese
whole mint leaves, for garnish

Application:

Minty Syrup
- In a small saucepan, combine sugar, water, mint, and ginger.
- Bring to a boil; then reduce heat to a simmer.
- Simmer for 5 minutes to thicken slightly.
- Set aside to cool.

Fruit Salad
- Place all the fruit in a large bowl and toss with lime juice.
- Once syrup mixture is cool, add to fruit mixture in large bowl.
- Toss very gently to coat fruit evenly.
- Add crumbled feta into salad bowl and stir gently to integrate cheese into salad.
- Serve immediately in bowls with fresh mint leaf for garnish.

Supermodel Hint
Miss Divina has a few tips for when making a fresh fruit salad.
1: always choose in-season fruits. 2: avoid mushy fruits. 3: cut fruit into
medium-sized pieces. And lastly, add juice from a fresh-squeezed lemon.

Strong and Warmhearted Spinach Salad

Makes 4 salads.

Makeup:

1 pound spinach, washed and drained
2 cups red cabbage, washed and drained
4 slices thick-cut bacon or pancetta
1 clove garlic, finely chopped
4 green onions, chopped
1 small red onion, sliced
salt, pepper, and garlic powder to taste
4 hard-boiled eggs
3 tablespoons extra-virgin olive oil
3 tablespoons sherry vinegar
1 cup grated parmesan cheese

Application:

- Cut spinach and chop red cabbage and set aside.
- Heat olive oil in a large skillet over medium-high heat.
- Fry bacon until crispy and chop into small pieces.
- Remove bacon from skillet and set aside.
- Add chopped red cabbage and garlic to pan. Cook 3–4 minutes.
- Put spinach into pan and wilt down a bit but do not fully cook.
- Remove and place this salad mixture in a large bowl.
- Season with salt, pepper, and garlic powder.
- Finely chop 3 hard-boiled eggs and add to salad mixture.
- In the previously used skillet, over medium heat, heat olive oil and vinegar and sauté half the bacon bits.
- Pour this mixture over salad in large bowl.
- Add remaining bacon bits, green and red onion slices to bowl and toss.
- Transfer salad to a large serving platter or individual plates.
- Slice remaining egg and add to top of salad, garnish with cheese, and serve.

Supermodel Hint

Spinach salad goes way back, just like my secrets about Miss Divina. If you want to dress up this spinach salad for a holiday gathering, add cranberries and walnuts.

Swimsuit–Issue Salad

Makes 4 salads.

Makeup:

2–3 large peaches, peeled, pitted, and cut in half
2 avocados, slightly firm, peeled, pitted, and sliced
   into large wedges
1/3 cup extra-virgin olive oil, divided
1/4 cup honey
2 tablespoons balsamic vinegar
1 teaspoon pepper, plus additional to taste
1 teaspoon salt
2 cups romaine lettuce, chopped
2 cups baby spinach
2 cups arugula
1/4 cup toasted pine nuts

Application:

- Prepare outdoor grill according to your specific grill instructions.
- Brush the peach halves and avocado slices with about 2 tablespoons olive oil. Set remaining olive oil to the side.
- Place peach halves and avocado slices on hot grill and sear each side until slightly charred, about 2–4 minutes per side.
- Carefully remove peach halves and avocado slices from grill and set aside.
- Slice grilled peaches into wedges.
- In a small mixing bowl, combine honey, vinegar, pepper, and salt and mix well to create dressing.
- Add remaining olive oil and mix well.
- Combine romaine, spinach, and arugula in a large bowl and toss.
- Add about 1/2 cup of the dressing and toss to evenly coat the salad greens.
- Divide salad onto four serving plates.
- Top with grilled avocado, grilled peaches, and pine nuts.
- Add more dressing and pepper if desired.

Supermodel Hint

*Nothing screams summer like fresh peaches and avocados in a salad. They're sweet and juicy
and the perfect salad additions. Peaches and avocados are rich and creamy and taste even better grilled.
The honey will bring out the peaches' natural sweetness.*

Entertaining Entrées

Dinner need not be a drag!

Luscious Lobster Risotto alla Parmigiana (p. 205)

Vaina Black's Côte de Boeuf

Stiletto Spaghetti with Clam Sauce

After cocktails and hors d'oeuvres, as dinner is served in the dining room, your helpers should dash into the living room to collect all the debris—the leftover canapés, the glasses, and any discarded clothes on the floor. This would be a good time to release any children on hand. They can get some air and get a little housework exercise. And it wouldn't hurt if they emptied the dirty ashtrays and plumped up the pillows. I always say, "A tidy home is a happy home!"

Have you been serving boiled steaks or fried spaghetti to your guests? Well, those days are over! A few tips from Miss Divina and you'll be fine. Start with a buffet. Miss Divina insists on having two hot entrées. Some entrée possibilities are Charlie's Chicken and the Sea, Oh Man! The Naughty Man-I-Caught-i, or the Sultan's Harem Lamb Kebabs, with all their interesting accompaniments. Miss Divina indulges her guests with a wide variety of enticing selections. If you're going to be a relaxed host, consider recipes that can be made the day before. Many of these entrées improve with reheating. Any of these recipes are perfect for an evening of enchantment and seduction.

Some like it haute! Hot food must be on warm plates. Before serving your hot entrée, like Hollie Woode's Roasted Chicken with Herbs, place the serving plates in the warm—not hot—oven. When meat is put onto a serving platter, there are bound to be a few little splatters. Though the splatters may be inevitable, that's no excuse to ignore them. Wipe the edges of your platters clean before bringing them to the table. Time the presentation of your entrées so too much time does not lapse between the soup or salad portion of your meal and the entrée. No guest wants to sit for twenty minutes waiting for Miss Divina's Prosciutto-Stuffed Triple-D Chicken Breast, Vaina Black's Côte de Boeuf, or Luscious Lobster Risotto alla Parmigiana.

Poultry Dishes

Endora's Cornish Game Hens (p. 153)

Adobo Lourdes's Fabulous Skillet Chicken

Makes 4–8 servings.

Makeup:

1 tablespoon extra-virgin olive oil
12 chicken wings or boneless thighs
2 medium yellow onions, chopped
3 fresh garlic cloves, peeled and finely chopped
2 cups fresh mushrooms, chopped
1 cup soy sauce
1/4 cup white vinegar
1 teaspoon salt, or to taste
1 teaspoon pepper, or to taste
1 teaspoon ground rosemary, or to taste
1/4 cup chicken stock, plus additional as needed
white or brown rice, cooked, for serving
fresh rosemary sprigs, for garnish

Application:

- Heat olive oil over medium heat in a large skillet.
- Rinse chicken, pat dry, and place in a large skillet. Brown for 2–3 minutes, turning chicken periodically to brown on all sides.
- Remove chicken to a plate and set aside.
- Put yellow onions, garlic, and mushrooms in same skillet.
- Add soy sauce and white vinegar. You want enough that the vegetables can simmer in it—adjust the amounts accordingly.
- Season chicken with salt, pepper, and rosemary.
- Return chicken to skillet.
- Add chicken stock to skillet.
- Be sure to baste chicken while it cooks, stirring occasionally.
- Turn chicken pieces over every 4–5 minutes to evenly coat and cook.
- Cook, covered, over low heat for 20–25 minutes, keeping an eye on liquid content.
- Add more chicken stock if needed.
- When chicken is fully cooked and golden, remove and serve over rice.
- Garnish with fresh rosemary sprigs.

One of the world's shorter supermodels, Missy Lourdes of the Philippines storms the stage with her larger-than-life style and grace! Good thing she is under 5'5" in height! Otherwise she might give Miss Divina a run for the money!

Makes 6–8 servings.

Makeup:

4 boneless, skinless chicken breasts
3 medium russet potatoes
1 (10.5-ounce) can cream of celery soup
1 (8-ounce) can water chestnuts, sliced and drained
1 cup (4 ounces) sliced sharp cheddar cheese
   (regular or white cheddar), divided
1 cup grated parmesan cheese, divided
1 cup milk
2 tablespoons chopped pimiento

Application:

- Preheat oven to 350 degrees F.
- Place chicken on a cookie sheet with sides and bake for 20 minutes, or until breasts are fully cooked.
- Set chicken aside to cool. Once cool, cut into small pieces.
- Peel and slice potatoes thinly and set aside.
- In a mixing medium bowl, mix soup, water chestnuts, 1/2 cup cheddar cheese, 1/2 cup parmesan cheese, milk, and pimiento.
- In a buttered casserole dish, place layer of potatoes, layer of chicken, and then layer of soup/cheese mixture.
- Repeat layers until you reach just below the top of the casserole dish and the ingredients are used up (end on a layer of soup/cheese mixture).
- Top with remaining 1/2 cup cheddar cheese and 1/2 cup parmesan cheese.
- Bake for 45 minutes, or until potatoes are cooked and cheese is golden.
- Remove from oven and let cool slightly before serving.

Supermodel Hint

Miss Divina thinks you should also try this recipe with turkey breast.
The tryptophan just may relax your man enough to sleep cuddled in your arms all evening!

Blue Velvet Cheese, Bacon, and Avocado, Turkey Burger

Makes 4 burgers.

Makeup:

8 thick bacon slices
1/4 cup sliced almonds
1 tablespoon salted butter, room temperature
   (enough to toast the almonds and butter the buns)
2 pounds ground turkey
1 fresh egg
1/4 cup seasoned bread crumbs
1 tablespoon dijon mustard
1/2 teaspoon salt, plus additional to taste
1/2 teaspoon garlic powder
1/4 teaspoon pepper, plus additional to taste
1/2 cup chopped red onions
1/2 cup crumbled blue cheese
4 sourdough hamburger buns, sliced
1/4 cup mayonnaise
1 1/2 cups fresh baby spinach leaves (or your favorite lettuce)
1 medium tomato, sliced
1 ripe avocado, sliced

Application:

- Prepare outdoor grill according to your specific grill instructions.
- Cut bacon slices into halves. Fry until slightly crisp and set aside.
- Toast sliced almonds in a little butter for 3 minutes. Remove to a small bowl and set aside.
- In a medium mixing bowl, combine ground turkey, egg, bread crumbs, mustard, salt, garlic powder, and pepper.
- Shape turkey into 8 thin patties.
- In a small mixing bowl, combine onions and blue cheese.
- Spoon the blue cheese / onion mixture onto the center of 4 patties.
- Top with remaining patties and press edges together firmly to seal.
- Sprinkle additional salt and pepper over patties to taste.
- Grill burgers over medium heat or broil in oven for 5–7 minutes on each side, or until meat is browned.
- Butter and grill hamburger buns on grill or in skillet for 1–2 minutes, depending on grill type and temperature.
- Serve burgers on buns with mayonnaise, spinach, tomato, avocado, bacon, and almonds.

Supermodel Hint

They say that all messy foods are delicious. Well, I know all foods Miss Divina makes are finger-licking good.
But one problem always arises. Who is lucky enough to lick Miss Divina's fingers?

Makes 4 servings.

Makeup:

Chicken
cooking spray
4 boneless, skinless chicken breast halves
salt and pepper to taste
1 cup all-purpose flour
1/2 teaspoon paprika
1/2 teaspoon garlic salt
2 tablespoons butter
1 tablespoon extra-virgin olive oil

Mushroom Sauce
1 tablespoon butter
4 cups sliced fresh mushrooms
1 cup chicken broth
1/2 cup sour cream
1/4 teaspoon lemon zest
1 tablespoon freshly squeezed lemon juice
2 tablespoons all-purpose flour
1 teaspoon salt
1 teaspoon pepper
2 tablespoons chopped fresh parsley, for garnish
freshly cracked black pepper, for garnish

Application:

Chicken
- Preheat oven to 375 degrees F.
- Lightly spray a 11 x 7–inch baking dish with cooking spray. Set aside.
- Flatten each chicken breast half to 1/2-inch thickness.
- Season chicken with salt and pepper.
- Place flour, paprika, and garlic salt in a resealable plastic bag.
- Add chicken, a few pieces at a time. Seal bag and shake to coat. Remove chicken to plate, making sure to shake off excess flour.
- Heat butter and olive oil in a large pan over medium-high heat.
- Once pan is hot, add chicken and brown for 2 minutes on each side.
- Transfer chicken to baking dish.

Mushroom Sauce
- In same skillet used for chicken, add butter and sauté mushrooms for about 3 minutes.
- Meanwhile, in a separate small mixing bowl, combine broth, sour cream, lemon zest, lemon juice, flour, salt, and pepper. Whisk to combine.
- Add mixture to sauté pan with mushrooms and stir to combine.
- Cook 2–3 minutes, or until sauce thickens slightly.
- Add mushroom sauce to top of chicken and bake, uncovered, for 20–30 minutes, or until chicken is no longer pink inside.
- Serve with a little parsley and freshly cracked pepper on top.

Charlie's Chicken and the Sea

Makes 4 servings.

Makeup:

4 boneless, skinless chicken breasts
1/2 pound crab meat, washed, drained, and chopped
  or shredded
1 cup grated Havarti cheese
1 teaspoon salt
1 teaspoon ground black pepper
2 cups béarnaise sauce (see p. 311 for recipe)
1 teaspoon paprika, for garnish
3 green onions or chives, finely chopped, for garnish

Application:

- Preheat oven to 375 degrees F.
- Clean chicken breasts and flatten with kitchen mallet (meat tenderizer).
- Evenly place crab on half of flattened chicken breast.
- Add cheese, salt, and pepper.
- Wrap side of breast over filled side and use wooden toothpick to keep together if needed. Repeat process for each breast.
- Place breasts in lightly greased square casserole dish tightly so each breast is just barely touching.
- Bake uncovered for 15 minutes, or until tops of breasts are golden brown.
- Remove and cover with foil and bake for additional 15 minutes.
- Prepare béarnaise sauce while chicken is cooking.
- When chicken is finished, place on serving plate and remove toothpicks.
- Spoon a little sauce over each breast.
- Serve remaining sauce in ramekins or gravy boat.
- Sprinkle paprika lightly over chicken and sauce, and garnish with fresh chives.

Serving note: Serve with rice or pasta, and sautéed mushrooms
(chanterelle or portabella, if available).

Supermodel Hint
*Use a mallet to rid yourself of any everyday aggressions
(even divas have them!) and to flatten the chicken.
Think of it as kitchen therapy.*

Makes 4–6 servings.

Makeup:

1 pound dried cannellini beans
3 quarts water
3 tablespoons salt
1 quart chicken stock
2 tablespoons bacon fat
6–8 chicken thighs and drumsticks
freshly ground black pepper to taste, divided
1 pound cooked garlic pork sausage or smoked pork
    kielbasa, cut crosswise into 1/3-inch-thick slices
1 large onion, finely diced
2 celery stalks, finely diced
1 whole head garlic, peeled and divided
4 sprigs parsley
2 bay leaves
2 teaspoons fennel
2 teaspoons celery salt
kosher salt to taste

Application:

- In a large bowl, soak the beans overnight at room temperature in 3 quarts water and 3 tablespoons salt.
- Drain and rinse beans in a colander; then set aside.
- Adjust an oven rack to lower-middle position and preheat oven to 300 degrees F.
- Heat bacon fat in a large skillet over high heat until shimmering.
- Season chicken pieces with pepper and place skin side down in skillet.
- Cook over medium heat without moving until well browned, 6–8 minutes.
- Flip chicken pieces and continue cooking until lightly browned on second side, about 3 minutes longer.
- Place chicken on plate and set aside.
- In a skillet, add sausage (or kielbasa) and cook, turning occasionally, until well browned on both sides.
- Transfer to a separate plate from chicken.
- Add onions to skillet and cook, stirring and scraping up browned bits from bottom of pan. Cook until onions are translucent but not browned, about 4 minutes.
- To a dutch oven, add beans, onions, celery, garlic, parsley, bay leaves, fennel, celery salt, kosher salt, pepper, and chicken stock. Bring to a simmer over high heat.
- Reduce to low heat, cover dutch oven, and cook until beans are almost tender but retain a slight bite, about 45 minutes.
- Remove bay leaves and discard.
- Add meats to pot and stir to incorporate, making sure chicken pieces end up on top of beans with skin facing upward. Beans should be almost completely submerged.
- Transfer to oven and cook, uncovered, until thin crust forms on top, about 1 hour, adding more water to pot as necessary to keep beans mostly covered.
- Cook undisturbed until beans are completely cooked, approximately 30 minutes.
- Serve immediately.

Makes 4 servings.

Makeup:

1/2 cup grated, unsweetened coconut
1/2 cup fresh bread crumbs
1 tablespoon salt, divided
1 tablespoon freshly ground white pepper, divided
1/4 cup chopped onion
1 1/2 teaspoons cumin seeds
4 boneless, skinless chicken breast halves
1/4 cup all-purpose flour
1/3 cup buttermilk
6 tablespoons extra-virgin olive oil, divided
4 cups fresh, clean baby spinach

Application:

- Preheat oven to 375 degrees F.
- Combine coconut, bread crumbs, 1/2 tablespoon salt, 1/2 tablespoon pepper, onion, and cumin seeds in a food processor.
- Pulse for 1 minute, until mixture is slightly ground.
- Remove mixture from food processor and place in a large pan.
- Place flour, buttermilk, and coconut / bread crumbs mixture into individual shallow dishes. Evenly coat each chicken breast with flour, then buttermilk, and then coconut / bread crumbs mixture.
- Place breasts in a large skillet with ovenproof handle.
- Add 2 tablespoons olive oil and heat over medium.
- Brown chicken breasts on each side for 2–3 minutes.
- Place skillet in oven and cook chicken for 5 minutes.
- Pour 1 tablespoon olive oil over each chicken breast.
- Cook in oven for additional 5–10 minutes, or until breasts are golden brown.
- Place 1 cup spinach on each serving plate.
- Remove chicken from oven and place on individual serving plates or a serving platter.
- If there are any juices left in the pan from cooking, dribble a little of that over each piece of chicken.

Serving note: Serve with Wild-Nights Rice with Golden Raisins (see p. 245) as side.

Supermodel Hint
When Miss Divina was last in Northern Africa, she subdued her unruly host with this fabulous dinner and a warm body to cling to in the cool desert evening.

Makes 6 servings.

Makeup:

6 chicken breast halves with skin
4 tablespoons butter, room temperature
3 tablespoons minced garlic
1 teaspoon fennel seeds
1/4 teaspoon crushed red pepper
1 teaspoon salt, divided
1 teaspoon freshly ground black pepper, divided
2 cups fresh mushrooms, finely chopped
2 cups fresh spinach, finely chopped
3/4 cup almonds, finely chopped
1/2 cup greek yogurt

Application:

- Preheat oven to 375 degrees F.
- Clean and bone chicken breasts; do not remove skin.
- Run fingers between chicken skin and meat to loosen skin.
- Dry breasts on paper towels.
- Mix butter, garlic, fennel, and crushed red pepper in a small bowl.
- Season butter mixture with a pinch of salt and pepper.
- Spoon 1 teaspoon of garlic-butter mixture into a medium skillet over medium heat.
- Set remaining garlic butter aside.
- Add mushrooms to skillet and sauté until all the butter has evaporated.
- Add spinach and sauté until it is just slightly wilted.
- Remove from heat and cool slightly.
- Stir in almonds and yogurt.
- Divide stuffing between breasts, spreading evenly under skin.
- Using wooden toothpicks, skewer skin to chicken to enclose stuffing.
- Place chicken in a baking dish.
- Spread remaining garlic butter over the top of each chicken breast.
- Season with salt and pepper over skin.
- Cover dish with foil and cook for 40–45 minutes, or until skin has browned and chicken is cooked thoroughly.
- Remove foil for last 5–10 minutes to brown skin.
- Be careful to avoid burning the skin.
- Remove from oven and place on serving plates or platter.

Endora's Cornish Game Hens

Makes 2 servings.

Makeup:

2 whole fresh Cornish game hens
1/2 cup sesame oil
1 teaspoon rosemary
1 teaspoon basil
1 teaspoon french thyme
1 teaspoon freshly ground pepper
1 teaspoon salt
1 clove garlic, freshly chopped
1/4 cup white wine

Application:

- Preheat oven to 425 degrees F.
- Remove giblets and clean hens. Discard giblets or save for another use.
- Place both hens on a roasting rack and place rack in a baking dish.
- Line baking dish bottom with aluminum foil if desired.
- Brush sesame oil evenly over both hens.
- Evenly coat hens with rosemary, basil, thyme, pepper, salt, and garlic and pour wine in bottom of dish.
- Cover with foil and bake in oven for 25 minutes, depending on size of chicken.
- After 25 minutes, remove foil and cook uncovered until hens are fully cooked.
- Remove chicken every 10 minutes and baste with juices to help brown the hens.
- When finished, remove hens from oven and let stand for 5 minutes before serving.

Serving note: Serve with Wild-Nights Rice with Golden Raisins (see p. 245) or Mr. Atkin's Herbed Bambino Potatoes (see p. 236), and steamed fresh asparagus.

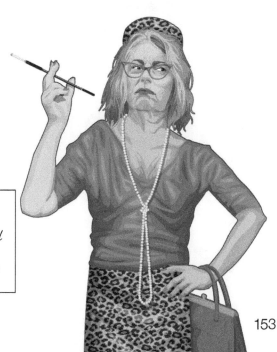

Supermodel Hint

Endora really isn't much of a looker, but she does seem to cast a spell over everyone she meets. She can whip up a delicious meal faster than anyone I know! Now, her daughter—she is the bewitching one!

Makes 8 servings.

Makeup:

8 large (8-ounce) red, orange, green and yellow bell
  peppers (2 of each)
4 tablespoons extra-virgin olive oil, divided
2 cups chopped onions
1/4 cup fresh parsley, chopped
3 garlic cloves, chopped
2 cups cooked white rice, cooled
1 tablespoon paprika
2 teaspoons salt
2 teaspoons ground black pepper
1 teaspoon ground allspice
3 cups tomato sauce, divided
1 large egg
1 1/4 pounds lean ground turkey
1 cup shredded parmesan cheese

Application:

- Preheat oven to 425 degrees F.
- Cut off top 1/2 inch of peppers. Discard the tops (or save for presentation later on).
- Clean and scoop seeds from cavities.
- Heat 2 tablespoons olive oil in a large skillet over medium-high heat.
- Add onions, parsley, and garlic.
- Sauté until onions soften, about 5–6 minutes.
- After onions are translucent, transfer mixture to a large bowl.
- In the bowl, mix onion mixture, rice, paprika, salt, pepper, and allspice.
- Mix in 1/2 cup tomato sauce, egg, and then ground turkey (uncooked). Mix thoroughly.
- With a tablespoon, fill each pepper cavity with turkey mixture.
- Coat ovenproof casserole dish with remaining 2 tablespoons of olive oil.
- Stand filled peppers in casserole dish.
- Sprinkle small amount of parmesan on top of each bell pepper.
- Bake uncovered for 30–45 minutes, or until meat is fully cooked.
- In a small saucepan, bring remaining 2 1/2 cups tomato sauce to a soft boil over medium-high heat.
- When bell peppers are fully cooked, remove and place on individual plates or on a serving platter.
- Pour tomato sauce over peppers just before serving.

Serving note: Serve with a green salad and fresh french bread.

Supermodel Hint

When Miss Divina was just a wee bit of a thing, her lovely mama made this with only green bell peppers.
Miss Divina added the festive pairing of red, orange, yellow, and of course green bell peppers to this family recipe.

Freida "Frenchy" Frye's Poulet avec Crème des Herbes

Makes 4 servings.

Makeup:

1/4 cup packed fresh parsley leaves
1/4 cup packed fresh tarragon leaves
1/4 cup shallots, thinly sliced
4 tablespoons salted butter, divided
4 whole boneless chicken breasts
2 tablespoons flour
1/2 cup chicken broth
1/2 cup heavy cream
1/4 cup capers
2 tablespoons dijon mustard

Application:

- Chop parsley, tarragon, and shallots in a blender or food processor.
- In a large skillet, sauté chicken in 2 tablespoons butter over medium heat.
- Heat until chicken breasts are browned lightly on each side and fully cooked.
- Transfer chicken to plate.
- Return skillet to heat. Add remaining 2 tablespoons butter and flour. Mix until smooth paste is formed.
- Whisk in broth and cook mixture until it thickens.
- Stir in cream, parsley mixture, capers, and mustard. Stir until mixed thoroughly.
- Add chicken breasts and cook for 5–6 minutes on each side over medium heat.
- Transfer chicken to clean serving plate.
- Pour sauce over chicken.

Serving note: Serve with pasta or potatoes, and steamed fresh artichokes or brussels sprouts.

Supermodel Hint
Miss Divina always tests her chicken, especially thick slices, to assure it's thoroughly cooked.

Hearty Man's Chicken Potpie

Makes 4–6 servings.

Makeup:

Crust
2 cups all-purpose flour
2 teaspoons baking powder
1 teaspoon salt
1 tablespoon butter
1/2 cup water
2 eggs, lightly beaten

Filling
1 large onion, finely chopped
2 tablespoons butter, divided, 1 tablespoon melted
1 teaspoon ground french thyme
1 teaspoon pepper
1/2 cup chicken broth
3 tablespoons cornstarch
5 cups cooked chicken breast chunks
1 (10-ounce) package mixed frozen vegetables (peas, corn, carrots, green beans, baby white onions, etc.)
1/4 cup all-purpose flour
1 teaspoon salt

Photo of individual potpie shown.

Application:

Crust
- Preheat oven to 425 degrees F.
- Grease and flour a 9-inch pie dish.
- In a large bowl, combine flour, baking powder, and salt.
- Add butter and mix together with your fingers or process in a food processor until mixture resembles coarse meal.
- Add water and mix or process until manageable dough forms.
- Transfer dough to a lightly floured surface and knead 1 minute, or until smooth.
- Divide dough in half; set half aside.
- Roll dough into a 10-inch-diameter circle (1 inch larger than the diameter of the pie dish).
- Repeat, rolling remaining dough for second crust. Save second crust for top.
- Place one piecrust in pie dish.
- With a fork, prick the bottom of piecrust for ventilation.
- Bake for 5 minutes and then remove. Patch crust where needed. Return crust to oven for 3 additional minutes.

Filling
- In a large pan over medium heat, combine onion, 1 tablespoon butter, thyme, and pepper.
- Cook, stirring, until onion is golden brown.
- Add 1/4 cup water; cook until most of the liquid evaporates.
- Mix broth and cornstarch in a small bowl.
- To pan, add cooked chicken, frozen vegetables, flour, and cornstarch/broth mixture. Cook, stirring, until boiling.
- Spoon mixture into pie shell, cover with second crust, and fold in edges.
- Brush top with remaining 1 tablespoon melted butter and slightly salt.
- Cut two small holes into crust for ventilation.
- Bake in oven for 35–50 minutes.
- Brush with beaten egg now and then to prevent crust burn.
- Remove pie from oven and let cool for 5–10 minutes before serving.

Hollie Woode's Roasted Chicken with Herbs

Makes 6–8 servings.

Makeup:

1 whole chicken (3–5 pounds)
1 cup extra-virgin olive oil
1 teaspoon garlic powder
1 teaspoon rosemary
1 teaspoon basil
1 teaspoon french thyme
1 teaspoon freshly ground pepper
1 teaspoon salt
1/2 cup white wine

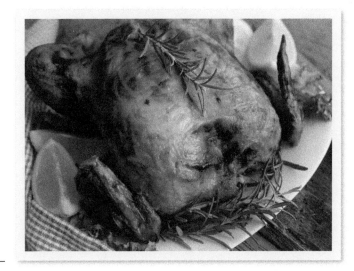

Application:

- Preheat oven to 425 degrees F.
- Clean chicken and cut in half.
- Place both sides on roasting rack; place rack in a large, oblong baking dish.
- Line baking dish with aluminum foil if desired.
- Pour olive oil evenly over entire chicken.
- Evenly coat chicken with seasonings (garlic powder, rosemary, basil, thyme, pepper, and salt) and pour wine in bottom of dish.
- Cover with foil and bake in oven for 30–45 minutes, depending on size of chicken.
- Remove chicken every 10 minutes and baste chicken with juices.
- After 30 minutes, remove and discard foil over chicken, baste, and return to oven to brown skin, approximately 10–15 minutes.
- When finished, remove and let stand for 5–10 minutes; cut into pieces and place on individual serving plates or serve on platter.

Serving note: Pair with cooked wild rice or Mr. Atkin's Herbed Bambino
Potatoes (see p. 236).

Supermodel Hint

*Butter up your chicken! Gently work your fingers between the
skin and the meat of the breasts and legs, separating the two
from one another, and work in additional butter or oil.
This will enhance the flavor and help moisten the bird.*

Makes 4 servings.

Makeup:

1/4 cup fresh parsley, finely chopped
1 teaspoon lemon zest
4 boneless, skinless chicken breasts
1 tablespoon dijon mustard
1 garlic clove, minced
1 teaspoon salt
1 teaspoon freshly ground black pepper
1 teaspoon freshly ground white pepper
2 tablespoons sesame oil
juice of 1 lemon
kalamata olives, for garnish

Application:

- Mix parsley, lemon zest, and garlic in a small bowl.
- Clean and pat dry chicken breasts.
- Brush each breast with mustard; then sprinkle with parsley mixture.
- Season with salt, black pepper, and white pepper.
- Heat sesame oil in a large skillet over medium heat.
- Add chicken and brown for 5–8 minutes on each side, or until cooked through.
- As you cook chicken, squeeze juice from leftover lemon over each breast.
- When breasts are cooked, remove from skillet and place on individual plates or a serving platter.
- Pour any leftover sauce over chicken.
- Garnish with fresh kalamata olives.

Serving note: Serve with freshly cooked pasta with light extra-virgin olive oil and seasonings, and your choice of vegetable.

Supermodel Hint

Jackie is hard to please but loves to dine out with Miss Divina. Miss Divina thinks that this recipe will impress even the most finicky diva. She's one, so she should know!

Makes 4 servings.

Makeup:

1 tablespoon butter
1 cup fresh chanterelle mushrooms, sliced
3/4 cup chicken broth
2 tablespoons all-purpose flour
1/2 cup chardonnay wine
2 teaspoons minced tarragon leaves
3 tablespoons extra-virgin olive oil
4 boneless, skinless chicken breast halves
2 tablespoons whipping cream

Application:

- Sauté mushrooms with butter in a medium skillet over medium heat for 5–10 minutes, or until tender and golden brown.
- When mushrooms are done, add broth and flour.
- Cook, mixing well, for about 5 minutes.
- Add wine and tarragon and cook over medium heat until liquid is reduced to 1/2 cup.
- In a separate large skillet, brown chicken in olive oil until meat is no longer pink in center (cut to test if done; about 10 minutes may suffice).
- Transfer chicken breasts to plate and keep warm.
- Add mushroom mixture and cream to chicken skillet; stir until bubbling over medium-high heat.
- Spoon sauce over chicken just prior to serving.

Serving note: Serve with pasta and green salad.

Supermodel Hint
Miss Divina fondly remembers her mama making this wonderfully comforting dish on many a cold winter night.

Miss Hottkiss's Honey-Sweet Balsamic Chicken

Makes 4–6 servings.

Makeup:

1/4 cup balsamic vinegar
6 tablespoons honey
3 tablespoons extra-virgin olive oil, divided
2 cloves garlic, minced
1 tablespoon dried french thyme
1 tablespoon dried rosemary
1 tablespoon crushed red pepper
2 tablespoons salt, divided
2 tablespoons ground black pepper, divided
2 pounds boneless, skinless chicken breasts
1 pound baby red potatoes, quartered
1 pound fresh green beans, trimmed

Application:

- Preheat oven to 425 degrees F.
- Make the marinade: in a medium bowl, combine vinegar, honey, 1 tablespoon olive oil, garlic, thyme, rosemary, crushed red pepper, 1 tablespoon salt, and 1 tablespoon pepper. Stir well to mix.
- Place chicken breasts in a large, resealable plastic bag and pour marinade over the top.
- Seal and toss chicken to evenly coat.
- Marinate for at least 30 minutes.
- Coat large casserole dish with butter or olive oil. Use a cooking brush if you have one.
- Remove marinated chicken breasts from plastic bag, reserving remaining marinade in the bag.
- Place chicken in center of casserole dish and surround chicken with potatoes.
- Drizzle with remaining 2 tablespoons olive oil, season with remaining 1 tablespoon each of salt and pepper, and stir to coat.
- Bake uncovered for 25 minutes.
- Meanwhile, steam green beans until they are cooked but still bright green and firm, about 10 minutes.
- Remove casserole dish from oven and set aside.
- Toss steamed green beans in with potatoes.
- Rearrange chicken breasts so they are spaced evenly in the casserole dish, on top of the vegetables.
- Pour remaining marinade over the top of the chicken and vegetables.
- Bake for additional 5–7 minutes.
- Remove from oven and serve.

Pardoned-Turkey Tacos

Makes 12 tacos.

Makeup:

2 cups seedless red or green grapes, halved
1 red onion, finely chopped
2 jalapeño chiles, seeded and finely chopped
1/3 cup cilantro
juice of 1 lime
salt, pepper, and garlic powder to taste
12 corn tortillas
canola oil (to fry tortillas)
1 (15-ounce) can black beans, drained and rinsed
1 1/2–2 pounds roasted turkey breast, shredded
  (cooked ground turkey may be substituted)
1 cup shredded jalapeño Monterey Jack cheese
1/2 cup coleslaw
hot sauce (optional)
sour cream, for garnish (optional)

Application:

- In a medium saucepan, combine grapes, onion, jalapeño chiles, cilantro, and lime juice.
- Season with salt, pepper, and garlic powder.
- Cook over medium heat for 5–7 minutes. Set aside and keep warm.
- In a small skillet, heat oil over medium heat.
- Fry tortillas to desired crispness in canola oil.
- Remove cooked tortillas to a paper towel and lightly pat off excess oil with another paper towel.
- Fold tortillas in half and place on a plate to set but keep warm.
- Heat black beans in microwave until warm, about 1 minute. Drain excess moisture.
- Heat turkey in microwave until warm, about 1 minute.
- Assemble tacos in the following order: beans, turkey, and jalapeño jack cheese.
- Place small amount of coleslaw on top of turkey.
- Top with grape/jalapeño sauce.
- For a spicier taco, add hot sauce.
- Top with a small dab of sour cream if so desired and serve.

Supermodel Hint

Your turkey may have been pardoned by the president at Thanksgiving, but that was before the unfortunate bird met Miss Divina!

161

Makes 6–8 servings.

Makeup:

Chicken
6 boneless, skinless chicken breasts, cut into halves
2 celery stalks, chopped
4 carrots, peeled and chopped
1 medium yellow onion, diced
1 (15-ounce) can chicken broth
2 tablespoons dried parsley
2 teaspoons chicken bouillon granules
1 1/2 teaspoons salt, plus additional to taste
1 1/2 teaspoons pepper, plus additional to taste
1/4 cup all-purpose flour or cornstarch
1/4 cup cold water (or cold chicken broth), for slurry

Dumplings
2 cups all-purpose flour or biscuit flour
4 teaspoons baking powder
1 teaspoon salt
3/4 cup milk
1/4 cup canola oil

Application:

Chicken
- On the stovetop in a large ovenproof pan or dutch oven, combine chicken, celery, carrots, onion, chicken broth, parsley, chicken bouillon granules, salt, and pepper; add enough water to cover chicken.
- Bring to a boil, reduce heat, cover, and simmer for 1 hour, or until chicken is done.
- In a measuring cup, add flour (or cornstarch) and cold water to create slurry. (If you want, use cold chicken broth for richer flavor.)
- Add slurry to ovenproof pan or dutch oven to thicken the gravy. If gravy is too thin, create and add more slurry.
- Taste sauce and add more salt and pepper to taste, if desired.

Dumplings
- Preheat oven to 425 degrees F.
- In a large mixing bowl, combine dumpling ingredients and mix well to form stiff dough.
- When chicken and gravy is ready, drop large tablespoonful of dough on top of simmering sauce. Repeat until all the dough is used.
- Cover and simmer for 15 minutes.
- Move pan to oven and cook, uncovered, for 5–10 minutes, just enough time for dumplings to brown on top.
- Remove from oven and place dumplings on a plate.
- Place chicken on individual serving plates and pour sauce over chicken.

Supermodel Hint
Grandma Grasso (Gammy) on Miss Divina's father's side was renowned for this recipe. She was aptly named, for she was all gams and no legs!

Makes 4 servings.

Makeup:

4 boneless, skinless chicken breasts, flattened
1 1/2 teaspoons fresh rosemary
1 teaspoon sage
1 teaspoon french thyme
1 teaspoon salt
1 teaspoon pepper
1/3 cup pesto sauce
1/3 cup sundried tomatoes
8 ounces prosciutto, very thinly sliced
1/2 cup finely chopped fresh chives, divided
4 teaspoons extra-virgin olive oil
1 teaspoon paprika, for garnish

Roasted Red Pepper Mayonnaise
1/2 cup roasted red peppers
1/2 cup mayonnaise
4 sage leaves

Application:

- Preheat oven to 350 degrees F.
- Wash and dry chicken breasts and flatten with kitchen mallet (meat tenderizer).
- Season chicken with rosemary, sage, thyme, salt, and pepper.
- Spread small amount of pesto sauce to evenly cover each chicken breast.
- Evenly layer sundried tomatoes and then prosciutto on one half of each chicken breast.
- Sprinkle 1/4 cup chives over prosciutto. Save remainder for garnish.
- Fold each chicken breast over filling and use wooden toothpick to keep together.
- Place breasts in roasting pan with small amount of olive oil and so each breast is just barely touching.
- Bake covered for 15 minutes.
- Remove cover and bake for another 10 minutes, or until tops of breasts are golden brown.
- When chicken is finished, place on cutting board and remove toothpicks.
- Slice chicken breasts into two equally sized pieces.
- Place each breast in the center of a serving plate.

Roasted Red Pepper Mayonnaise
- Place roasted red peppers, mayonnaise, and sage into a blender or food processor and process until smooth.
- Transfer to a small bowl.
- Dribble roasted red pepper mayonnaise over each chicken breast.
- Sprinkle paprika on top of each breast and garnish with remaining 1/4 cup chives.

Serving note: Serve with steamed brown rice and a variety of sautéed mushrooms.

Supermodel Hint

Miss Divina forgives you if you stuff these breasts. But she hopes that you are not so unfortunate for the need to "accent" your bras with extra stuffing. But she's seen enough skinny models to know it's a cruel joke of mother nature.

Makes 6–8 servings.

Makeup:

2 tablespoons extra-virgin olive oil, divided
2 pounds boneless, skinless chicken breasts
salt, pepper, and garlic powder to taste
1–2 (28-ounce) can(s) enchilada sauce, mild to hot,
  divided
1 package (12–30 count) corn tortillas
1 (15-ounce) can black beans, rinsed
1 (14.5-ounce) can black olives, chopped
1 bunch green onions, chopped
1 (15-ounce) can corn, drained
6 hard-boiled eggs, chopped
2 pounds extra-sharp cheddar cheese, grated
sour cream (optional)

Application:

- Preheat oven to 375 degrees F.
- Season chicken with salt, pepper, and garlic powder to taste, and brown in 1 tablespoon olive oil in a large skillet over medium heat.
- Once chicken is browned and cooked fully, set aside in a bowl and let cool.
- Once chicken is cool, shred it into small pieces.
- Coat large casserole dish with remaining 1 tablespoon olive oil.
- Place small amount of enchilada sauce in bottom of dish and distribute evenly over the bottom.
- Place a layer of tortillas over enchilada sauce.
- Layer some black beans, chicken, olives, green onions, corn, and eggs onto tortillas.
- Cover with some cheese and sauce, and season with small amount of salt, pepper, and garlic powder.
- Repeat layers until dish is filled (2–3 layers of each), ending with cheese and enchilada sauce. Reserve some green onions for garnish if desired.
- Bake uncovered for 1–1 1/2 hours.
- Serve with a dab of sour cream and sprinkle on some chopped green onions (optional).

Supermodel Hint

Pair this easy dish with a nice green salad and a pitcher of margaritas! Nothing beats a nice, warm evening on the patio with this delicious meal and a good tequila cocktail! ¡Olé!

Makes 4 servings.

Makeup:

1/4 cup honey
2 tablespoons soy sauce
2 teaspoons freshly grated ginger
2 tablespoons sesame oil
minced garlic to taste
4 skinless, boneless chicken breast halves
1 tablespoon sesame seeds

Application:

- Combine honey, soy sauce, ginger, sesame oil, and garlic in a small bowl; stir well and set aside.
- Flatten chicken breasts and marinate in honey / soy sauce mixture for 2 hours.
- Prepare outdoor grill according to your specific grill instructions.
- Remove chicken, saving the honey / soy sauce mixture.
- Grill chicken on outdoor grill or in a pan, about 5–6 minutes each side.
- Flip chicken every few minutes and brush with honey / soy sauce mixture frequently.
- Pour sesame seeds onto a plate.
- Remove chicken from grill, brush with final coating of honey / soy sauce mixture, and roll chicken in the sesame seeds.
- Remove and place on a warm plate.

Serving note: This dish tastes great with steamed white rice and steamed broccoli.

Supermodel Hint

Like a good wine or preparing for a promising date, marinating shouldn't be rushed. An extra few hours in the right sauce makes a memorable mouthful later on. Plan ahead. Consider letting it go overnight!

Show–Us–Your–Bourbon Chicken and Sausage Jambalaya

Makes 4–6 servings.

Makeup:

8 cups cooked rice, cooled completely
2 tablespoons extra-virgin olive oil
3 pounds chicken breast, cooked and cubed
1/2 cup bourbon
1/4 cup finely chopped yellow onion
1/4 cup finely chopped celery
1/4 cup finely chopped red bell pepper
1/4 cup finely chopped parsley
2 cloves garlic, finely chopped
1 pound smoked sausage, sliced
1 (14.5-ounce) can stewed tomatoes
1 1/2 cups chicken stock, plus additional as needed
2 tablespoons black pepper, or to taste
2 tablespoons salt, or to taste
2 tablespoons cayenne pepper, or to taste
1/2 teaspoon sugar, or to taste
1/2 teaspoon french thyme, or to taste
1 bay leaf
1/4 cup chopped green onions, for garnish

Application:

- In a large, high-sided, covered pan, over medium heat, heat olive oil, and brown chicken on both sides.
- Remove chicken, chop, add bourbon, and set aside to marinate.
- In same pan, sauté onion, celery, red bell pepper, parsley, and garlic.
- Add sausage and brown for 5 minutes.
- Add chicken and bourbon.
- Add stewed tomatoes, chicken stock, pepper, salt, cayenne, sugar, thyme, and bay leaf.
- Bring to a boil and reduce heat to a simmer.
- Cook uncovered until chicken is thoroughly cooked, about 25 minutes.
- Stir occasionally and make sure there is always enough liquid. Add more water or stock if needed.
- Taste carefully and adjust seasonings to your taste.
- Remove and discard bay leaf and stir in rice.
- Mix completely until mixture is thick but neither soupy nor dry.
- Taste again and correct seasonings as desired.
- Warm together for 5 minutes on simmer and serve with green onions on top.

Supermodel Hint
Be sure to add just as much cayenne as you can take. Once cayenne gets into your system, it makes you sweat, so wear plenty of deodorant!

Makes 4–6 servings.

Makeup:

1/4 cup extra-virgin olive oil
1/4 cup soy sauce, or to taste
2 boneless, skinless chicken breasts (or 3 thighs), diced
1 package stir-fry Szechuan-style sauce mix
crushed red pepper to taste
1/4 cup each freshly cut vegetables (broccoli, green onions, mushrooms, etc.)
1 can water chestnuts, drained
cooked wild rice, for serving
sesame seeds, for garnish

Application:

- Heat olive oil and soy sauce in a large skillet or stir-fry pan over medium-high heat.
- Place diced chicken into the skillet and brown until tender.
- Add stir-fry sauce mix, crushed red pepper, and more soy sauce as needed.
- When chicken and sauce are mixed well, add vegetables and water chestnuts.
- Stir constantly so all ingredients are mixed well.
- Cook about 5–7 minutes. Keep vegetables firm; don't overcook them.
- Serve over wild rice and sprinkle sesame seeds on top.

Supermodel Hint

The premier of China convinced Miss Divina (with an offer she couldn't refuse) to make this dish just for him. Needless to say, she refuses to model in China again!

Fish and Seafood Dishes

Heavenly Sent Cod with Jesus-Walked-on-Water-cress Sauce (p. 175)

Baked Trout with Mango Striptease Salsa

Makes 4 servings.

Makeup:

Mango Salsa
2 fresh serrano chili peppers
2 large mangos, peeled and diced
2 teaspoons minced red onion

Fish
4 rainbow trout fillets
1 teaspoon salt
1 teaspoon freshly ground black pepper
1/4 cup chopped green onions, for garnish
1 lime, quartered, for garnish
8 (6-inch) flour tortillas, for serving

Application:

• Preheat oven to 425 degrees F.

Mango Salsa
• Grill serrano chili peppers on hot grill or under broiler and cook for 4 minutes, turning frequently.
• Remove peppers when finished and charred on all sides; set aside to cool.
• When peppers are cool, remove skin, halve, seed, and dice into small pieces.
• Combine mangos, peppers, and onions; mix well and cool in refrigerator.

Fish
• Line baking sheet with aluminum foil, and lightly grease the foil with butter.
• Place cleaned trout on foil and lightly brush fish with salsa.
• Season fish with pepper and salt.
• Bake for 10 minutes per inch of thickness.
• Fish will be done when it turns opaque and flakes easily with a fork.
• Use spatula to carefully place fish on serving plate and garnish with green onions.
• Serve with lime slices, side ramekins of mango salsa, and warmed tortillas.

Supermodel Hint
Remember Mango? One of the hottest stars of the striptease stage? Oh dear, where is she now? These one-night wonders come and go so quickly!

169

Makes 4 servings.

Makeup:

Béarnaise Sauce Divine
2 tablespoons finely chopped shallots
1 tablespoon red vinegar
1 tablespoon water
3 large egg yolks, room temperature
1 tablespoon fresh tarragon
1/4 teaspoon salt
1 pinch cayenne pepper
1/2 cup butter, room temperature and cut into small
   pieces, divided

Fish
4 thick cod fillets (6–8 ounces each)
4 tablespoons sesame oil, divided
salt and pepper to taste

Application:

• Preheat oven to 400 degrees F.

Béarnaise Sauce
• In a thick-bottomed saucepan, mix shallots and vinegar.
• Cook over low heat until vinegar is evaporated.
• Add water, yolks, tarragon, salt, and cayenne.
• Beat with whisk until just blended.
• Improvise a double boiler by bringing 1/2 inch of water to a simmer in a large pan and setting the saucepan with egg mixture in it.
• Beating constantly, gradually add 1/4 cup butter.
• Cook for 1–2 minutes, until yolks thicken.
• Beating constantly, gradually add remaining 1/4 cup butter.

Fish
• Rinse fillets under cold water and pat dry.
• Brush fillets with 2 tablespoons sesame oil.
• Sprinkle with salt and pepper.
• Coat baking pan with remaining 2 tablespoons sesame oil and place fillets on it.
• Bake for 5–7 minutes. Turn fillets over and bake additional 5 minutes. Keep an eye on the fish, being careful not to overcook.
• Once fillets are browned on both sides, remove from oven.
• Place fillets on serving plates, spoon béarnaise sauce over the fish, and serve.

Supermodel Hint
*In this case, your fish being flaky is just wonderful,
but you must be an interesting host at all times and never flaky!*

Countess De Payne Oyster Bake with Havarti Cheese

Makes 4–6 servings.

Makeup:

1/2 cup butter
2 tablespoons flour
2 cups whipping cream
2 teaspoons anchovy paste
grated rind of 1 lemon
1 teaspoon salt
1 teaspoon white pepper
3 tablespoons minced pimiento
36 large oysters, shucked and drained, divided
1 cup plain cracker crumbs, divided
1 cup shredded Havarti cheese, divided
4 tablespoons minced fresh parsley, divided, plus
   additional for garnish

Application:

- Preheat oven to 395 degrees F.
- Melt butter in a medium saucepan over low heat.
- Stir in flour to form smooth paste.
- Remove from heat and gradually stir in cream until smooth.
- Cook over medium heat, stirring until thickened.
- Blend in anchovy paste, lemon rind, salt, pepper, and pimiento.
- Spread a quarter of the sauce in a buttered 2-quart baking dish.
- Arrange 18 oysters over sauce.
- Sprinkle with layer of 1/3 cup cracker crumbs, 1/2 cup cheese, and 1 tablespoon parsley.
- Add another quarter of sauce and remaining 18 oysters.
- Sprinkle with another layer of 1/3 cup crumbs, remaining 1/2 cup cheese, and 1 tablespoon parsley.
- Add remaining sauce and top with remaining 1/3 cup crumbs.
- Bake 15–20 minutes; sprinkle with remaining 2 tablespoons parsley just before serving.

Serving note: Serve with rice and fresh vegetables.

Supermodel Hint

*The countess was renowned for her unusual parties. She usually filled you with tasty treats
and then whipped you if you didn't show her the respect she was entitled to!*

Makes 6 servings.

Makeup:

8 slices dried french bread, torn into small pieces
1/4 cup milk (or half-and-half for a creamier
  consistency), plus additional as needed
4 tablespoons butter, divided
1 red onion, finely chopped
4 celery stalks, finely chopped
1 green bell pepper, finely chopped
2 eggs, beaten
1 1/2 pounds of crab meat, chopped
1/2 teaspoon crushed red pepper
1/2 teaspoon dry mustard
1 teaspoon salt
1 teaspoon freshly ground white pepper
3 tablespoons bread crumbs
6 teaspoons mayonnaise
1/4 cup parmesan cheese

Application:

- Preheat oven to 425 degrees F.
- Place bread pieces in a large bowl and add milk (or half-and-half).
- Set aside for 5 minutes.
- Press milk into bread with a fork and make a paste, adding more milk if needed.
- Heat 2 tablespoons butter in a large skillet over medium heat.
- Add onion, celery, and green bell pepper.
- Cook until vegetables soften.
- Stir in remaining 2 tablespoons butter until melted.
- Pour mixture over bread paste.
- Stir in eggs, crab meat, crushed red pepper, mustard, salt, and pepper.
- Stir to combine all ingredients.
- Divide crab mixture evenly into six greased individual-size casserole dishes or ramekins.
- Sprinkle bread crumbs over crab mixture.
- Top each individual casserole with 1 teaspoon mayonnaise.
- Bake for 10 minutes in oven.
- Remove and spread the hot mayonnaise over the casseroles with knife.
- Sprinkle tiny bit of parmesan cheese on each casserole and bake for 3 additional minutes.

Serving note: Serve warm with steamed asparagus.

Supermodel Hint

Dungeness crabs are from the Pacific Northwest; blue crabs are from the East Coast. Both are best boiled or steamed.

Frita Lay's Crab Enchiladas

Makes 6 servings.

Makeup:

2 tablespoons unsalted butter
3 tablespoons all-purpose flour
2 tablespoons lobster stock (seafood, vegetable, or chicken stock may be substituted)
2 cups whole milk
1 teaspoon salt
1 teaspoon white pepper
1 pound freshly cracked crab
12 corn tortillas
1 (12-ounce) can enchilada sauce, green or red
1/2 cup grated white cheddar
1/2 cup grated Monterey Jack cheese
1/2 cup sour cream

Application:

- Preheat oven to 350 degrees F.
- Melt butter in a small saucepan over medium heat.
- Stir in flour and lobster stock and cook for 2 minutes.
- Pour in milk and cook, stirring continuously, until mixture comes to a light boil.
- Continue to cook and stir for 2 minutes.
- Season with salt and pepper.
- Remove from heat and chill.
- Butter a 9 x 13-inch baking dish.
- Combine crab and 1/2 cup of chilled sauce in a medium mixing bowl.
- Spread a quarter of the crab/sauce mixture on the bottom of the buttered dish.
- In a dry skillet, no oil, over medium heat, heat tortillas for 1 minute on each side.
- Spoon 2–3 teaspoons of crab mixture down the center of a tortilla and roll up. Repeat procedure with remaining tortillas.
- Place tortillas seam side down in the baking dish.
- Spoon remaining sauce over tortillas, drizzle enchilada sauce over tortillas, and sprinkle with cheese.
- Bake for 15–20 minutes.
- Garnish with a dab of sour cream.

Supermodel Hint

Here is another nontraditional way to have crabs.
Look for lobster base at gourmet food stores.
Yes, you too can have the whole enchilada!

Makes 4 servings.

Makeup:

Mustard Sauce
1/4 cup dijon mustard
1/4 cup nonfat plain greek yogurt
1/4 cup lemon juice
3 tablespoons minced fresh dill weed
1 tablespoon honey

Fish
4 fresh center-cut swordfish fillets (8–10 ounces each)
2 tablespoons extra-virgin olive oil
1 teaspoon salt
1 teaspoon freshly ground black pepper

Application:

- Prepare outdoor grill. (I prefer charcoal grilling, but you can use an indoor grill if you don't have an outdoor grill.)
  - If using a charcoal grill, mound coals to one side, allowing for an area of indirect heat.
  - If using a gas grill, turn on only a few of the burners and leave the rest off for indirect heat.

Mustard Sauce
- While grill heats, combine mustard, yogurt, lemon juice, dill weed, and honey in a small bowl.
- Stir until mixture is smooth.
- Place in a serving bowl and chill.

Fish
- Rinse fish under cold water and pat dry.
- With pastry brush, lightly coat fish with olive oil.
- Oil or butter the grilling rack for the swordfish just prior to grilling.
- Place fish on grilling rack and sprinkle with salt and pepper.
- Cook on grill until fish flakes with a fork, about 4–5 minutes each side.
- Remove fish from rack and place on serving plates.
- Serve mustard sauce on the side.

Serving note: Serve with fresh salad and freshly grilled vegetables.

Supermodel Hint
British supermodel Lady Wilde was of landed gentry, but her language spoke of no lady! She was all East Ender! That tongue could certainly cut like a sword! Just goes to show title doesn't always mean class!

Makes 4 servings.

Makeup:

1 cup fresh watercress, washed and drained
1 tablespoon finely chopped parsley
1/2 teaspoon paprika
1/2 teaspoon crushed red pepper
2 cloves garlic, finely chopped
2 tablespoons extra-virgin olive oil
1/4 cup butter
4 cod fillets
2 tablespoons grated lemon zest, for garnish
1 lemon, sliced, for garnish

Application:

- Preheat oven to 375 degrees F.
- In a small mixing bowl, combine watercress, parsley, paprika, and crushed red pepper.
- Add garlic and olive oil to a medium skillet over medium heat.
- Sauté until garlic is fragrant, and then remove the pan from the heat.
- Add watercress mixture to garlic and mix thoroughly.
- Melt butter in a small pan over medium heat or in microwave for 15 seconds.
- Spread melted butter on the bottom of a shallow baking dish.
- Place cod fillets in baking dish and spoon on half of the watercress/garlic mixture.
- Bake in oven for about 8 minutes.
- Remove dish from oven and spoon on remaining watercress/garlic mixture.
- Return to oven and bake for another 8–12 minutes, or until the cod flakes easily with a fork.
- Place on serving platter, squeeze some lemon juice over the fish, and garnish with lemon zest.

Serving note: Serve over Mother-Agent Mashed Potatoes (see p. 235).

Supermodel Hint

Miss Divina's mother once grew watercress by her own reflecting pool at home. Hoping to dissuade the resident ducks from ruining her prized produce, she also installed a tiny hand-lettered sign instructing the waterfowl not to eat or trample her little crop.

175

Hottie Butte (a Hell—of—a—Butt) Grilled Halibut

Makes 4 servings.

Makeup:

4 (1 1/2-pound) halibut fillets, thickly sliced
2 cups red-grapefruit juice, divided
1 tablespoon garlic powder
1 tablespoon salt
1 tablespoon pepper
1 teaspoon dill weed
1 teaspoon fennel
1 teaspoon *herbes de provence*
1 teaspoon crushed red pepper
1 teaspoon french thyme
2 tablespoons extra-virgin olive oil
1 cup half-and-half
1/2 cup dry white wine, preferably chardonnay
1 cup vegetable broth
2 tablespoons all-purpose flour
1/4 cup sun-dried tomatoes
1 zucchini, diced
1 cup chopped green onions, for garnish

Application:

- In a shallow bowl, marinate halibut fillets in 1 1/2 cups of grapefruit juice for 2 hours, turning every 30 minutes.
- Season both sides of fillets with garlic powder, salt, pepper, dill weed, fennel, herbes de provence, red pepper, and thyme.
- Prepare outdoor grill according to your specific grill instructions.
- Place seasoned fillets on center of oiled grill.
- Cook fillets until first side is slightly golden, approximately 5 minutes, depending on thickness.
- Turn over and grill the second side until slightly golden and fish flakes when tested with a fork, approximately 3–5 minutes, depending on thickness.
- Transfer fillets to a plate.
- In skillet, stir together remaining 1/2 cup grapefruit juice, half-and-half, wine, and broth.
- Add flour to thicken and mix thoroughly.
- Stir and bring to low boil.
- Sauce should be consistency of a light cream sauce.
- Add sun-dried tomatoes and zucchini.
- Cook for 3–5 minutes.
- Pour sauce into side dish.
- Place halibut onto serving plates.
- Pour small amount of sauce on halibut. Place remainder of sauce in a side dish.
- Garnish with green onions.

Serving note: Serve with steamed rice or risotto.

Supermodel Hint

Miss Divina likes to use pepper mixture. She gets hers in jars at the local market, but you can also make your own. Just buy pepper varieties and mix them! Fun for the whole family!

Jumbo Prawns, Scallops, and Sautéed Leeks to Stuff Your Cheeks

Makes 2–4 servings.

Makeup:

2 fresh leek stalks, thinly sliced and cleaned
1/4 cup sesame oil
2 teaspoons Thai seasoning
2 teaspoons lemon juice
2 teaspoons freshly ground pepper, divided
1 teaspoon finely chopped fresh garlic
1 teaspoon dill weed
1 pound jumbo prawns, shelled and cleaned
1 pound large scallops
1/4 cup chicken stock
1/4 cup sliced almonds, for garnish
1 (8-ounce) can mandarin orange slices, chilled,
   for garnish

Application:

- Let leeks sit in a large bowl of cold water for 1 hour before preparation.
- In a large sauté pan or wok at medium-high temperature, add sesame oil, Thai seasoning, lemon juice, 1 teaspoon pepper, garlic, and dill weed.
- Place cleaned and shelled jumbo prawns and scallops in pan or wok and sauté until they are cooked, or about 5 minutes. Cover and remove from heat.
- Drain the leeks and rinse under cold water if they need more cleaning.
- Place leeks in a large skillet with chicken stock and remaining 1 teaspoon freshly ground pepper.
- Sauté leeks over medium-high heat for 5–7 minutes, or until all stock has evaporated.
- When leeks are cooked, with a slotted ladle, place evenly in the center of the serving plates, removing as much stock as possible in the process. Next place the prawns and scallops (optional) over the leeks.
- Garnish with sliced almonds and chilled mandarin orange slices.

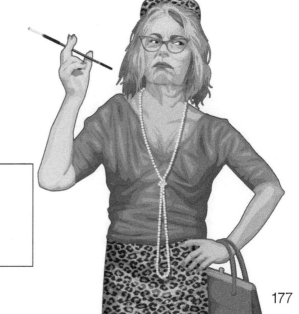

Supermodel Hint

*Leeks tend to have a lot of soil within their stalks.
Cutting and soaking in a large pot or bowl should rid you
of all those dirty thoughts.*

Sizzling Garlic Shrimp with Sesame and Ginger

Serves 4–6 people.

Makeup:

Marinade
1/4 cup soy sauce
3 garlic cloves, minced
2 teaspoons brown sugar
2 tablespoons extra-virgin olive oil
1 teaspoon dark sesame oil
1 tablespoon grated ginger

Shrimp
1 pound (16/20-count) shrimp, peeled and deveined
1 tablespoon canola oil
3 green onions, sliced on the diagonal, divided
1 tablespoon toasted sesame seeds, for garnish
soba noodles or rice noodles, for serving

Application:

Marinade
• In a medium bowl, whisk together soy sauce, garlic, and brown sugar until the sugar has dissolved.
• Then whisk in olive oil, sesame oil, and grated ginger.

Shrimp
• Place shrimp in the bowl with the marinade.
• Toss to coat with the marinade and chill until ready to cook.
• Heat canola oil in a large nonstick sauté pan or wok over high heat.
• When oil is hot, move shrimp from the marinade into the hot pan.
• Stir-fry shrimp for 2 minutes, turning the individual shrimp, until they are cooked through.
• Add half of the sliced green onions and fry for 1 minute.
• Transfer shrimp and onions to a bowl.
• Place leftover marinade in hot sauté pan and simmer until it reduces to a syrup.
• Pour marinade over shrimp. Toss to coat.
• Transfer shrimp to a serving plate.
• Sprinkle shrimp with toasted sesame seeds and remaining green onions.
• Serve over soba noodles or rice noodles.

Supermodel Hint
Straight shrimp are undercooked, shrimp that have just curled into a C shape are perfectly cooked, and shrimp that have twisted into an O shape are terribly overcooked. Overcooked shrimp will be rubbery.

Makes 2–4 servings.

Makeup:

1 1/2 pounds large sole or flounder fillets
20 ounces small shrimp, peeled and deveined
1 teaspoon salt, or to taste
1 teaspoon pepper, or to taste
1 teaspoon paprika, or to taste
15–20 black olives, pitted
8–10 shelled large shrimp
1/2 cup chardonnay wine
1 tablespoon lemon juice
2 tablespoons chopped green onion
1 clove garlic, minced
1 tablespoon butter
1 tablespoon flour

Application:

- Preheat oven to 350 degrees F.
- Clean fillets and place on work surface.
- Place an equal amount of shrimp across one end of each fillet.
- Roll each fillet to enclose shrimp and secure with wooden toothpick.
- Place in a lightly greased baking dish.
- Sprinkle with salt, pepper, and paprika, adjusting to taste.
- Evenly place olives and large shrimp in baking dish.
- In a small bowl, combine wine, lemon juice, green onions, and garlic.
- Pour wine mixture over fish and bake covered with aluminum foil for 25 minutes.
- While fish cooks, melt butter in a small saucepan.
- Stir in flour and cook until bubbly.
- When fish is done, transfer to a plate; reserve liquid.
- Remove toothpicks, cover fish, and keep warm.
- Stir small spoonfuls of reserved liquid into the sauce. Continue to stir and cook until thickened.
- Pour sauce over fillets.

Serving note: Serve with steamed asparagus, rice, and lemon quarters. Chardonnay, a fruity selection, goes well with this dish.

Supermodel Hint

When cooking the sole fillets, keep a close eye on the cooking time to avoid drying them out.
Most fish sold as "sole" in the United States is actually flounder, so if you want authentic sole,
ask your grocer or seafood market for Dover sole.

Makes 2–4 servings.

Makeup:

1 pound sea scallops, thickly sliced
1 tablespoon flour
1 tablespoon salt
1 tablespoon pepper
2 tablespoons extra-virgin olive oil
1 tablespoon clam juice
2 tablespoons minced shallots
1 teaspoon grated grapefruit peel
1/2 cup pink-grapefruit juice
1/2 teaspoon sugar
3 tablespoons butter
1/2 cup dry white wine, preferably chardonnay
1 tablespoon thinly sliced scallions, for garnish

Application:

- Rinse scallops under cold water and pat dry.
- In a large bowl, toss together scallops, flour, salt, and pepper.
- In a large skillet, heat olive oil over medium heat until hot.
- Sauté scallops, flipping, for 2–3 minutes, or until firm and slightly golden on each side.
- Transfer scallops to a separate plate.
- To skillet, add clam juice, shallots, grapefruit peel, grapefruit juice, and sugar.
- Boil until mixture is reduced to 1/2 cup.
- Add butter; sauce should be consistency of a light cream sauce.
- Add wine, scallops, and any juices on the scallops' plate. Cook for 5 minutes.
- Evenly divide scallops onto plates and garnish with shallots.

Serving note: Serve with steamed rice and lightly steamed and buttered snow peas or asparagus.

Supermodel Hint

Miss Divina's sleuthing doesn't stop at the supermarket, fishery shop, or deluxe walk-in freezer. Be careful with buying or ordering sea scallops; shark meat cut into circles is often sold as scallops. Check with your local fish shop.

Temptation Tilapia with Lemon–Butter Sauce

Makes 4–6 servings.

Makeup:

2 pounds skinless, boneless tilapia fillets
1 teaspoon salt
1 teaspoon freshly ground black pepper,
  plus additional for garnish
4 tablespoons finely minced green onions, divided
1 teaspoon paprika
3/4 cup dry white wine, divided
1/3 cup water, divided
6 tablespoons butter
3 teaspoons freshly squeezed lemon juice
2 tablespoons all-purpose flour
2 teaspoons finely minced chives (dill weed or parsley
  may be substituted)

Application:

- Preheat oven to 375 degrees F.
- Lightly grease a glass baking dish with small amount of butter.
- Rinse fillets under cold water and pat dry with paper towels.
- Season fillets lightly with salt and pepper.
- Sprinkle 2 tablespoons green onions on the bottom of the baking dish.
- Place fillets in dish and sprinkle remaining 2 tablespoons green onions on top.
- Sprinkle with paprika.
- Pour in wine and water in equal amounts, just enough to halfway cover the fillets; reserve the remaining liquid for later.
- Place baking dish in oven and cook for about 15 minutes, or until fish turns opaque or milky white.
- Remove from oven and carefully drain cooking liquid into a medium saucepan.
- Cover fish to keep warm.
- Add any remaining wine and water, butter, and lemon juice to **saucepan.**
- Whisk until mixture thickens. Create a slurry (see "Supermodel **Hint**" below) to thicken if needed.
- Garnish with fresh chives and freshly ground pepper if desired.
- Pour sauce over fish and serve hot.

Supermodel Hint

*Slurry is a mixture of equal parts cold water and flour
used to thicken sauces and gravies. You can also use cornstarch
in place of flour. Simply mix the cornstarch or flour with
an equal amount of cold water and then whisk the mixture
slowly into the hot sauce or gravy.*

Meat Dishes

The Sultan's Harem Lamb Kebabs (p. 201)

Makes 6–8 servings.

Makeup:

1 (3–5 pound) beef chuck roast
1/4 cup salt, plus additional to taste
1/4 cup freshly ground black pepper, plus
   additional to taste
1/4 cup extra-virgin olive oil
2 whole onions, peeled and sliced
3 cups beef stock (more or less may be needed
   according to the size of the chuck roast)
6 whole carrots, unpeeled, cut into pieces
3 medium red or white potatoes, unpeeled, cut into
   large pieces
2 or 3 sprigs fresh rosemary
2 or 3 sprigs fresh french thyme
1 cup red wine

Application:

- Preheat oven to 325 degrees F, or use a slow cooker on low heat (meat is more tender when slow cooked).
- Rinse meat and pat dry with paper towel. Move to a large skillet
- Generously salt and pepper the chuck roast.
- Brown the meat in olive oil for 5–10 minutes each side.
- Once meat is browned on both sides, move it to a dutch oven or slow cooker.
- In a medium skillet, over medium heat, sauté onions until slightly golden brown, approximately 10 minutes.
- Remove the onions to a plate.
- Add beef stock to dutch oven or slow cooker, adding enough to cover the meat halfway.
- Cook for 1 1/2–2 hours.
- Add onions, carrots, potatoes, rosemary, thyme and red wine to the pot.
- After 30 minutes, taste gravy and add additional salt and pepper if necessary (but don't overdo it!).
- Carefully stir every 10 minutes or so, scraping the sides of the pot.
- When roast is done, remove meat to a serving platter and thicken gravy with slurry (equal parts flour and cold water) if needed.
- The roast is ready when the meat falls apart and is tender.
- Serve the carrots and potatoes on the side.

Serving note: Serve with a green salad and fresh french bread.

Supermodel Hint

Miss Divina is fickle sometimes. From time to time, she feels a need for mashed potatoes. If you prefer, you can leave out the red or white potatoes in the pot roast and serve mashed potatoes as a side instead.

Makes 6–8 servings.

Makeup:

Cranberry Sauce
1 cup white sugar
1 cup orange juice
1 1/2 cups fresh cranberries

Meatloaf
1 small yellow onion, chopped
2 tablespoons butter
1 pound lean ground beef
1 pound lean ground Italian sausage
1 fresh egg
1/2 cup bread crumbs
1/2 cup sun-dried tomatoes, finely chopped
12 ounces dried cranberries, finely chopped
1 cup béarnaise sauce (see p. 311 for recipe)
1/4 cup worcestershire sauce
1 teaspoon chopped fresh sage leaves
2 tablespoons Italian seasoning
1 teaspoon salt
1 teaspoon ground rosemary
1 teaspoon ground mustard
1 teaspoon freshly ground black pepper
1 teaspoon garlic powder

Application:

Cranberry Sauce
- In a medium saucepan over medium heat, dissolve sugar in orange juice.
- Stir in cranberries and cook until they start to pop, about 10 minutes.
- Remove from heat and place sauce in a bowl. Sauce will thicken as it cools.

Meatloaf
- Heat oven to 350 degrees F.
- Sauté onions in butter until translucent, about 7–10 minutes.
- In a large mixing bowl, mix ground beef and ground sausage thoroughly.
- Add sautéed onions, egg, bread crumbs, sun-dried tomatoes, cranberries, béarnaise sauce, and worcestershire sauce.
- Mix in Italian seasoning, salt, rosemary, ground mustard, pepper, and garlic powder and mix well.
- Spread meat mixture in ungreased loaf pan.
- Bake uncovered 60 minutes.
- Remove loaf from oven and spread cranberry sauce over the top.
- Cover loaf with foil and cook for additional 10 minutes.
- Remove from oven, slice, and serve.

Supermodel Hint

Think meatloaf is something only for the downtrodden and serving it for dinner is like child abuse? Well, you haven't tried Miss Divina's recipe! The Japanese have a word for it—umami. Umami can be translated as "pleasant savory taste."

Gayle-Force-Winds Tortilla al Horno

Makes 6–8 servings.

Makeup:

Meat
3 pounds pork butt or beef chuck roast
2 tablespoons salt
2 tablespoons pepper
2 tablespoons garlic powder
2 tablespoons canola oil
1 large yellow onion, chopped
1 (24-ounce) jar pepperoncinis
juice of 2 limes
1 cup rice (white rice works best)
1 (16-ounce) can red beans, drained

Salsa Verde
3–4 tomatillos, depending on size
1–2 jalapeños, diced (remove seeds for less heat)
1/2 bunch of cilantro, chopped
1 (4–8-ounce) can green chilies
2 tablespoons cayenne pepper
2 tablespoons cumin
10 (8-inch) flour tortillas or 20 (6-inch) corn tortillas
1 (16-ounce) bag shredded Mexican cheese blend
guacamole, for garnish (optional)
lime wedges, for garnish (optional)

Application:

Meat
- Season meat with salt, pepper, and garlic powder.
- Heat oil for 3 minutes in a large skillet over high heat.
- Sear meat on all sides in skillet, browning the outside.
- Remove meat and set aside.
- Using the same pan, sauté onions.
- Add meat, onions, pepperoncinis (including liquid), and lime juice to a slow cooker.
- Cook on high for 8 hours. If starting the night before going to bed, turn to low in the morning.
- When meat is fully cooked, shred it with two forks.
- Drain liquid into a large measuring cup. Add as much meat liquid as you have and then add additional water to reach 2 cups. Set aside and reserve for rice.

Salsa Verde
- Preheat oven to 400 degrees F.
- Peel outside skin off tomatillos and chop. Add to a blender.
- Squeeze juice of 1 lime into blender.
- Add jalapeño, cilantro, green chilies, cayenne, and cumin to blender and puree.

Assembly
- On cutting board, lay 1 flour or 2 corn tortillas flat and fill with meat. Roll and put fold side down in a glass baking dish. Repeat until dish is filled.
- Pour salsa verde over entire dish and then cover with cheese.
- Bake uncovered on middle rack for 20–25 minutes.
- Prepare rice while tortillas are in the oven:
  - Bring reserved 2 cups liquid to a boil in a large saucepan over high heat.
  - Add rice and stir. Bring back to a boil while stirring.
  - Reduce heat to low and cover, cooking for 20–25 minutes.
- When rice is cooked, gently mix in red beans.
- When tortillas are done baking, remove from oven and let cool for 5 minutes.
- Garnish with guacamole (optional) and lime wedges (optional), and serve over the rice or with the rice on the side, however you prefer.

Makes 6–8 servings.

Makeup:

2 pounds top round steak
1 cup all-purpose flour
2 teaspoons extra-virgin olive oil
2 tablespoons garlic salt
2 tablespoons black pepper
2 tablespoons cayenne pepper
1 (28-ounce) can hot enchilada sauce
3 (8-ounce) cans tomato sauce
2–3 fresh garlic cloves, chopped

Application:

- Cut round steak into small cubes.
- Lightly coat the meat in flour.
- In a large skillet, heat olive oil over medium heat.
- Brown and season meat with garlic salt, pepper, and cayenne.
- When meat is browned, add chili sauce and tomato sauce.
- Add garlic to sauce.
- Simmer over low heat until meat is tender, about 3 hours.

Serving note: Serve over white or brown rice and with steamed broccoli.

Supermodel Hint

Miss Divina's mama always wants to know when her darling girl is coming home for a visit and what meal she wants that first night home at the villa. This dish is often at the top of the list!

Makes 8–10 servings.

Makeup:

2 pounds beef stew meat, cubed
2 tablespoons all-purpose flour
1 medium yellow onion, diced
6 cups beef stock
1 teaspoon salt
1 teaspoon pepper
1 teaspoon garlic salt
1 teaspoon garlic powder
3 red potatoes, diced
6 medium carrots, diced
6 celery stalks, diced

Application:

- Lightly coat meat in flour.
- Brown beef with onion in a large pan over medium-high heat.
- Drain off any excess grease if necessary.
- Place meat in a medium to large pot.
- Add beef stock and salt, pepper, garlic salt, and garlic powder.
- Simmer over low heat until meat is tender, approximately 3–4 hours.
- When meat is tender, add potatoes, carrots, and celery.
- Cook over low heat until vegetables are tender, approximately 30 minutes.
- Thicken gravy with slurry (equal parts flour and cold water) if needed.

Serving note: Serve with freshly sliced french bread.

Supermodel Hint

Brown your beef! Flavor comes from a good sear. Scraping up those caramelized brown bits from the bottom of your pot is going to give your stew a deep, rich flavor. Also, give each piece of meat enough room to get really browned.

Hunnie Fay Baker Ham with Grand Marnier Glaze

Makes 10–15 servings.

Makeup:

1 (10–20 pound) ham
2 cups honey
2 cups Grand Marnier
1 cup fresh orange juice with pulp
salt, pepper, garlic powder, and nutmeg to taste
20–30 fresh whole cloves
2 cups brown sugar
1 can sliced pineapple

Application:

- Preheat oven to 425 degrees F.
- Place ham in a large baking pan.
- To create the glaze, mix honey, Grand Marnier, orange juice, salt, pepper, garlic powder, and nutmeg in a medium mixing bowl. Set aside.
- Evenly spread cloves around top and sides of ham, pushing pointed side of cloves into ham.
- With a pastry brush, glaze ham with glaze mixture.
- Next, with your hands, coat top of ham with even coating of brown sugar.
- Cover with tin foil and bake for 15–20 minutes per pound.
- Baste ham every 15 minutes with glaze from bottom of pan.
- After about 1 1/2 hours, remove tin foil and bake uncovered for remaining time (according to poundage).
- Continue to baste ham regularly and evenly.
- When 20 minutes of cook time remain, place pineapple slices over and around ham. Use wooden toothpicks to secure pineapple in place if needed.
- When ham is cooked, remove from oven and let stand for 10 minutes before carving.
- Remove toothpicks, place pineapples in a serving side dish, and carve ham. Cover ham and pineapples with foil and keep warm until served.

Serving note: Serve with Just-Peachy Applesauce (see p. 234) on the side.

Supermodel Hint

*Our dear friend Hunnie was just that—a honey! She was a bit overzealous in her religion and, oh, that makeup!
The poor dear was so misunderstood! But we love her ham recipe nonetheless!*

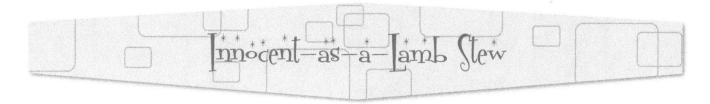

Make 6–8 servings.

Makeup:

2 medium onions, chopped
1 tablespoon butter
1 sprig dried french thyme
1/4 cup canola oil
2 1/2 pounds leg of lamb, cut into large pieces
7 carrots, chopped or sliced lengthways into 2-inch
  pieces
2 bay leaves
24 small red potatoes, halved, peeled or unpeeled as
  desired
5 cups beef stock (chicken or vegetable stock may
  be substituted)
1 tablespoon salt
freshly ground black pepper to taste
1 pinch parsley
1 pinch french thyme
1 bunch chives, chopped

Application:

- In a large skillet, sauté onions in butter over medium-high heat until they are translucent.
- Add dried thyme and stir.
- Add canola oil and lamb and brown meat over high heat to seal in juices.
- Add carrots, bay leaves, and potatoes.
- Pour in stock so that it almost covers the meat and vegetables.
- Season with salt, pepper, parsley, and thyme.
- Cover and simmer over low heat for 2 1/2 hours, being careful not to boil.
- Stirring occasionally, cook until potatoes are tender.
- Serve stew in large soup bowls, garnishing with chives.

Supermodel Hint

Leaving the skin on potatoes provides lots of added minerals to your food.
Just make sure you clean the potatoes well prior to cutting.

Makes 2 servings.

Makeup:

2 (1 1/2-inch-thick) bone-in rib eye steaks
  (about 1 1/4 pounds each)
2 teaspoons coarse kosher salt
black pepper to taste
extra-virgin olive oil, as needed
2 ounces blue cheese
1 tablespoon unsalted butter
2 teaspoons finely chopped chives
hot sauce to taste

Application:

- Season steaks with salt and pepper at least 30 minutes and up to 1 hour before you plan to cook them.
- Cover loosely with plastic wrap and let stand at room temperature.
- Heat grill to high.
    - If using charcoal grill, mound coals to one side, allowing for an area of indirect heat.
    - If using gas grill, turn on only a few of the burners and leave the rest off for indirect heat.
- Lightly oil steaks.
- Place on hottest part of grill.
- Cook, covered, until they develop a golden-brown crust, 2–3 minutes per side.
- Move steaks to indirect heat and crumble blue cheese over the top.
- Cover with foil and continue cooking 2–5 minutes longer, depending on desired doneness.
- Transfer steaks to a cutting board to rest, loosely covered with foil, for 10 minutes.
- While steaks rest, stir together butter, chives, and hot sauce.
- Pour sauce over steak before serving.

Supermodel Hint

Miss Divina knows the way to a man's heart and how to get him in the mood. Just cook him a big, juicy steak, and you may get a big, juicy diamond!

Jeanne's Old-Fashioned-Girl Honeycombed Tripe Stew

Makes 6–8 servings.

Makeup:

1 pound honeycomb tripe, cut into squares
   (cuts easier when partially frozen)
1 (16-ounce) can tomato sauce
1 (12-ounce) can fried onion chips
1 bay leaf
salt, pepper, garlic powder, and parsley to taste
1 (16-ounce) can stewed tomatoes
8 medium red potatoes, cut into squares
4 carrots, diced

Application:

- Combine tripe, tomato sauce, onion chips, bay leaf, salt, pepper, garlic powder, and parsley in a stewing pot.
- Add sufficient water to cover all ingredients.
- Simmer for 2–3 hours.
- Add stewed tomatoes, potatoes, and carrots and simmer for 30 minutes.
- Either serve immediately or store in refrigerator for up to a day.

Serving note: Serve with green salad, french bread, and French cheese. This dish is best if made the day before, stored in the refrigerator overnight, and heated on low for 30 minutes before serving the next day.

Supermodel Hint

Tripe has long been called the stepchild of meats, but Miss Divina identifies with the downtrodden. Give her credit. It takes guts to cook this for company.

Makes 8–10 servings.

Makeup:

2 pounds ground turkey
2 pounds Italian sausage
2 cloves garlic, chopped
2 (8-ounce) cans tomato sauce
1 (15-ounce) can kidney beans, drained
1 (15-ounce) can pinto beans, drained
1 (28-ounce) can hot enchilada sauce
2 tablespoons chili powder, or to taste
1 teaspoon ground cumin, or to taste
1 teaspoon ground oregano, or to taste
1 teaspoon salt, or to taste
1/4 teaspoon cayenne pepper, or to taste
1/4 cup masa harina (corn flour)
1/2 cup water
1 cup chopped red and yellow onions, for garnish
shredded white or yellow extra-sharp cheddar cheese,
    for garnish
1 fresh avocado, cubed, for garnish

Application:

- Brown ground turkey and Italian sausage in a large pot over medium-high heat.
- When meat is browned, drain off excess fat.
- Add garlic to meat mixture.
- Pour in tomato sauce, kidney beans, pinto beans, enchilada sauce, chili powder, cumin, oregano, salt, and cayenne.
- Stir together well, cover, and reduce heat to low.
- Simmer for 1 hour, stirring occasionally and mashing beans (this will help create a thicker chili). If chili becomes overly dry, add 1/4–1/2 cup water at a time as needed.
- After chili has been simmering for 1 hour, place masa harina and 1/2 cup water in a small bowl and stir together to form paste.
- Add masa harina mixture to chili and stir well to thicken as desired. Add more masa harina paste and/or water to get chili to preferred consistency.
- Taste and adjust seasonings as desired.
- Simmer for additional 1–2 hours, stirring occasionally. The longer you simmer, the more tender the meat will become.
- Serve topped with onions, cheese, and avocado.

Supermodel Hint

Miss Divina likes things hot and steamy. If you prefer your chili less spicy, reduce the amount of hot and spicy seasonings and substitute a medium or mild enchilada sauce for the hot variety.

Killed-the-Rabbit Stew

Makes 6–8 servings.

Makeup:

2 tablespoons all-purpose flour
1 teaspoon salt
1 teaspoon pepper
1 whole rabbit, boned if available, cut into pieces
2 cups chicken stock (vegetable stock may be
   substituted)
1 cup white wine
10 ounces fresh mushrooms, chopped
1/2 cup chopped yellow onion
1 tablespoon chopped fresh parsley

Application:

- Mix flour, salt, and pepper thoroughly in a small bowl.
- Cut rabbit into pieces if necessary; remove fat and bone as much as possible.
- Coat rabbit in seasoned flour mixture.
- Over medium heat, brown rabbit in a large skillet until golden brown, approximately 10 minutes. Be sure to turn rabbit pieces over to brown all sides.
- Add stock, wine, mushrooms, onion, and parsley.
- Simmer over low heat, covered, for 1–1 1/2 hours, or until rabbit is well cooked.
- Thicken sauce to gravy-like consistency with slurry (equal parts flour and cold water) if necessary.

Serving note: Serve with Mother-Agent Mashed Potatoes (see p. 235) and freshly chopped leeks sautéed in butter, salt, and pepper.

Supermodel Hint

If you can't find rabbit in your local gourmet market, try this recipe with chicken. It will taste just as delicious.

Makes 4 servings.

Makeup:

Meat
4 (4-ounce, 1-inch-thick) sliced pork chops
2 tablespoons salt
2 tablespoons pepper
2 tablespoons rosemary
2 tablespoons extra-virgin olive oil

Glaze
1 tablespoon butter
2 chives, minced
1/4 cup pine nuts (optional)
1/2 cup red wine
1/2 cup beef stock

Application:

Meat
- Season pork chops with salt, pepper, and rosemary.
- Heat olive oil in a large skillet over medium-high heat.
- Add chops and cook until browned and cooked through, about 5–7 minutes per side.
- Remove chops to a serving platter and cover to keep warm.

Glaze
- Heat butter in same skillet as the meat. Add chives and pine nuts (optional) and sauté until golden.
- Add wine and beef stock, scraping to remove any browned bits from bottom of pan.
- Cook about 7 minutes, until liquid is reduced by half.

Assembly
- Place chops on individual plates and pour sauce from pan over each chop.

Serving note: Serve with your favorite vegetable and freshly steamed rice.

Supermodel Hint

Down in the ole south, Mrs. Sippie was infamous for her pork chops and a good round of steamy gossip about the neighbors. I sure do miss those nights drinking mint juleps on the front porch with that dear ole gal!

Nagatha's Crispy Sesame-Beef-on-the-Orient Stir-Fry

Makes 4–6 servings.

Makeup:

1/4 cup soy sauce
3 tablespoons light-brown sugar
3 tablespoons rice vinegar
2 tablespoons hoisin sauce
1 tablespoon finely chopped fresh ginger
4 teaspoons sesame oil, divided
2 teaspoons cornstarch
1 teaspoon crushed red pepper
2 cups water
2 (3-ounce) beef-flavor ramen noodles
   with seasoning packets)
1/4 cup scallions
1 pound boneless sirloin, thinly sliced
2 tablespoons minced garlic
1/2 cup chopped fresh asparagus
1/2 cup chopped green beans
3 teaspoons sesame seeds, for garnish

Application:

- In a small mixing bowl, mix soy sauce, brown sugar, vinegar, hoisin sauce, ginger, 2 teaspoons sesame oil, cornstarch, and crushed red pepper.
- In a medium saucepan, mix water, ramen noodles and packet seasonings, and scallions; bring to a boil.
- Remove from heat.
- Drain beef broth into soy sauce mixture.
- Set noodles aside but keep covered and warm.
- In a large skillet or wok, stir-fry sirloin and garlic in remaining 2 teaspoons sesame oil for 5 minutes.
- Add asparagus and green beans and stir-fry for additional 2–3 minutes.
- Add beef broth / soy sauce mixture to skillet and stir-fry for 3 minutes, or until broth has thickened and mostly evaporated.
- Evenly divide warm noodles on individual plates and place meat over **noodles**.
- Sprinkle with sesame seeds for garnish.

Supermodel Hint

Nagatha never knew when to mind her own business.
But she traveled extensively around the Far East and just killed
Miss Divina with her scandalous suspense stories!

Makes 8–10 servings.

Makeup:

Lamb
1 leg of lamb, bone in (about 6–7 1/2 pounds)
1/4 cup freshly squeezed lemon juice
8 cloves garlic, minced
3 tablespoons chopped fresh rosemary leaves
1 tablespoon salt
2 teaspoons coarsely ground black pepper

Sauce
2 cups diced onions
1 cup chopped fresh herbs (rosemary, chives, and parsley)
2 cups chicken stock (vegetable stock may be substituted)
1 cup red wine

Application:

Lamb
- Preheat oven to 375 degrees F.
- Using your hands, rub lemon juice all over lamb.
- Pat garlic and rosemary evenly all over lamb.
- Season meat with salt and pepper.
- Place lamb in a roasting pan and roast for approximately 25–30 minutes per pound. Baste occasionally to help crisp outside of roast.
- Reduce oven heat to 350 degrees F and cook for about 1 hour longer for medium-rare, or until meat thermometer inserted into center of roast registers 145–150 degrees F. (Be careful that the thermometer does not touch the bone.)
- Remove lamb from pan and allow to rest for 10–15 minutes before carving.

Sauce
- In a small to medium saucepan, add pan drippings, onions, and herbs and stir to combine.
- Add chicken stock and wine to deglaze the pan, scraping the bottom with a wooden spoon. Reduce over high heat until sauce consistency is slightly thin.
- Strain sauce before serving, if desired.

Assembly
- Slice lamb and drizzle sauce over the top when serving.

Supermodel Hint
The most important thing to remember about cooking a roasted lamb is to not overcook it.
If you do, just shoot yourself! Your life is over anyway!

Pork Sausage Kiss—adillas

Makes 4–6 servings.

Makeup:

1 pound ground pork chorizo sausage
1/2 cup water
1 red onion, chopped
1 (1.25-ounce) package taco or enchilada sauce mix
10–12 (8-inch) flour tortillas, slightly warmed
1 cup grated sharp cheddar cheese
1 head iceberg lettuce, finely chopped
1 large tomato, chopped
1 jar salsa, mild to hot
hot sauce, such as Tabasco

Application:

- Preheat oven to 350 degrees F.
- Brown sausage in a large skillet over medium heat; drain grease.
- Return sausage to skillet; add water, onion, and taco or enchilada sauce mix.
- Let simmer, stirring occasionally, until water has evaporated, approximately 10–12 minutes.
- Place equal amounts of meat into warmed tortilla shells.
- Evenly place a small amount of cheese, lettuce, and tomato over meat in tortillas.
- Spoon on salsa and shake on hot sauce.
- Roll each tortilla and use a wooden toothpick to keep together.
- Place rolled tortillas in a glass baking dish.
- Pour small amount of salsa over each tortilla.
- Sprinkle remaining cheese on top.
- Bake tortillas for 5 minutes, or until cheese melts.

Serving note: Serve with refried beans and rice as well as salsa and sour cream on the side.

Makes 6–8 servings.

Makeup:

1 pound ground beef
2 eggs
1/4 cup dried onion flakes
2 tablespoons salt
2 tablespoons pepper
2 tablespoons garlic powder
1/2 cup bread crumbs, plus additional as needed
1/4 cup all-purpose flour
1 tablespoon vegetable oil
2 cups beef stock
8 ounces sour cream
1/4 cup ground tarragon
2 tablespoons cornstarch or flour, for thickening, if needed
1 package extra-wide egg noodles

Application:

- Thoroughly mix together meat, eggs, dried onion flakes, salt, pepper, and garlic powder.
- Add bread crumbs to bind.
- Roll into medium-size meatballs.
- Dredge meatballs in flour.
- Heat oil in a large skillet over medium heat and brown meatballs.
- Once meatballs are browned, drain excess oil.
- Add beef stock and cook until meatballs are cooked through, 30 minutes or so over low heat.
- Add sour cream and heat through.
- Add the tarragon and mix well.
- If sauce needs thickening, add cornstarch or flour.
- Prepare noodles as instructed on package.
- Serve meatballs in sauce on a bed of noodles.

Supermodel Hint

Miss Divina's makeup artiste, "Missy" Randi Reade, is a wiz at getting her to look perfect at every shoot.
As a reward, Miss Divina makes up a special batch of these meatballs just for Missy.
Downside? Missy Reade is getting a bit too "hippy" lately.

Makes 6–10 servings.

Makeup:

4 cups grilled and chopped chicken breast
2 cups grated sharp cheddar cheese, divided
1 (15-ounce) can black beans
1 (15-ounce) can corn, drained
1 (15-ounce) can chili con carne with beans
1 (14.5-ounce) can enchilada sauce, mild to hot
1 (8-ounce) can tomato paste
1 cup minced yellow onions
1/2 cup water
12–16 ounces corn chips, crushed, divided
1 cup sour cream, for serving

Application:

- Preheat oven to 375 degrees F.
- Combine chicken, 1 1/2 cups cheese, black beans, corn, chili con carne, enchilada sauce, tomato paste, onion, water, and all but 1 cup of crushed corn chips.
- Pour into lightly greased oblong baking dish.
- Bake uncovered in oven for 30 minutes.
- Remove and sprinkle remaining 1/2 cup cheese on top.
- Make a circle of remaining 1 cup corn chips around edges.
- Bake additional 5 minutes.
- Remove and let cool for 5 minutes.
- Serve with sour cream on the side.

Supermodel Hint

Irish supermodel Shannon O'Ennis, formerly known in professional wrestling circles as "Meatball Murphy," knows how to throw a party and a punch! Get yourself invited to her gatherings! But hold on to your margarita! She has a taste for the "sauce."

Makes 4–6 servings.

Makeup:

2 tablespoons canola oil
6–8 (1/2-pound, 3/4-inch-thick) swiss steaks (also known as cube steaks)
1/4 cup all-purpose flour
2 cups beef stock, room temperature, plus additional as needed to fully cover meat
8 large, fresh gourmet mushrooms (any variety is fine), chopped
1 medium yellow onion, finely chopped
1 teaspoon salt
1 teaspoon pepper
1 teaspoon garlic salt
1 cup red wine

Application:

- Heat oil in a large skillet over medium-high heat.
- Lightly coat steak with flour, place in skillet, and brown for 7–10 minutes.
- Remove and place in a large simmering pan with lid.
- Add warm beef stock; make sure liquid covers meat.
- Mix in mushrooms and onions.
- Add salt, pepper, and garlic salt and blend in well.
- Cover and simmer over low heat for 2 hours, or until meat is tender.
- Add wine and mix. Simmer for additional 30 minutes.
- Thicken gravy with slurry (equal parts flour and cold water) if needed.

Serving note: Serve with Mother-Agent Mashed Potatoes (see p. 235) and a fresh vegetable.

Supermodel Hint

I shouldn't tell you, but dear Miss Divina always has some of this dish stashed away in the freezer for a rainy day. It's her secret comfort food, and she tells no one about it—not even her laundry lady.

The Sultan's Harem Lamb Kebabs

Makes 6–8 servings.

Makeup:
Marinade
1/3 cup extra-virgin olive oil
1/4 cup white wine vinegar
3 tablespoons minced garlic
2 tablespoons dijon mustard
2 tablespoons soy sauce
2 tablespoons honey
1 tablespoon french thyme
1 tablespoon rosemary
1 tablespoon oregano
1/4 teaspoon salt

Kebabs
2 thick-cut, boneless lamb chops, cut into 1 1/2-inch cubes
1/2 pound fresh whole mushrooms
3 bell peppers, red, orange, and yellow, cut into 1-inch squares

Application:
Marinade
- In a medium mixing bowl, stir together olive oil, vinegar, garlic, mustard, soy sauce, honey, thyme, rosemary, oregano, and salt.
- Divide marinade into two medium bowls.

Kebabs
- Place lamb cubes into one bowl of marinade and mix, coating lamb with marinade.
- Mix mushrooms and peppers into second bowl of marinade.
- Let both bowls marinate for at least 1–2 hours at room temperature or up to 4 hours in refrigerator.
- Thread lamb and vegetables alternately on 6-inch skewers.
- Prepare outdoor grill according to your specific grill instructions. I recommend your grill be on medium heat so kebabs will not burn or dry out.
- Grill (or broil) kebabs until meat is browned on one side, approximately 3–5 minutes. Rotate and follow same procedure until lamb is cooked. Avoid overcooking, or the meat will be dry and the vegetables burnt.

Serving note: Serve with Wild-Nights Rice with Golden Raisins (see p. 245) and Phi Beta Tomato and Cucumber Salad (see p. 133).

Supermodel Hint

Lamb, like pork, can often be overcooked. Checking the internal temperature often will help prevent dry meat. Cook these meats until the internal temperature reaches between 145–160 degrees F.

Vaina Black's Côte de Boeuf

Makes 4 servings.

Makeup:

4 (3–5-pound, 3-inch-thick) rib steaks with one rib left
   on, tied
3 teaspoons salt
3 teaspoons coarsely ground black pepper
1 teaspoon ground french thyme
1 teaspoon sage
6 tablespoons extra-virgin olive oil
steamed vegetables, for serving

Application:

- Preheat oven to 450 degrees F.
- Season both sides of steaks with salt, pepper, thyme, and sage. Set aside.
- In a large skillet, heat olive oil over high heat until it ripples.
- Sear steaks for 3 minutes each side to form a brown crust.
- Arrange a rack inside a large, high-sided roasting pan.
- Place steaks on rack and roast in oven for 30–40 minutes, depending on how rare you prefer your steaks.
- Remove from oven and let stand for 10 minutes before removing string.
- Place and serve on platter surrounded by steamed vegetables of your choice.

Supermodel Hint

*Every beefy man wants a good, juicy steak. If this meat doesn't get your cowboy in the mood,
bury him — he died on the trail!*

You Big Oxtail Stew

Makes 6–8 servings.

Makeup:

2 cups all-purpose flour
2 tablespoons salt
2 tablespoons pepper
6 pounds oxtails
1/4 cup extra-virgin olive oil
4 cloves garlic, sliced and mashed in salt to puree
 consistency
1 red onion, chopped
4 cups beef stock
1 cup red wine
3 cups crushed tomatoes with juice
3 bay leaves
1 pound carrots, peeled and chopped into large chunks
2 pounds potatoes, peeled and chopped into large chunks

Application:

- In a shallow bowl, add flour, salt, and pepper.
- Dredge meat in flour, shaking off any excess.
- Heat olive oil in a large stockpot or Dutch oven over medium-high heat.
- When oil is hot, add meat and brown on all sides, about 3 minutes per side.
- When meat is browned, remove from pot and set aside.
- Add garlic and red onion to pot and sauté.
- Add beef stock and wine to pot.
- Add browned meat back into pot and add crushed tomatoes.
- Add enough water to cover meat and add bay leaves.
- Simmer over low heat for 2 1/2–3 hours.
- Add carrots and potatoes and simmer for another 45 minutes.
- Remove from heat and serve.

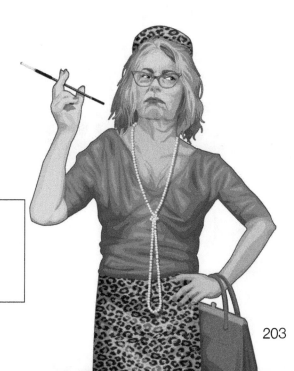

Supermodel Hint

*Whether your man is a slim-jim or a big ox, this hearty stew
pleases all that are fortunate enough to land an invitation
to sit at Miss Divina's beautifully bountiful table.*

Pasta Dishes

Stuff Your Man with This Turkey Manicotti (p. 213)

Luscious Lobster Risotto alla Parmigiana

Makes 8–10 servings.

Makeup:

12 ounces fresh lobster (crab or shrimp may be
  substituted for cheaper option)
6 cups chicken stock
3 tablespoons butter, divided
2 tablespoons extra-virgin olive oil
2 tablespoons finely chopped onion
2 cups Italian short-grain rice (arborio)
1/2 cup frozen petite peas
1/2 cup grated parmesan cheese
2 tablespoons freshly ground black pepper
2 tablespoons white pepper
1 teaspoon salt

Application:

- Steam lobster in a medium steamer until lobster is fully cooked, about 10 minutes.
- Remove lobster meat from shells and chop into small pieces. Cover and set aside.
- Bring chicken stock to a simmer in a small pot.
- In a wide, heavy-bottomed saucepan, add 1 tablespoon butter, olive oil, and onion.
- Over medium heat, sauté onion until translucent.
- Add rice and stir quickly until each grain is coated.
- Add 1/2 cup hot chicken stock and cook until liquid is absorbed. Stir constantly with wooden spoon and scrape sides of pot regularly so rice is evenly cooked.
- Add another 1/2 cup stock and stir until all is absorbed.
- Continue to add broth, always stirring, until rice is tender but still firm to the bite (al dente).
- Start tasting rice to check for doneness at 7 minutes. Rice is usually done around 8–10 minutes.
- Once rice reaches al dente stage, stir in remainder of broth.
- When rice is done, it should be tender, creamy, and moist but not runny.
- Add lobster, peas, parmesan, black pepper, white pepper, and salt. Stir until cheese is dissolved, about 1 minute.
- Remove from heat and serve immediately.

Supermodel Hint

*If you do not serve this dish immediately, the rice will get sticky and dry. Your dinner will be ruined,
and you might as well move to Alaska, because no one will care if you fall off the face of the earth!*

Missy's Comfort Mac and Cheese

Makes 10–12 servings.

Makeup:

16 ounces elbow macaroni (or favorite specialty pasta shells)
6 tablespoons unsalted butter
2 cups chicken stock
2 cups half-and-half
1 1/2 cups whole milk
2 teaspoons salt
1/4 teaspoon freshly ground black pepper
1/4 teaspoon freshly grated nutmeg
1/4 teaspoon cayenne pepper
2 cups (8 ounces) grated romano cheese, divided
5 cups (20 ounces) grated extra-sharp white cheddar cheese, divided
2 cups Italian bread crumbs, divided

Photo of individual serving in ramekins shown.

Application:

- Preheat oven to 375 degrees F.
- Cook pasta until outside is cooked but inside is slightly underdone.
- Drain water and rinse pasta under cold water. Set aside.
- Butter a 3-quart casserole dish and set aside.
- Melt butter in a large saucepan over medium heat.
- Add chicken stock, half-and-half, and milk to saucepan and cook for 5–7 minutes.
- Remove from heat and add salt, pepper, nutmeg, cayenne, 1 cup romano cheese, and 2 1/2 cups cheddar cheese.
- Stir pasta into cheese sauce and add 1 cup bread crumbs. Mix well.
- Pour into casserole dish.
- Sprinkle remaining 1 cup romano cheese, 2 1/2 cups cheddar cheese, and 1 cup bread crumbs over the top.
- Bake for 30 minutes, or until crumbs are golden brown; avoid burning top crust.
- Let cool for 5 minutes before serving.

Supermodel Hint

*Even supermodels need a little comfort food now and again. Just don't overdo it,
or your modeling agent may start promoting you as a "plus-size" or "curvy" model!*

Makes 4–6 servings.

Makeup:

2 (8-ounce) cans tomato sauce
1 (8-ounce) can tomato paste
2 shallots, chopped
2 cubes beef bouillon
1/4 teaspoon garlic
1/4 teaspoon salt
1/4 teaspoon pepper
1/4 teaspoon oregano
1 cup diced tomatoes
8 ounces cream cheese
1 (16-ounce) package whole wheat fettuccine
grated parmesan cheese, for garnish
1/2 cup pine nuts, for garnish

Application:

- To a large saucepan, add tomato sauce, tomato paste, shallots, bouillon, garlic, salt, pepper, and oregano.
- Mix well and cook over medium heat until slightly boiling.
- Add diced tomatoes and cream cheese to sauce. Mix cream cheese into sauce until it is completely melted.
- Reduce heat and simmer over low for 15 minutes.
- Prepare pasta as instructed on package, making your desired amount. Pasta serving amounts vary per personal preferences. Some like more pasta than others.
- Serve sauce over fettuccine.
- Sprinkle with parmesan cheese and pine nuts for garnish.

Serving note: Serve with freshly made That-Furry-Italian Garlic Bread (see p. 241).

Supermodel Hint

Wine is a great addition to add flavor to tomato sauce. Red wine gives the sauce added richness and robustness, while white gives a fruity flavor. Let the wine cook down and reduce almost all the way. The alcohol will cook off while the wine's wonderful flavors are left behind.

Makes 8–10 servings.

Makeup:

1 (9-ounce) package lasagna noodles
1 (32-ounce) can chopped spinach
16 ounces tomato sauce, preferably My Italian Cousin
René's Sauce di Pomodoro (see p. 207)
1 cup Italian bread crumbs
1 teaspoon salt
1 teaspoon pepper
1 teaspoon garlic powder
1 teaspoon basil
1 teaspoon rosemary
4 cups shredded mozzarella cheese
1 (15-ounce) tub ricotta cheese (or cottage cheese)

Application:

- Preheat oven to 375 degrees F.
- Prepare lasagna noodles according to package directions. Drain and set aside to cool.
- Drain spinach well; squeeze as much water out as possible.
- In mixing bowl, combine tomato sauce, bread crumbs, salt, pepper, garlic powder, basil, and rosemary.
- In greased oblong pan, layer lasagna noodles, tomato sauce mixture, spinach, mozzarella cheese, and ricotta cheese. Continue until you have 5 or 6 layers (depending on the depth of your dish), or until all the noodles and other ingredients are used. On last layer, cover with remaining shredded mozzarella cheese.
- Bake for approximately 35–45 minutes.
- Keep an eye on crust to make sure cheese does not burn. Cover with aluminum foil if needed.
- Remove from oven and let cool for 5–10 minutes.

Serving note: Serve with freshly made That-Furry-Italian Garlic Bread (see p. 241).

Supermodel Hint

*Miss Divina's grandmother Nana teased Mussolini one night over spinach lasagna before
he became dictator of Italy. He begged for this recipe, but she withheld it and fled to Corfu by yacht,
not breaking a nail as she ordered the crew to set sail.*

Makes 8-10 servings.

Makeup:

6 slices thick bacon
3 tablespoons salt
1 (16-ounce) jar garlic Alfredo sauce
2 tablespoons extra-virgin olive oil
2 tablespoons minced garlic
2 (16-ounce) packages potato gnocchi
2 tablespoons fresh basil, finely chopped
1/4 cup crumbled gorgonzola cheese
1/2 cup parmesan cheese, divided
1/2 cup minced chives

Application:

Fry bacon, finely chop, and set aside.

- Fill a medium pan halfway with water, add salt, and bring to a rolling boil over high heat.
- While waiting for the water to boil, in a separate saucepan, heat Alfredo sauce over medium heat. Do not bring to a boil.
- In a small skillet, add olive oil and garlic. Sauté garlic for 2 minutes over medium heat.
- When water is boiling, add gnocchi and, stirring occasionally, boil for approximately 10 minutes, or until gnocchi float to the top.
- When garlic is done, add to Alfredo sauce. Mix well.
- Add bacon, basil, gorgonzola, and three-quarters of parmesan cheese to Alfredo sauce. Mix well.
- When gnocchi are cooked, remove from heat, drain in a colander, and rinse under cold water for 15 seconds. You can check to see if the gnocchi are fully cooked by either biting or cutting one in half to see the center.
- Return gnocchi back to pot, add Alfredo sauce, and gently mix.
- Remove gnocchi to a serving platter or individual serving plates.
- Sprinkle chives and remaining parmesan cheese on top.

Supermodel Hint

In Italy, gnocchi are usually served after appetizers as a first course (or primo piatto), instead of pasta. When Italians eat gnocchi as an appetizer, the portions are usually on the small side. Gnocchi can just as easily be served as a main course, as suggested here.

Makes 4–6 servings.

Makeup:

butter-flavored cooking spray
12 large manicotti shells
4 cups shredded mozzarella cheese, divided
2 cups ricotta cheese
6 tablespoons chopped fresh basil
16 ounces tomato sauce, preferably My Italian Cousin
   René's Sauce di Pomodoro (see p. 207), divided
   (Alfredo pasta sauce may be substituted)
1/2 cup grated parmesan or romano cheese

Application:

- Preheat oven to 350 degrees F.
- Spray 13 x 9–inch baking dish with cooking spray.
- Cook manicotti until slightly firm. Do not overcook.
- Drain and rinse pasta under cold water so shells will not stick together.
- Let pasta dry on paper towels.
- In a medium mixing bowl, stir 3 cups mozzarella with ricotta cheese and basil.
- Using a teaspoon, very carefully stuff pasta with cheese mixture.
- Pour 1/2 cup pasta sauce into prepared baking dish and spread evenly on bottom.
- Arrange stuffed pasta over sauce.
- Pour remaining sauce over shells.
- Sprinkle pasta with remaining 1 cup mozzarella.
- Bake for 15–20 minutes.
- Remove from oven and sprinkle with parmesan or romano cheese.
- Bake for additional 10 minutes.
- When fully cooked, carefully dish pasta shells onto individual plates.

Serving note: Serve with freshly made That-Furry-Italian Garlic Bread (see p. 241).

Supermodel Hint

As a sweet, innocent child, this was one of Miss Divina's favorite foods! This dish makes plenty, it's filling, completely family-friendly, and the leftovers are sometimes even better than the freshly made batch.

Rosie's Salmon with Black-Tie Pasta

Makes 4–6 servings.

Makeup:

1 cup white wine
3 tablespoons water
2 (8-ounce) skinless salmon fillets
8 ounces asparagus
1 cup frozen peas, thawed
1/2 cup extra-virgin olive oil
2 tablespoons snipped fresh chives
1 tablespoon finely grated lemon zest
1 teaspoon salt
1 teaspoon freshly ground black pepper
12 ounces uncooked bow-tie pasta
1 cup diced ripe plum tomatoes
3 tablespoons freshly squeezed lemon juice
parmesan or romano cheese, for garnish
fresh basil leaves, for garnish

Application:

- Bring wine and water to a boil in a medium saucepan.
- Reduce heat to medium; add salmon and cook, partly covered, for 5–7 minutes each side, or until fish flakes easily when tested with a fork.
- Remove salmon and set aside to cool. Discard wine/water mixture.
- In a medium saucepan, cook bow-tie pasta according to package directions. Drain water when pasta is done.
- Trim and discard tough stem ends of asparagus and cut stalks into 1-inch pieces.
- Blanch asparagus until tender.
- Drain and place in a large bowl with peas, olive oil, chives, lemon zest, salt, and pepper; toss together.
- Break salmon into small pieces and gently mix salmon, tomatoes, and lemon juice with vegetables.
- Gently mix in pasta.
- Place pasta on a large serving platter and garnish with parmesan or romano cheese and fresh basil.

Serving note: Serve with freshly made That-Furry-Italian Garlic Bread (see p. 241).

Supermodel Hint

Rosie is one of my favorite "street" fashion designers. Rumor has it that she once lived under a bridge and that her "designs" are nothing more than a bunch of secondhand clothes she picked up out of the mud.

211

Makes 4–6 servings.

Makeup:

1 pound freshly steamed clams or 16 ounces canned
    chopped or minced clams
1/4 cup salted butter
1 small onion, finely chopped
1/4 cup fresh parsley, chopped
1 teaspoon freshly chopped garlic
1 (12-ounce) bottle clam juice, divided
1 (12-ounce) package spaghetti
freshly grated parmesan or romano cheese, for garnish

Application:

- Clean and drain clams; then set aside.
- In a small skillet, sauté onions, parsley, and garlic in butter over medium heat for 3–5 minutes.
- After onions are golden brown, add 1/2 cup clam juice.
- Simmer for 30 minutes over low heat.
- Add more bottled clam juice if needed.
- A few minutes prior to serving, mix in clams and more extra juice if needed.
- Prepare spaghetti according to package directions and drain.
- Fold clam mixture into spaghetti.
- Serve with freshly grated parmesan or romano cheese on top.

Serving note: Serve with freshly made That-Furry-Italian Garlic Bread (see p. 241).

(see p. 241)

Supermodel Hint

*As a general rule, the smaller the clams, the more tender they are. And, no matter what they say,
larger is not always better! Try this recipe with freshly steamed mussels! Miss Divina loves mussels!*

Stuff Your Man with This Turkey Manicotti

Makes 4–6 servings.

Makeup:

butter-flavored cooking spray
1 (8-ounce) package manicotti pasta
1 pound ground turkey, cooked
2 eggs
1 (15-ounce) can spinach, drained
12 ounces ricotta cheese
1 teaspoon salt
1 teaspoon pepper
1 teaspoon garlic powder
16 ounces tomato sauce, preferably My Italian Cousin
   René's Sauce di Pomodoro (see p. 207), divided
1 cup freshly grated parmesan or romano cheese

Application:

- Preheat oven to 375 degrees F.
- Spray a 13 x 9–inch baking dish with cooking spray.
- Cook manicotti until slightly firm. Do not overcook.
- Drain and rinse pasta under cold water so shells will not stick together.
- Let pasta dry on paper towels.
- Combine cooked ground turkey, eggs, spinach, ricotta cheese, salt, pepper, and garlic powder in a large mixing bowl and mix well.
- Using a piping bag, stuff pasta shells with meat mixture.
- Coat bottom of baking dish with 1/2 cup tomato sauce.
- Lay stuffed pasta in rows in baking dish.
- Cover with remaining pasta sauce.
- Sprinkle parmesan or romano cheese on top and bake for 40 minutes.
- When fully cooked, carefully dish pasta shells onto individual plates.

Serving note: Serve with freshly made That-Furry-Italian Garlic Bread (see p. 241).

Supermodel Hint

If you don't have a piping bag, put all the meat filling into a large ziplock freezer bag. Cut a large enough hole in one bottom corner for the meat filling to easily come out to fill the manicotti shells.

Pizza Dishes

Veneziano Paradiso Pizza (p. 221)

Chauffeur's Choice Pizzeria Crust

Makes 2 pizza crusts.

Makeup:

3/4 cup warm water
2 teaspoons or 1 (0.25-ounce) packet yeast
1/2 teaspoon sugar
2 cups all-purpose flour, divided, plus additional
   for dusting
1 teaspoon salt
cooking spray
cornstarch (optional)
extra-virgin olive oil

Photo of uncooked pizza crust shown.

Application:

- Adjust oven rack to highest position. Preheat oven to 500 degrees F.
- Dissolve sugar and yeast in warm water and let sit until foamy, about 5 minutes.
- While yeast is soaking, combine 1 cup flour and salt in a separate large bowl. Stir until salt is evenly mixed into flour.
- Pour yeast water into bowl of flour and stir with wooden spoon until fairly smooth. Stir in additional 1/2 cup flour.
- Turn dough out onto a floured surface and knead for 5 minutes, slowly adding up to 1/2 cup more flour as you go. Be sure to add flour slowly while kneading to prevent dough from becoming too dry and stiff.
- Let dough rest for 5 minutes.
- Divide dough into two equal portions and form each piece into a ball. (See "Supermodel Hint" below.)
- Press dough balls down into flattened circular disks. Using a rolling pin, roll them out into thin circles, about 12 inches in diameter and 1/8 inch thick.
- Prepare pizza pans with either nonstick cooking spray or a combination of cooking spray and cornmeal. Then carefully place dough onto pans.
- Bake crusts for 5 minutes, or until edges develop just a hint of golden brown.
- Remove crusts from oven.
- Brush crust edges with olive oil.
- Add toppings and bake for additional 7–10 minutes, or until cheese is bubbly and crusts are a medium golden brown.

Supermodel Hint

If making your own dough, leave it in the refrigerator for at least two hours before rolling it out. Use cornmeal on the baking sheet; it will keep the crust from clinging. Be sure to move the dough, not your hands or pin, to get it to an even thickness.

Farm—Fresh Goat Cheese and Caramelized Onion Pizza

Makes 6–8 servings.

Makeup:

1 freshly made pizza crust (see p. 215 for recipe) or
  1 ready-made thin pizza crust
1/2 cup extra-virgin olive oil or butter, divided, plus
  additional as needed
1 large white onion, cut into thin rings
salt and pepper to taste
1 (15-ounce) jar garlic Alfredo pasta sauce
3 ounces goat cheese
fresh basil, for garnish (optional)

Application:

- Prepare freshly made pizza crust (see p. 215 for recipe) or ready-made pizza crust. If using a pizza stone, place stone in oven as it preheats.
- Reduce oven heat to 395 degrees F and position a rack low in the oven.
- Sauté onion in 1/4 cup olive oil or butter over medium heat, stirring frequently. Season with salt and pepper and cover to keep moisture in. Sauté for 5–7 minutes, or until onions are soft, translucent, and golden in color. Set aside once cooked.
- Place crust on pizza stone (removed from oven) or baking sheet.
- Brush crust edges with remaining 1/4 cup olive oil.
- Spread small amount of Alfredo sauce over entire crust.
- Evenly spread caramelized onions and clumps of goat cheese over crust.
- Bake for 10–12 minutes, or until edges appear crisp and onions and goat cheese have warmed through.
- Slice and serve topped with fresh basil leaves (optional).

Supermodel Hint

If you're making fresh pizza dough and are preparing only one pizza, wrap the second ball of dough in plastic and store in the refrigerator for up to two days or in the freezer for up to three months.

Gorgonzola and Apricot Pizza—Boy Roberto

Makes 6–8 servings.

Makeup:

1 freshly made pizza crust (see p. 215 for recipe) or
   1 ready-made thin pizza crust
1/4 cup extra-virgin olive oil
4 ounces tomato sauce, preferably My Italian Cousin
   René's Sauce di Pomodoro (see p. 207)
8 ounces romano or parmesan cheese, freshly grated
1 teaspoon pepper
1 teaspoon garlic salt
1 teaspoon tarragon
1 teaspoon oregano
1/4 medium red onion, thinly sliced
10–15 dried apricots, chopped
1/2 cup crumbled gorgonzola cheese

Application:

- Prepare freshly made pizza crust (see p. 215 for recipe) or ready-made pizza crust. If using a pizza stone, place stone in oven as it preheats.
- Reduce oven heat to 395 degrees F and position a rack low in the oven.
- Place crust on pizza stone (removed from oven) or baking sheet.
- Brush crust edges with olive oil.
- Evenly spread tomato sauce over crust.
- Evenly spread romano and parmesan cheese over crust.
- Season with pepper, garlic salt, tarragon, and oregano.
- Evenly distribute sliced red onions, apricots, and gorgonzola over crust.
- Bake 10–12 minutes, or until cheese is melted and crust is crisp.
- Slice and serve.

Supermodel Hint

Miss Divina got this recipe from her dear friend Roberto. They go way back to the days when they modeled diapers.
New York was where all the best diaper models worked. Now, Roberto is a frustrated husband in Hotlanta.

Makes 6–8 servings.

Makeup:

1 freshly made pizza crust (see p. 215 for recipe) or
   1 ready-made thin pizza crust
8 ounces fresh jumbo shrimp
1/4 cup extra-virgin olive oil
4 ounces tomato sauce, preferably My Italian Cousin
   René's Sauce di Pomodoro (see p. 207)
8 ounces mozzarella cheese, freshly grated
8 ounces romano cheese, freshly grated
8 ounces parmesan cheese, freshly grated
1 teaspoon pepper
1 teaspoon garlic salt
1 teaspoon oregano
1 medium red onion, diced
1/4 cup diced broccoli, uncooked
15–20 small black olives
1 (2-ounce) can anchovies
2 teaspoons minced garlic
melted butter, as needed (for brushing crust)

Application:

- Prepare freshly made pizza crust (see p. 215 for recipe) or ready-made pizza crust. If using a pizza stone, place stone in oven as it preheats.
- Reduce oven heat to 395 degrees F and position a rack low in the oven.
- Steam shrimp with shells on. Cool under cold water, shell, and remove tails.
- Place crust on pizza stone (removed from oven) or baking sheet.
- Brush crust edges with olive oil.
- Evenly spread tomato sauce over crust.
- Evenly spread mozzarella cheese over crust.
- Evenly spread romano and parmesan cheese over crust.
- Season with pepper, garlic salt, and oregano.
- Evenly distribute onion, broccoli, cooked shrimp, olives, anchovies, and garlic over crust.
- Bake 10–12 minutes, or until crust is golden brown and cheese is melted.
- Brush crust with melted butter to keep from burning if needed.
- Slice and serve.

Paparazzi Prosciutto Pizza

Makes 6–8 servings.

Makeup:

1 freshly made pizza crust (see p. 215 for recipe) or
   1 ready-made thin pizza crust
1/4 cup salted butter
8 ounces fresh mushrooms, sliced
1 garlic clove, minced
1 teaspoon chopped fresh french thyme
2 teaspoons sherry vinegar
1/4 cup extra-virgin olive oil
1/2 cup pesto sauce
1/3 cup shredded fontina cheese
2 ounces prosciutto, cut into thin strips
1/4 cup finely chopped shallots
fresh basil, for garnish (optional)

Application:

- Prepare freshly made pizza crust (see p. 215 for recipe) or ready-made pizza crust. If using a pizza stone, place stone in oven as it preheats.
- Reduce oven heat to 395 degrees F and position a rack low in the oven.
- Add butter to a medium skillet and sauté mushrooms over medium-high heat until mushrooms are tender.
- Add garlic and thyme; sauté 1 minute.
- Stir in sherry vinegar; remove from heat.
- Place crust on pizza stone (removed from oven) or baking sheet.
- Brush crust edges with olive oil.
- Spread pesto sauce over entire pizza crust.
- Top crust with fontina cheese, prosciutto, mushrooms, and shallots, in that order.
- Bake 10–12 minutes, or until cheese is melted and crust edges are golden brown.
- Top with fresh basil for garnish, slice, and serve.

Supermodel Hint

Miss Divina goes low! For the best browning, put a rack in the lowest position in the oven and use a pizza stone if you have one. Be sure to preheat the oven; you want it as hot as it can get for a crisp crust.

219

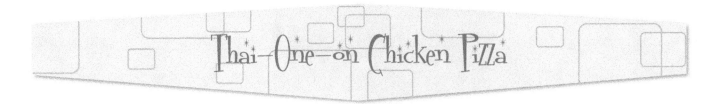

Makes 6–8 servings.

Makeup:

1 freshly made pizza crust (see p. 215 for recipe) or
   1 ready-made thin pizza crust
1 large boneless, skinless chicken breast, cubed
1/4 cup Thai peanut sauce
2 tablespoons sesame oil
1 teaspoon coriander
1 teaspoon Thai chili powder
1 teaspoon galangal
1 teaspoon green peppercorns
1 teaspoon lemongrass
1 teaspoon turmeric
1/4 cup extra-virgin olive oil
2–3 cups shredded mozzarella cheese
1/2 cup julienned carrots
1/2 cup bean sprouts
1/2 cup peanuts
1/4 cup fresh cilantro, chopped
1/4 cup diced green onions
6 large mushrooms, sliced
sesame seeds to taste

Application:

- Prepare made pizza crust (see p. 215 for recipe) or ready-made pizza crust. If using a pizza stone, place stone in oven as it preheats.
- Reduce oven heat to 395 degrees F and position a rack low in the oven.
- Marinate chicken in peanut sauce for 1 hour.
- In a small saucepan, stir together sesame oil, coriander, Thai chili powder, galangal, green peppercorns, lemongrass, and turmeric and let simmer over medium heat for 2 minutes.
- Add chicken to saucepan and cook over medium heat for 5 minutes.
- Place crust on pizza stone (removed from oven) or baking sheet.
- Brush crust edges with olive oil.
- Top crust with cheese, chicken, carrots, bean sprouts, peanuts, cilantro, and onions.
- Bake 10–12 minutes, or until cheese is melted and crust edges are golden brown.
- Sprinkle sesame seeds over pizza.
- Slice and serve.

Serving note: Serve with a good dry chardonnay wine.

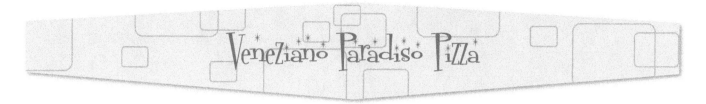

Makes 6–8 servings.

Makeup:

1 freshly made pizza crust (see p. 215 for recipe) or
  1 ready-made thin pizza crust
4 tablespoons extra virgin olive oil
4 ounces tomato sauce, preferably My Italian Cousin
  René's Sauce di Pomodoro (see p. 207)
1 cup shredded mozzarella cheese
4 ounces prosciutto, cut into thin strips
1 (6 ounce) jar marinated artichokes, chopped
4 tablespoons roasted garlic, minced
4 ounces kalamata olives, pitted and chopped
1/2 cup shredded asiago cheese
fresh thyme or basil, for garnish

Application:

- Prepare freshly made pizza crust (see p. 215 for recipe) or ready-made pizza crust. If using a pizza stone, place stone in oven as it preheats.
- Reduce oven heat to 395 degrees F and position a rack low in the oven.
- Place crust on pizza stone (removed from oven) or baking sheet.
- Brush crust edges with olive oil.
- Spread tomato sauce over entire crust.
- Top crust with mozzarella, prosciutto, artichokes, garlic, olives, and asiago cheese, in that order.
- Bake 10–12 minutes, or until cheese is melted and crust edges are golden brown.
- Top with fresh thyme or basil for garnish, slice, and serve.

Supermodel Hint

Miss Divina believes that pizza is like your facial powder foundation. She prefers to apply the mozzarella cheese before other toppings, but finicky eaters may prefer it on top.

Makes 6–8 servings.

Makeup:

1 freshly made pizza crust (see p. 215 for recipe) or
 1 ready-made thin pizza crust
1/4 cup extra-virgin olive oil
1 (8-ounce) package cream cheese, room temperature
1/2 cup sour cream
1 tablespoon crushed red pepper
1 teaspoon dried dill weed
1 teaspoon salt
1 teaspoon pepper
1 teaspoon garlic powder
8 ounces mozzarella cheese, freshly sliced
8 ounces romano cheese, freshly grated
2 cups fresh baby spinach
1 cup sliced zucchini
1/2 cup small, fresh chopped broccoli florets, steamed
1 roma tomato, chopped
4 ounces kalamata olives, pitted and chopped
1/4 cup shredded carrot

Application:

- Prepare freshly made pizza crust (see p. 215 for recipe) or ready-made pizza crust. If using a pizza stone, place stone in oven as it preheats.
- Reduce oven heat to 395 degrees F and position a rack low in the oven.
- Place crust on pizza stone (removed from oven) or baking sheet.
- Brush crust edges with olive oil.
- In a small bowl, mix cream cheese, sour cream, crushed red pepper, dill weed, salt, pepper, and garlic powder until smooth.
- Spread mixture evenly over crust.
- Top with mozzarella and romano cheese.
- Evenly spread spinach, zucchini, broccoli, tomato, olives, and carrot on top.
- Bake 10–12 minutes, or until vegetables are cooked and cheese is melted.
- Slice and serve immediately.

Sensational Sides

I am here to be admired, maybe even seduced!

Zucchini Sliced-up-the-Side Dress (p. 247)

What woman is complete without a cherished, loving partner on her arm? For that matter, what entrée is complete without a side dish? There are so many things you can make to accompany the main course of the dinner menu—more than Miss Divina can put in this book. But that's not to say Miss Divina doesn't have a few tried-and-true recipes she can rely on to take your taste buds on a wild and crazy journey!

As you already know, your menu selections should complement each other. Never serve a chicken stock–based rice with a beef entrée! Hasn't Miss Divina taught you better than that? I simply adore Miss Divina's Sam Francisco's Double-Stuffed Potato and her Gra-Tintin's Little-Reporter Potatoes. Just can't get enough of those carbs! Of course, not all her side recipes are potatoes. Try String of Pearl Onions, Green Peas, and Bacon, a recipe courtesy of her mama, Yvonne. So buttery and delicious! If you are serving Beauty-Shot Baked Cod with Béarnaise Sauce Divine, I suggest you try Wild-Nights Rice with Golden Raisins as a side dish. That might get your man wild for you! I know it does Miss Divina's beaux! I'm keeping a photographic record of all those men in case she decides someday to cut off my liquor-store charge account! Honey, it's not blackmail; it's "insurance"!

Gra-Tintin's Little-Reporter Potatoes

Viva-Italia Vegetable Torte

Blanche Itche
celebrating … again.

Mother-Agent Mashed Potatoes (p. 235)

Betsey's Better Buttery and Crusty Croutons

Makeup:

half to full loaf day-old french bread
1/4 cup extra-virgin olive oil
2 tablespoons butter
1 teaspoon salt
1 teaspoon freshly ground black pepper
1/4 teaspoon crushed red pepper

Application:

- Preheat oven to 400 degrees F.
- Cut bread into cubes and place in a large bowl.
- Drizzle cubes with olive oil, butter, salt, pepper, and crushed red pepper. Mix well.
- Spread seasoned bread onto a sheet pan and bake for about 15 minutes.
- Remove from oven and let cool.
- Set aside for when you are ready to use. Store no more than 3–4 days.

Makes 12–18 biscuits.

Makeup:

10 slices bacon
3 cups all-purpose or biscuit flour, plus additional for
  flouring baking sheet
3 tablespoons sugar
4 teaspoons baking powder
1 1/2 teaspoons salt
1 teaspoon baking soda
3/4 cup unsalted butter, room temperature, plus
  additional for serving
2 cups shredded cheddar cheese
1/2 cup chopped fresh chives
1 cup buttermilk

Application:

- Preheat oven to 425 degrees F.
- Sprinkle flour on a baking sheet and set aside.
- Fry bacon until crisp and brown.
- Transfer bacon to a paper towel and drain grease.
- When bacon is cool, chop into small- to medium-size pieces and set aside.
- In a large bowl, combine flour, sugar, baking powder, salt, and baking soda and mix well.
- Add butter to dry ingredients and mix well.
- Add cheese, fresh chives, and chopped bacon and mix evenly.
- Add buttermilk and stir just until moistened.
- Using 1/2 cup dough for each biscuit, drop biscuits onto prepared baking sheet, spacing them about 2 inches apart.
- Place no more than 6 biscuits per baking sheet.
- Bake until biscuits are golden brown on top, about 15–20 minutes.
- Repeat baking sequence again until all the dough is used.
- Split and serve biscuits warm with butter.

Supermodel Hint

Miss Divina bakes only six biscuits at a time in the oven. It takes more time to bake, but she feels it results in more evenly baked biscuits. And more-contented gentlemen callers!

228

Cheesy Broccoli, Mushrooms, and Rice Casserole

Makes 8 servings.

Makeup:

2 cups chicken stock
1/2 cup uncooked wild rice
6 slices thick-cut applewood bacon
1 large yellow onion, finely chopped
1/4 cup salted butter
1 1/2 pounds fresh broccoli, chopped
1 (12-ounce) can condensed cream of mushroom soup
1 (8-ounce) can condensed milk
1 (6.5-ounce) can sliced mushrooms
2 cups grated extra-sharp cheddar cheese, divided
1 cup half-and-half
butter-flavored cooking spray
1/2 cup seasoned bread crumbs

Application:

- Preheat oven to 350 degrees F.
- In a medium saucepan, bring chicken stock to a boil.
- Add rice and stir.
- Reduce heat to a simmer, cover, and cook for 20 minutes, or until rice is cooked.
- Fry bacon until medium brown. Drain and let cool.
- Crumble bacon when it is cool and set aside.
- Sauté chopped onions in butter over medium heat until light golden brown.
- In a large mixing bowl, add cooked rice, bacon, sautéed onions, broccoli, soup, condensed milk, mushrooms, 1 1/2 cups cheese, and half-and-half. Mix well.
- Spray 8 large ramekins with butter-flavored spray.
- Transfer mixture to individual ramekins and smooth out evenly.
- Sprinkle bread crumbs over entire surface. Sprinkle remaining cheese on top.
- Cook in oven for 15 minutes, or until top cheese is golden brown.
- When casseroles are fully cooked, remove from oven and let cool slightly.
- Flip ramekins over onto serving plates and garnish with chives sprinkled on top before serving.

Serving note: Serve with Mrs. Sippie's Glazed Pork Chops (see p. 194 for recipe) or any other meat or chicken entrée.

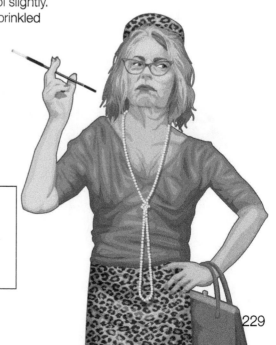

Supermodel Hint

You can bake this dish in one large casserole dish or in individual ramekins as Miss Divina likes to. Just make sure your cookery is always oven-safe! It's all about protection, darling!

Chunky Plus–Size–Girl Blue Cheese Salad Dressing

Makeup:

1 cup mayonnaise
1 cup sour cream
1/2 cup buttermilk
1/4 cup dried onion flakes
2 tablespoons freshly squeezed lemon juice
2 tablespoons worcestershire sauce
1 tablespoon white pepper
1 tablespoon coarsely ground black pepper
2 teaspoons minced garlic
2 teaspoons sugar
1 teaspoon chili powder
1 teaspoon salt
1 teaspoon hot sauce, such as Tabasco
12 ounces crumbled blue cheese

Application:

- Combine mayonnaise, sour cream, and buttermilk in a large mixing bowl and mix thoroughly.
- Add dried onion flakes, lemon juice, worcestershire sauce, white pepper, black pepper, garlic, sugar, chili powder, salt, and hot sauce and mix thoroughly.
- Using a hand mixer on low speed, add in crumbled blue cheese and mix well.
- Refrigerate for at least 24 hours before serving.

Supermodel Hint

Miss Divina is a sucker for a good blue cheese, and she's sure you'll enjoy this fabulous salad dressing more than the expandable-waist pants you may need to buy if you indulge in too much of this dressing!

Eastern Bloc Potato Salad

Makes 8–10 servings.

Makeup:

6 slices thick-cut applewood bacon
6 cups red potatoes, peeled or not
6 green onions or chives, chopped, divided
1/2 cup chopped red onion
2 tablespoons all-purpose flour
2 tablespoons sugar
1 1/2 teaspoons salt
1 teaspoon celery seed
1 teaspoon pepper
1 cup vinegar
1/4 cup water

Application:

- Fry bacon until crisp in a large skillet. Drain, reserving 1/4 cup drippings. Crumble bacon when cool.
- Wash potatoes and peel if desired.
- Evenly cube potatoes into medium-size pieces.
- Place potatoes in a large pan and cover with enough water to submerge them.
- Cook them in simmering water until just tender, usually about 10 minutes.
- Drain potatoes in a colander but do not rinse.
- In a large mixing bowl, combine bacon, potatoes, and 3 chopped green onions or chives.
- Sauté onions in reserved drippings in large skillet until tender.
- Add flour, sugar, salt, celery seed, and pepper to pan and blend in.
- Add vinegar and water; cook and stir until thickened and bubbly.
- Remove from heat and transfer to mixing bowl, tossing lightly into potato mixture.
- Transfer to a large serving bowl, and refrigerate, covered, for 2–4 hours or overnight.
- Serve cold or room temperature as preferred.
- Top with remaining 3 chopped green onions or chives for garnish.

Supermodel Hint

Don't boil the potatoes over high heat; instead let them cook over medium heat. For best results, start the potatoes in cold, salted water and bring them to a boil. Then lower to a simmer until cooked through.

Gra-Tintin's Little-Reporter Potatoes

Makes 12–15 servings.

Makeup:

2 cups heavy cream
1 cup whole milk
7 cloves garlic, minced
2 tablespoons rosemary
1 tablespoon french thyme
1 teaspoon salt
1 teaspoon white pepper
3 pounds russet potatoes, washed and unpeeled
4 tablespoons butter, divided
2 cups extra-sharp white cheddar cheese

Application:

- Preheat oven to 375 degrees F.
- In a medium saucepan, combine cream, milk, garlic, rosemary, thyme, salt, and pepper.
- Simmer mixture for 10 minutes.
- While mixture is simmering, slice potatoes into 1/8-inch-thick slices.
- Grease a 10 x 14-inch gratin dish with 1 tablespoon butter.
- Overlapping the potatoes in rows, arrange first layer of potatoes along bottom of dish.
- Pour about 1/2 cup of cream over each layer.
- Evenly sprinkle some cheese over each layer, saving some for the top of the dish later.
- Repeat the process until you have 3–4 layers, depending on the depth of dish.
- Pour any remaining cream on top.
- Dot top with remaining 3 tablespoons butter.
- Cover dish with aluminum foil.
- Bake for 45 minutes.
- Remove from oven and remove the foil.
- Sprinkle remaining cheese on top.
- Return to oven uncovered and continue to bake until top is golden brown, or 25–30 minutes.

Italiano Paesano Riso

Makes 10–12 servings.

Makeup:

1 1/2 cups uncooked long-grain white rice
3 cups chicken broth
2 tablespoons Italian seasoning, crushed
2 tablespoons salt
1 cup chopped fresh spinach
1 (8-ounce) can white beans
1 cup chopped fresh mushrooms
1/4 cup fresh green peas
1 cup heavy cream
1/2 cup grated parmesan cheese, plus additional
  for garnish

Application:

- Place rice in a fine-mesh strainer and rinse under cold running water. Shake to drain.
- Bring broth and Italian seasoning to a boil in a 2-quart saucepan over medium-high heat.
- Add rice and salt to saucepan.
- Reduce heat to low.
- Simmer for 45 minutes. Check the rice and stop cooking when the grains are tender.
- Stir spinach into broth. Add white beans, mushrooms, and green peas.
- Cover and cook for 10 minutes.
- Add cream and cook for additional 10 minutes.
- Stir in parmesan cheese.
- Serve with additional parmesan cheese grated on top if desired.

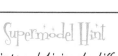

Supermodel Hint

Plain rice turns into a deliciously different side when it's cooked in broth and accented with spinach, cream, and parmesan cheese. You'll be goose-stepping at every bite!

Just–Peachy Applesauce

Makeup:

10–15 Granny Smith apples (about 4 pounds), peeled, cored, and cut into chunks
1/2 cup pear or apple cider
1/4 cup sugar, plus additional to taste
peel of 1 lemon
1 tablespoon lemon juice
1 tablespoon ground cinnamon, plus additional to taste
1/2 teaspoon ground cloves
8 fresh peaches (about 4 cups), peeled and chopped (2 [15-ounce] cans peaches may be substituted if fresh peaches are not available)
1/4 cup cognac
cinnamon sticks, for garnish

Application:

- Mix apples, pear or apple cider, sugar, lemon peel, lemon juice, cinnamon, and ground cloves in a large saucepan or medium pot.
- If desired, add more sugar or cinnamon to taste.
- Heat over medium heat, stirring occasionally, until apples are soft. Be careful not to burn the bottom of the pan; burning will ruin the taste of the applesauce.
- Remove and discard lemon peel.
- With a potato masher, mash apples slightly so sauce is slightly chunky.
- Add peaches and mix thoroughly; cook for additional 15 minutes over low heat.
- Mash peaches ever so slightly but keep them chunky.
- Add cognac and mix thoroughly.
- Serve either hot or preserve in a glass jar and refrigerate for later use.

Note: This recipe can also be made by substituting cranberries, apricots, pears, or any fruit of your choice for the peaches.

Mother-Agent Mashed Potatoes

Makes 6–8 servings.

Makeup:

6 large russet (or Yukon Gold) potatoes
4 cups cauliflower
1 tablespoon extra-virgin olive oil
1 teaspoon salt
1 teaspoon pepper
1 teaspoon garlic powder
1/2 cup greek yogurt
1/2 cup grated parmesan cheese
2 tablespoons butter
4 teaspoons minced fresh chives, divided
2 teaspoons minced fresh parsley
2 teaspoons minced freshly roasted garlic
gravy, for serving (optional)

Application:

- Preheat oven to 375 degrees F.
- Clean and peel potatoes and cut into thirds.
- In a large pot, add potatoes and sufficient water to cover.
- Bring to a boil.
- Clean and chop cauliflower into medium-size pieces.
- Pour olive oil on cauliflower.
- Season with salt, pepper, and garlic powder.
- Roast cauliflower on greased baking sheet for 20 minutes, or until slightly golden.
- Remove from oven and mash and set aside.
- When potatoes are fully cooked (when a fork inserted goes in easily), drain water and return potatoes to pot.
- Mash potatoes to desired consistency. Some like their potatoes lumpy; others, very smooth.
- Add mashed cauliflower to potatoes.
- Add yogurt, parmesan cheese, butter, 2 teaspoons chives, parsley, and garlic.
- Mix well until potatoes are smooth.
- Sprinkle remaining 2 teaspoons chives on potatoes as garnish before serving. Serve with or without your favorite gravy.

Supermodel Hint

When making mashed potatoes, always use starchy (russet) or all-purpose (Yukon Gold) potatoes. Never use waxy potatoes (i.e., red bliss, fingerlings, and so on). Starchy potatoes break down better, resulting in a creamier mash.

Makes 8–12 servings.

Makeup:

24–30 small new potatoes
4 teaspoons salt
4 teaspoons black pepper
4 teaspoons garlic powder
1/4 cup extra-virgin olive oil
1/4 cup butter, melted
4 teaspoons minced fresh parsley
4 teaspoons minced fresh chives

Application:

- Preheat oven to 450 degrees F.
- Clean potatoes and peel if desired, or leave nutritious peels on.
- Halve potatoes.
- Season potatoes with salt, pepper, and garlic powder.
- Coat baking sheet or large, oven-safe glass baking dish with olive oil.
- Place potatoes on sheet or in dish and roast until they are easily pierced by a fork but still firm, about 20–25 minutes.
- Remove potatoes and cover to keep warm.
- Place butter, parsley, and chives in a small bowl and mix well.
- Transfer potatoes to a serving dish.
- Pour butter mixture over potatoes and serve.

Serving note: If you are roasting a chicken or serving a beef roast, place the potatoes around the meat for a delicious roasted flavor. If you can find mixed varieties of potatoes in your store, they make for a beautiful color mixture.

Supermodel Hint

This is one of Miss Divina's famous side dishes that even those skinny supermodel friends of hers can't get enough of. Simple but delicious.

Papa Guglielmo's Summer Baked Beans

Makes 8–12 servings.

Makeup:

6 slices bacon, uncooked, chopped
1/2 medium sweet onion, chopped
1–2 cloves garlic, minced
2 (16-ounce) cans navy beans
1 cup dark brown sugar
1/4 cup molasses
1/4 cup ketchup
2 tablespoons worcestershire sauce
1 teaspoon prepared yellow mustard
1 cup chopped green bell peppers
1/2 cup chopped celery
1 teaspoon salt
1 teaspoon ground pepper
1 teaspoon ground cayenne pepper

Application:

- Preheat oven to 325 degrees F.
- In a medium skillet, add bacon, onion, and garlic.
- Sauté until bacon and onion are tender.
- Remove from heat and transfer to a large mixing bowl.
- Add navy beans, brown sugar, molasses, ketchup, worcestershire sauce, and yellow mustard.
- Stir to combine well.
- Add green bell peppers, celery, salt, pepper, and cayenne.
- Mix well and pour into deep oven-safe serving dish.
- Bake in oven for 45 minutes.
- Remove from oven and allow to cool about 5 minutes before serving.

Supermodel Hint

Every year after the grape harvest, Miss Divina's papa would host an outdoor celebration at the family villa for the local peasants. A warm summer breeze always reminds her of those al fresco meals and particularly this delicious warm bean dish.

Providence Buttery Lobster Dinner Rolls

Makes 12-15 rolls.

Makeup:

1 cup warm whole milk
3/4 cup salted butter, room temperature, divided
1 (1/4-ounce) packet of active dry yeast
1/4 cup granulated sugar
2 large eggs
1 teaspoon salt
4 cups all-purpose flour
6 ounces lobster meat, minced
2 tablespoons salted butter, melted, divided
2 teaspoons sea salt (for top of rolls)

Application:

- In a small bowl, mix milk and 1/2 cup butter together.
- Sprinkle yeast over milk/butter mixture and let it sit for 5 minutes to activate.
- Add milk/butter mixture to an electric stand mixer.
- Add sugar, eggs, 1 teaspoon salt, and flour.
- Mix until combined. Let mixture sit for 5 minutes.
- Sauté lobster in remaining 1/4 butter over medium heat for 5 minutes.
- Remove lobster from heat and add to dough in stand mixer.
- Switch the attachment of the mixer to the dough hook and knead on medium speed for 10 minutes.
- Cover dough with a damp, clean kitchen towel and let it rise in a warm place for 30 minutes, or until doubled in size.
- Divide and roll dough into 12–15 balls. You may have more or less depending on the size of your rolls.
- Place rolls in a greased 9 x 13–inch pan. Cover and let rise for 15–20 minutes.
- Preheat oven to 375 degrees F.
- Just prior to placing rolls in the oven, brush 1 tablespoon melted butter over rolls using a pastry brush.
- Bake in oven for 15–20 minutes, or until lightly browned.
- Remove from oven and coat the tops of the rolls with remaining 1 tablespoon melted butter.
- Sprinkle sea salt on top of each roll while butter is still moist and rolls are still hot.
- Serve warm.

Supermodel Hint

Don't have a stand mixer? You can make this bread without a stand mixer or a bread maker. Simply mix and knead by hand for 8-10 minutes. Be sure not to add extra flour when kneading by hand. The dough should be sticky.

Sam Francisco's Double-Stuffed Potato

Makes 1 serving.

Makeup:

1 large russet potato (baking potato)
1/4 cup sour cream
1/4 cup chopped ham, cooked
1/4 cup finely chopped fresh broccoli
1/4 cup grated sharp cheddar cheese
3 tablespoons cream cheese
2 green onions (or chives), chopped
1 teaspoon garlic powder
1 teaspoon paprika
1 teaspoon salt
1 teaspoon pepper

Application:

- Preheat oven to 450 degrees F.
- Wash potato to remove all dirt.
- Make a 2- to 3-inch slit for venting in the center of potato.
- Place potato in oven on rack and bake until cooked through. Do not cover potato with foil; skin should get hard but not burnt.
- After potato is cooked thoroughly, about 45–50 minutes, remove and let cool slightly.
- Gently squeeze sides of potato to open it along slit.
- Scoop out potato from inside with spoon, leaving shell of potato intact.
- In mixing bowl, mash potato and mix in all remaining ingredients, saving some cheese for later.
- Refill potato shell with potato mixture.
- Place potato on cooking sheet and bake additional 10–15 minutes.
- Remove from oven and sprinkle remaining cheese on top of potato.
- Bake additional 3–5 minutes, or until cheese melts.

Serving note: This dish can be served as an entrée or as a side with any meat dish. Multiply recipe ingredients per number of guests/potatoes.

Supermodel Hint

No one will try to pass on this hot potato. This one is a keeper! And yes, it's better than a San Francisco trick … oh, I mean treat!

Makes 10–12 servings.

Makeup:

10 slices thick-cut applewood bacon
1 (12-ounce) bag frozen pre-peeled pearl onions
2 (12-ounce) bags frozen petit pois (petite peas)
salt, pepper, and garlic powder to taste
1/4 cup salted butter

Application:

- Fry bacon in a skillet over medium-high heat until cooked but not crispy, about 6 minutes.
- Transfer bacon to a plate, leaving grease in skillet.
- Add onions to skillet and cook over medium-high heat, stirring often, until golden and translucent.
- Remove skillet from heat and set aside.
- Chop bacon into small pieces.
- Add bacon to skillet with onions.
- Cook peas according to package directions, until peas are tender but still bright green.
- Transfer onions and bacon to a large serving bowl.
- Drain cooked peas and fold into bacon and onions in serving bowl.
- Season with salt, pepper, and garlic powder.
- Fold in butter and mix carefully until butter is melted.

Serving note: Serve with Vaina Black's Côte de Boeuf (see p. 202 for recipe) or Hollie Woode's Roasted Chicken with Herbs (see p. 157 for recipe).

(see p. 202 for recipe) ... (see p. 157 for recipe)

Supermodel Hint

*Miss Divina adores pearl onions. If June Cleaver can wear 'em while cooking,
why not wear them while you cook? Real pearls that is, you silly!*

That-Furry-Italian Garlic Bread

Makes 6-10 servings.

Makeup:

1 fresh loaf italian bread
1/4 cup butter, room temperature
1/4 cup freshly minced garlic
1 teaspoon garlic powder, or to taste
1 teaspoon salt, or to taste
1 teaspoon freshly ground black pepper, or to taste
1 teaspoon cayenne pepper, or to taste
1 cup freshly grated romano cheese
1/4 cup fresh parsley, minced
1 teaspoon paprika

Application:

- Preheat oven to broil.
- On a flat surface, slice bread into 1/2-inch-thick slices.
- Spread butter on one side of bread slices.
- Spread freshly minced garlic over bread slices.
- Evenly season bread slices with garlic powder, salt, pepper, and cayenne, adjusting seasonings to taste.
- Sprinkle bread slices with romano cheese, parsley, and paprika.
- Broil in oven for 5–7 minutes, or until cheese is melted. Watch carefully to avoid burning the bread.
- Remove from broiler and let cool for 1 minute before serving.

Supermodel Hint

What Italian meal—or, for that matter, Italian stud—is complete without Miss Divina's fresh garlic bread with dinner?

Makes 10–12 servings.

Makeup:

2 tablespoons freshly chopped garlic
1 tablespoon extra-virgin olive oil
3 cups heavy cream or half-and-half
1 tablespoon sea salt, plus additional to taste
1 tablespoon freshly ground black pepper, plus
  additional to taste
2 1/2 pounds potatoes
1/4 cup minced fresh chives or green onions
1 1/2 cups coarsely crumbled blue cheese

Application:

- Preheat oven to 375 degrees F.
- In a medium saucepan, lightly sauté garlic in olive oil until golden.
- Add cream, salt, and pepper.
- Reduce heat to low.
- Warm mixture for 5 minutes, cover, and set aside.
- Peel potatoes and slice into 1/4-inch-thick slices.
- Generously butter a 2 1/2-quart baking dish with sides at least 2 inches high.
- Put one-third of the potato slices in baking dish; season with salt and pepper to taste.
- Sprinkle one-third of the chives over potatoes, followed by one-third of the blue cheese.
- Add another one-third of the potatoes, season with salt and pepper to taste, and sprinkle with one-third of the chives and blue cheese.
- Add final layer of potatoes, pour cream mixture over them, and press down gently to flatten potatoes.
- Season with salt and pepper to taste, and sprinkle on remaining chives and blue cheese.
- Put dish on an aluminum foil–lined baking sheet and bake for 1 hour, until it's bubbling and well browned on top. The acidic cheese may cause the cream to separate a little bit, which is normal.

Supermodel Hint

Scalloped potatoes are a must for any holiday menu. Miss Divina always doctors up drab, old-fashioned recipes with her own twist. Me, I think she should add some rum or tequila!

Twiggy Salty Breadsticks

Makes 12–16 breadsticks.

Makeup:

Breadsticks
1 1/2 cups warm water
2 tablespoons sugar
1 (1/4-ounce) packet active dry yeast
3 1/2 cups all-purpose flour
2 tablespoons salt, plus additional for tops
2 tablespoons unsalted butter, melted
butter-flavored cooking spray

Butter Topping
1/4 cup butter, melted
2 teaspoons salt
2 teaspoons garlic powder

Application:

Breadsticks
- In a large mixing bowl, dissolve sugar and yeast in warm water and allow to sit for 10 minutes to activate yeast.
- Add flour, salt, and melted butter to yeast mixture. Mix until fully combined.
- Knead dough for a few minutes just until dough is smooth in consistency.
- Spray a cookie sheet with cooking spray.
- Pull off pieces of dough and roll out into 12–16 strips, laying strips on cookie sheet.
- Cover dough with a towel and let sit for 45–60 minutes to allow dough to rise.
- Preheat oven to 395 degrees F.
- Bake breadsticks for 6–7 minutes.
- While breadsticks are baking, make butter topping by mixing melted butter, garlic powder, and salt.
- Remove breadsticks from oven and brush with half the butter topping.
- Turn breadsticks over and bake for additional 5 minutes, or until golden brown.
- Remove breadsticks from oven and immediately brush remaining butter topping on breadsticks.
- Immediately sprinkle the tops with salt while butter topping is still moist.
- Allow to cool for a few minutes before eating.

Supermodel Hint

These breadsticks are so yummy and don't require too much work! You'll definitely want to serve them the next time you're craving home-baked bread. The perfect addition to any meal!

Viva-Italia Vegetable Torte

Makes 8–10 servings.

Makeup:

butter-flavored cooking spray
20 ounces zucchini
20 ounces broccoli, finely chopped
20 ounces cauliflower, finely chopped
20 ounces carrots, finely chopped
5 tablespoons butter, divided
5 tablespoons all-purpose flour
1 1/2 cups heavy cream
2 tablespoons freshly ground pepper
2 tablespoons sea salt
2 tablespoons garlic powder
1 1/2 cups greek yogurt
10 fresh eggs
1 (1.5-ounce) package onion soup mix
1 cup grated parmesan cheese, divided
3/4 cup Italian-seasoned bread crumbs

Application:

- Preheat oven to 395 degrees F.
- Lightly grease 10-inch springform pan with 1 tablespoon butter or butter-flavored cooking spray.
- Thinly slice zucchini into rounds; set aside.
- Mix chopped vegetables (broccoli, cauliflower, and carrots) together in a bowl and set aside.
- Heat remaining 4 tablespoons butter in a medium saucepan over medium heat.
- When butter is melted, remove from heat, add flour, and whisk until blended.
- Return to heat and add cream.
- Cook, stirring constantly, until mixture thickens, or about 5 minutes.
- Remove from heat.
- Stir in pepper, salt, garlic powder, greek yogurt, eggs, soup mix, and 3/4 cup parmesan cheese; set aside.
- Line the sides of springform pan with sliced zucchini, saving some for the top of the torte.
- Add half the chopped vegetables to egg mixture.
- Add one-third of egg mixture to springform pan.
- Add remaining chopped vegetables to egg mixture and mix well.
- Carefully pour remaining egg mixture into springform pan as to not upset the zucchini on the sides.
- Place remaining zucchini slices around the top of the torte.
- Evenly sprinkle remaining 1/4 parmesan cheese and bread crumbs over the top layer.
- Bake uncovered for 45 minutes, or until torte is lightly browned and firm to touch. If torte begins to brown too much, cover with aluminum foil for last 10 or so minutes.
- Remove from oven and cool for 10–15 minutes.
- When torte has cooled sufficiently, carefully release and remove springform pan.
- With a large knife or spatula, carefully remove torte from the bottom of the springform pan and slide to a large serving plate.
- Slice and serve with your choice of entrée.

Makes 6–8 servings.

Makeup:

2 cups water
1 (16-ounce) package wild rice blend
2 cups beef stock
1 tablespoon butter
1 teaspoon salt
1 teaspoon pepper
1 teaspoon garlic powder
1 teaspoon parsley flakes
1 teaspoon basil
1 teaspoon oregano
1/2 cup golden raisins
1/2 cup seedless raisins
1/4 cup pecans, crumbled

Application:

- Rinse rice.
- Mix water, butter, and beef stock in a medium saucepan; bring to a boil over high heat.
- Add rice and stir.
- Add salt, pepper, garlic powder, parsley, basil, and oregano.
- Reduce heat and simmer covered for 45 minutes.
- When rice is cooked, add golden raisins, seedless raisins, and pecans.
- Remove from heat and let stand covered for 10 minutes.

Serving note: This dish goes well with any beef, pork, chicken, or fish entrée. Consider substituting chicken or vegetable broth for the beef broth if you are serving this with chicken or fish.

Supermodel Hint

There are different instructions for cooking rice depending on the type of method of cooking, such as stove top, oven, or slow cooker. Adjust the cooking instructions based on your preferred method of cooking.

Makes 10–12 servings.

Makeup:

4 medium zucchini
2 eggs, beaten
2 cups cracker crumbs, plus additional for garnish
1 cup grated parmesan cheese, divided
1 tablespoon salt, or to taste
1 tablespoon pepper, or to taste
1 tablespoon garlic powder, or to taste
1 tablespoon tarragon
1 tablespoon oregano
1 tablespoon cayenne pepper
1/4 cup parsley, finely chopped
1/4 cup butter, sliced

Application:

- Preheat oven to 375 degrees F.
- Wash and tip zucchini. Cut into medium-size chunks.
- Steam zucchini until cooked through and drain to remove excess water.
- Place zucchini in a large bowl and mash like potatoes.
- Add eggs and cracker crumbs to zucchini to bind.
- Add 3/4 cup parmesan cheese, salt, pepper, garlic powder, tarragon, oregano, and cayenne.
- Transfer zucchini mixture to a baking dish.
- Smooth top down and add more cracker crumbs to make it crispy.
- Sprinkle with remaining parmesan cheese and parsley and dot with pats of butter.
- Bake until solid in the middle, usually about 45 minutes.

Supermodel Hint

This is good as a vegetable side for any meat or fish dish and can be baked the day before.
Just pop into the oven to reheat and serve hot.

Zucchini Sliced-Up-the-Side Dress

Makes 4–6 servings.

Makeup:

3 large zucchini
2 tablespoons butter
1 clove fresh garlic, finely minced (garlic powder
    may be substituted)
1/2 tablespoon salt
1/2 tablespoon freshly ground pepper
1 cup freshly grated romano cheese
paprika, for garnish

Application:

- Place a rack in the center of the oven and preheat oven to 400 degrees F.
- Clean zucchini and cut off ends.
- Slice each zucchini lengthwise into two parts and score insides with crisscross cut.
- Spread butter evenly on each zucchini slice.
- Evenly spread garlic over each slice.
- Evenly sprinkle salt and pepper over each slice.
- Place zucchini in a baking dish and sprinkle romano cheese and then paprika over each slice.
- Bake in oven for 12–15 minutes.
- Turn oven to broil and broil for 3–5 minutes, or until cheese turns light brown and forms a melted crust.
- Remove and cut each slice into 2–3 pieces.

Supermodel Hint
*Wherever Miss Divina has lived, this side dish has always pleased the masses.
Even the most finicky vegetarian has stood up and given applause.*

Decadent Desserts

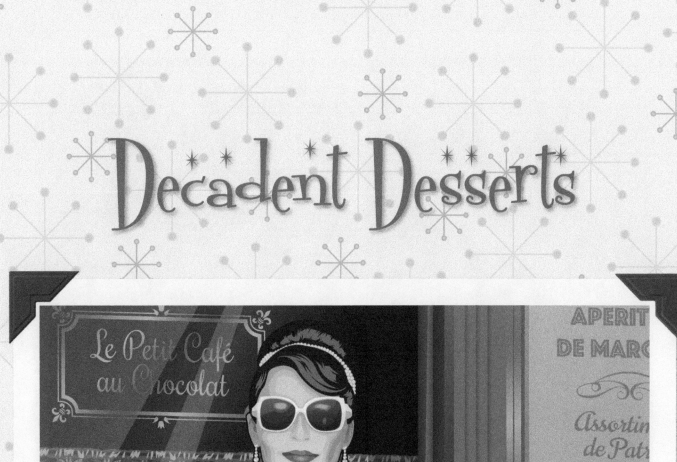

Le Petit Café
au Chocolat

APÉRIT
DE MARC

Assortin
de Patr

Pain F

Expres

Café au

Always enjoy la dolce vita!

Dark-Chocolate Miniskirt Cake with Dark-Cherry Sauce (p. 255)

How Sweet It Is!

No day is so bad that it can't be improved by one of Miss Divina's delicious desserts. If God wanted us to be thin, then why did He invent chocolates? Obviously God intended for Miss Divina to be thin, but that's between her and her God. Besides, what girl can do without a box of fine bonbons by her side while watching her favorite romantic movie or soap opera?

Sometimes when Miss Divina is on the road and needs a quick dessert, she stops off at the first five-star restaurant she can find. A sweet, dark, and fattening dessert is almost as good as a tall, dark, and handsome man. Lucky for her, the chauffeur is the latter. Some gals got it all! Damn her!

Maybe you don't have a private chauffeur, but I am willing to bet that you're thinking of dessert more than you will admit to! Everyone looks forward to and expects dessert at the end of a meal. Do you like tangy lemons? Try Signorina Divina's Tangy Lemon Cheesecake. If you want your guests

Miss Divina will teach you how to wear *tasteful hats* and clothes.

to kiss your feet, that's the dessert that will have them puckering up. Just make sure you've had a pedicure and painted your nails an appetizing color. Though I am not generally a dessert girl, unless it's a digestif, I do understand the importance of finishing off the evening with a bang. Perfectly Seductive Chocolate-Covered Strawberries can make for an especially sexy ending in front of a roaring fire with an equally hot man. If you want something a little more down to earth, something that makes you look and feel like Betty Crocker, try Baked Sin-a-Man Apples. If you are from the southern United States, you know that the bigger the hair, the closer to God. The same philosophy holds true for Strawberry Bouffant Cake. You will feel like you have gone to heaven while eating this dessert!

Lastly, close your eyes and image you are sitting in a Rome café, devouring a slice of Lennoxia's Café Cheesecake. That's the sweet life! But, no matter what dessert you make for your guests, if it's one of Miss Divina's creations, you're sure to come out looking like a star!

King Alfonso Cinnamon-Apple Pie

Lennoxia's Café Cheesecake

251

Cakes

Strawberry Bouffant Cake (p. 262)

Animal Crackers Strawberry Cake

Makes 16 servings.

Makeup:

Cake
2 cups white sugar
1/2 cup butter, room temperature
4 eggs
2 3/4 cups sifted cake flour
2 1/2 teaspoons baking powder
1 cup half-and-half
2 teaspoons vanilla extract
1 cup thawed frozen strawberries with juices, pureed
red food coloring

Strawberry Frosting
1 cup fresh strawberries
1/2 cup butter, room temperature
1 1/2 cups confectioners' sugar, sifted
1 teaspoon vanilla extract
red food coloring
pearl sprinkles, for garnish

Application:

Cake
- Preheat oven to 350 degrees F.
- Grease 9-inch springform pan.
- In a large bowl, cream together sugar and butter until light and fluffy.
- Beat in eggs one at a time, mixing well after each.
- Combine flour and baking powder; stir into batter alternately with half-and-half.
- Blend in vanilla, strawberry puree, and a few drops of food coloring.
- Pour into prepared springform pan.
- Bake for 25–30 minutes in oven, or until small knife inserted into the center of the cake comes out clean.
- Allow cake to cool in pan for at least 10 minutes before removing from pan to cool completely.

Strawberry Frosting
- Puree strawberries in a blender until smooth.
- Beat butter with an electric mixer in a large bowl until light and fluffy.
- Mix confectioners' sugar into butter until blended.
- Blend strawberry puree, vanilla, and a few drops of food coloring into butter mixture.
- Once frosting is completely blended into stiff consistency, frost cake according to your own personal style.
- Sprinkle generously with pearl sprinkles for decoration.

Supermodel Hint

The kiddies love this cake, and after the sugar rush subsides, you can lock them in their rooms for the night to sleep off their exhaustion! No animal crackers were harmed in the making of this cake.

Classic–Black–Dress Cheesecake

Makes 8–12 servings.

Makeup:

1 1/2 cups graham cracker crumbs
1 cup sugar, divided
1/4 cup butter, melted
5 (8-ounce) packages cream cheese, room temperature
3 tablespoons all-purpose flour
3 eggs
1/2 cup sour cream
2 teaspoons finely grated lemon peel
1 1/2 teaspoons vanilla extract
fresh fruit, for garnish (optional)

Application:

- Preheat oven to 350 degrees F.
- In a medium bowl, combine graham cracker crumbs and 2 tablespoons sugar.
- Add melted butter and stir to combine.
- Press crumb mixture into bottom and sides of a 9-inch springform pan.
- Chill for 30 minutes.
- In a large bowl, using an electric mixer on medium speed, beat cream cheese and remaining sugar until mixed fully.
- Gradually add flour and mix until combined.
- On low speed, mix in eggs until completely blended.
- Add sour cream, lemon peel, and vanilla; mix until completely blended.
- Pour into crust and bake for 1 hour and 15 minutes.
- Remove cake from oven and cool on wire rack.
- When completely cooled, remove from springform pan carefully and place on serving plate.
- Decorate with fresh fruit if so desired.

Supermodel Hint

*Wear only pearls when serving this scrumptious dessert. But don't spill,
because it'll be hard to remove the schmutz from the necklace.*

Dark–Chocolate Miniskirt Cake with Dark–Cherry Sauce

Makes 8 servings.

Makeup:

Dark-Cherry Sauce
1 (16-ounce) bag frozen pitted dark sweet cherries, thawed, undrained, and halved
1/2 teaspoon sugar
1/4 cup kirsch (clear cherry brandy)
1/4 teaspoon ground cinnamon

Cake
2/3 cup granulated sugar
6 tablespoons unsweetened cocoa powder
2 tablespoons all-purpose flour
3/4 cup butter
6 ounces semisweet chocolate chips
6 egg yolks
3 large whole eggs
1 teaspoon vanilla extract
powdered sugar, for garnish

Application:

Dark-Cherry Sauce
• Combine cherries, sugar, kirsch, and cinnamon in heavy medium saucepan.
• Stir over medium heat until sugar dissolves.
• Simmer until sauce thickens and is slightly reduced, about 10 minutes. Cover and keep warm.

Cake
• Preheat oven to 350 degrees F.
• Butter 8 (3/4-inch) ramekins.
• Whisk sugar, cocoa, and flour in a small bowl.
• Melt butter and chocolate in a double boiler or in a microwave until chocolate melts and mixture is smooth.
• Remove from heat and whisk into cocoa mixture.
• Add egg yolks, whole eggs, and vanilla. Blend **thoroughly**.
• Pour batter into prepared ramekins.
• Bake cakes uncovered until edges are set but center is still moist, about 15 minutes.
• Cut around warm cakes to loosen.
• Sift powdered sugar lightly on top.
• Serve with dark-cherry sauce poured over cakes.

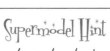

Supermodel Hint
This cake batter can be made a day in advance. Just chill and bring batter to room temperature before baking.

Lady Baltimore–Reade Cake

Makes 12–16 servings.

Makeup:

Filling
1 1/2 cups chopped nuts (hazelnuts, walnuts, and pecans)
1/2 cup dark rum

Cake
3 cups sifted cake flour
1 tablespoon double-acting baking powder
1/4 teaspoon salt
3/4 cup unsalted butter, room temperature
1 3/4 cups sugar
1 cup whole milk
1 teaspoon vanilla extract
1 teaspoon almond extract
6 egg whites, room temperature

Meringue
See p. 264 for ingredients

Application:

Filling
- In a small bowl, combine chopped nuts and rum; toss to coat.
- Cover and let stand overnight or at least a few hours.

Cake
- Preheat oven to 375 degree F.
- Grease and flour three 9-inch cake pans, 1 1/2 inches deep.
- Sift together cake flour, baking powder, and salt in a large bowl.
- In another bowl or in a food processor or mixer, cream butter until light.
- Add sugar to butter, 1/4 cup at a time, and continue to beat until light and fluffy.
- Add dry ingredients, alternating with milk, vanilla, and almond extract, and beat until smooth.
- Add egg whites and continue to beat until well blended.
- Pour mixture into cake pans, dividing batter evenly.
- Bake in the middle of oven for 25 minutes, or until cakes pull away from the sides of the pans.
- Turn cakes out onto racks to cool.

Meringue
See p. 264 for meringue instructions.

Assembly
- When cake layers are completely cool, place one layer on a plate.
- Spread about 1 cup of meringue on top.
- Cover meringue with 1/2 cup chopped nuts.
- Place another cake layer on top and repeat.
- After placing the last cake layer, spread a larger amount of meringue on top and then spread on the sides. Note that this cake is more attractive if the meringue isn't leveled smooth.
- If you have a kitchen flame torch, use it to brown the meringue.
- Garnish with walnut and pecan bits on top and around the sides.

Supermodel Hint

Lady Baltimore-Reade, as old as the colonies, loves to serve this to her oldest and dearest friends at her "salons."
It's a tradition with her going way back to the days when Baltimore was the place to be.

Lemon Meringue Triple-D Cupcakes

Makes 12 cupcakes.

Makeup:

Lemon Filling
3 egg yolks (reserve whites for meringue)
3/4 cup granulated white sugar
1/2 cup water
3 tablespoons all-purpose flour
2 tablespoons lemon zest, loosely packed
3 tablespoons lemon juice
2 tablespoons unsalted butter, melted
1 pinch salt

Cupcakes
1/2 cup unsalted butter
1 cup sugar
2 eggs
3 tablespoons lemon juice
2 teaspoons baking powder
1 teaspoon salt
1 1/2 cups all-purpose flour

Meringue
See p. 264 for ingredients

Application:

Lemon Filling
- In a small saucepan over low heat, whisk egg yolks, sugar, water, flour, lemon zest, lemon juice, melted butter, and salt; increase heat to medium, whisking constantly.
- Cook until lemon filling is smooth and thick, about 7 minutes.
- Remove from heat and set aside.

Cupcakes
- Preheat oven to 375 degrees F.
- Line 12-cup muffin tin with cupcake liners.
- In a medium bowl, beat butter and sugar until light and fluffy.
- Beat in eggs, lemon juice, baking powder, and salt.
- Beat in flour until just combined.
- Divide cupcake batter between 12 muffin cups.
- Bake 15 minutes, or until center of cupcakes firms up.
- Remove cupcakes from oven (but do not turn off oven) and cool 5–8 minutes.

Meringue
See p. 264 for meringue instructions.

Assembly
- With a sharp knife, remove center of each cupcake (about 1 inch in diameter), leaving a layer of cupcake beneath cutout; discard cupcake core.
- Fill each cupcake center with lemon filling.
- Divide dollops of meringue between cupcakes, spreading out to edges and gently tapping with back of spoon to form peaks.
- Return cupcakes to oven and bake additional 5 minutes, or until meringue peaks are golden brown. Or, if you have a kitchen flame torch, use it to brown the meringue.
- Remove cupcakes from oven and let cool for 20 minutes before serving.

Supermodel Hint

We all have crazy cravings at times. When Miss Divina feels the desire for something tangy, she often makes this recipe to satisfy those wild urges! And does she have some crazy urges at times!

Makes 12–16 servings.

Makeup:

Crust
1 (9-ounce) box chocolate wafer cookies
6 ounces semisweet chocolate, coarsely chopped
1/2 cup packed dark brown sugar
1/4 teaspoon ground nutmeg
1/4 teaspoon cinnamon
1/2 cup unsalted butter, melted

Ganache
1/2 cup whipping cream
20 ounces semisweet chocolate, chopped
1/4 cup coffee-flavored liqueur

Filling
4 (8-ounce) packages cream cheese, room temperature
1 1/3 cups sugar
1/4 cup coffee-flavored liqueur
2 tablespoons all-purpose flour
2 tablespoons dark rum
2 tablespoons instant espresso powder (or instant coffee crystals)
1 tablespoon vanilla extract
2 teaspoons molasses
4 large eggs

Topping
1 1/2 cups sour cream
1/3 cup sugar
1/4 cup cacao powder
2 teaspoons vanilla extract

Application:

Crust
- Finely grind cookies, chopped chocolate, brown sugar, nutmeg, and cinnamon in a food processor.
- Add butter and process until crumbs begin to stick together, scraping down bowl occasionally, about 1 minute.
- Transfer crumbs to 10-inch springform pan with 3-inch-high sides; set aside.

Ganache
- Bring whipping cream to a simmer in a large saucepan.
- Remove from heat; add chocolate and liqueur. Whisk until chocolate is melted and ganache is smooth.
- Pour 1 cup ganache over bottom of crust.
- Refrigerate until ganache layer is firm, about 30 minutes.
- Save residual ganache to drizzle on top of cake.

> ### Supermodel Hint
> *Miss Divina and Lennoxia created this recipe while sipping an aperitif at their favorite café in Milan, during a photo-shoot break. Girls have to do something when all the hot Italian men are inside watching a soccer game on TV!*

Filling
- Position a rack in the middle of the oven and preheat oven to 350 degrees F.
- Using an electric mixer, beat cream cheese and sugar in a large bowl until blended.
- In a small bowl, beat liqueur, flour, rum, espresso powder (or instant coffee crystals), vanilla, and molasses until instant coffee dissolves; beat into cream cheese.
- Beat in eggs one at a time, occasionally scraping down sides of bowl.
- Pour filling over cold ganache in crust.
- Place cheesecake on a rimmed baking sheet and bake until top is brown, puffed, and cracked at edges.
- Transfer cheesecake to rack and let cool 15 minutes while preparing topping (top of cheesecake will fall slightly). Do not turn off oven.

Topping
- Whisk sour cream, sugar, cacao powder, and vanilla in a medium bowl to blend.
- Pour topping over still-warm cheesecake, spreading to cover filling completely.
- Bake until topping is set, about 10 minutes. Transfer cheesecake to rack.
- Refrigerate cheesecake on rack until cool, about 3–4 hours.
- Run small, sharp knife between crust and pan sides to loosen cake; then release pan sides.
- Transfer cheesecake to platter and chill up to 1–2 days before serving.

Mocha Choco, She's-an-Angel Cake

Makes 12–16 servings.

Makeup:

1 cup cake flour
1/2 cup unsweetened cocoa powder
2 tablespoons instant espresso powder
1 teaspoon ground cinnamon
14 egg whites
2 teaspoons cream of tartar
1 1/2 cups granulated sugar
2 ounces white baking chocolate
powdered sugar, for garnish
1 cup fresh berries, any variety, for garnish (optional)
freshly whipped cream, for garnish (optional)

Application:

- Place a rack at lowest position in oven and preheat oven to 350 degrees F.
- Mix flour and cocoa powder in a medium bowl
- Add espresso powder and cinnamon; mix well.
- In a separate small bowl, beat egg whites until frothy.
- Beat in cream of tartar and then the sugar, 1 teaspoon at a time.
- Beat until soft peaks form.
- Mix flour mixture into egg whites.
- Spoon batter into ungreased nonstick 10-inch tube pan (also known as an angel food cake pan).
- Smooth surface of batter.
- Bake for 45 minutes, or until top is dry and cracked.
- Remove from oven and let cool for 5 minutes.
- Dust serving plate with powdered sugar.
- Invert cake pan over plate and remove cake carefully.
- Let cool for additional 30–45 minutes.
- When cake is cooled, melt white chocolate in a double boiler.
- Sprinkle very light dusting of powdered sugar over the top of the cake.
- Drizzle melted chocolate over the top of the cake in a back-and-forth pattern.
- Garnish with fresh berries and whipped cream if desired.

Supermodel Hint

A girl should always be light-handed when applying powder, whether it be on your face or a cake. Too much powder and you may come out looking like Baby Jane!

Pink Champagne and No-Caviar Cuppy Cakes

Makes 12–15 cupcakes

Makeup:

Cupcakes
2/3 cup butter
1 1/2 cups white sugar
2 3/4 cups all-purpose flour
3 teaspoons baking powder
1 teaspoon salt
3/4 cup pink champagne (the sweeter the better)
6 egg whites
4–5 drops red food coloring

Champagne Buttercream Frosting
3 1/4 cups powdered sugar
1/2 cup butter, room temperature
3 tablespoons pink champagne, room temperature
1/2 teaspoon vanilla extract
4–5 drops red food coloring
pink and white sugar pearls, for garnish

Application:

Cupcakes
- Preheat oven to 350 degrees F.
- Prepare a muffin tin with cupcake liners.
- In a large bowl, cream together butter and sugar until very light and fluffy.
- In a separate bowl, sift flour, baking powder, and salt together.
- Alternate adding flour mixture and champagne into the creamed mixture.
- In another large bowl, beat egg whites until stiff peaks form.
- Gently fold one-third of the whites into batter to lighten it. Then fold in remaining egg whites.
- Fill the cupcake liners about two-thirds full.
- Bake for 20 minutes, or until a wooden toothpick inserted into the cake comes out clean.

Champagne Buttercream Frosting
- In the bowl of a stand mixer, beat together powdered sugar and butter.
- Mix on low until well blended and then on medium for another 2 minutes.
- Add champagne, vanilla, and food coloring, beating on medium for another 1 minute.
- Transfer frosting into a decorating bag fitted with a large star tip, and decorate as desired.
- Sprinkle top with sugar pearls.

Supermodel Hint

*If decorating cupcakes with a swirl, using a larger amount of frosting, you'll need to double this frosting amount.
One batch of this frosting yields enough to cover up to 24 cupcakes with a flat top.*

Signorina Divina's Tangy Lemon Cheesecake

Makes 8–12 servings.

Makeup:

Crust
2 cups ground graham crackers
1/2 cup unsalted butter, melted

Filling
5 (8-ounce) packages cream cheese, room temperature
2 cups sugar
1/4 teaspoon salt
7 large eggs
3 cups (24 ounces) sour cream
2 tablespoons packed finely grated lemon peel
2 tablespoons freshly squeezed lemon juice

Lemon Curd Topping
1 (16-ounce) jar lemon curd
lemon leaves or twists, for garnish (optional)

Application:

Crust
- Preheat oven to 350 degrees F.
- Stir graham cracker crumbs and butter in a medium bowl until evenly moistened.
- Press mixture onto bottom of 10 1/2-inch-diameter springform pan with 3-inch-high sides.
- Bake crust until deep golden, about 12 minutes.
- Remove and cool completely.
- Reduce oven heat to 325 degrees F.

Filling
- Using an electric mixer, beat cream cheese in a large bowl until smooth and fluffy.
- Gradually beat in sugar, then salt, then eggs.
- Beat in sour cream, grated lemon peel, and lemon juice.
- Pour filling over graham cracker crust.
- Bake cake until filling is slightly puffed and moves only slightly when pan is shaken gently, about 1 1/2 hours.
- Cool cake in pan on a rack for 2 hours.
- Chill uncovered until cold; cover and keep chilled at least 1 day and up to 2 days.

Lemon Curd Topping
- Heat lemon curd on stove top over medium heat, stirring constantly to avoid burning, or heat for 1 minute in the microwave.
- Pour curd in the center of the cheesecake and spread evenly over the top of the cheesecake.
- Refrigerate for at least 1 hour prior to serving.

Assembly
- Cut around pan sides; carefully loosen pan bottom from sides and push up pan bottom to release cake.
- Carefully slide cake off its springform pan bottom, without breaking crust, onto a serving platter.
- If desired, garnish with lemon twists and/or cleaned lemon leaves.

Strawberry Bouffant Cake

Makes 12–16 servings.

Makeup:

Cake
butter-flavored cooking spray
3 cups all-purpose flour
2 1/2 teaspoons baking powder
1 teaspoon salt
4 large eggs
1 cup butter, melted
1 1/2 cups sugar
3/4 cup cranberry-strawberry juice
1 teaspoon vanilla extract
3 cups strawberries, sliced
whole fresh strawberries, for garnish
powdered sugar, for garnish

Strawberry Sauce
1/4 cup water
3 tablespoons sugar
3 tablespoons strawberry liqueur

Whipped Cream
1 1/2 cups whipping cream
3 tablespoons sugar
1 teaspoon strawberry liqueur (optional)

Application:

Cake
- Preheat oven to 350 degrees F.
- Coat two 8 x 2–inch round pans with cooking spray.
- In a medium bowl, mix flour, baking powder, and salt.
- In a separate bowl, beat eggs and add butter, sugar, cranberry-strawberry juice, and vanilla.
- Add flour mixture and mix until smooth.
- Pour into the two round baking pans, dividing evenly.
- Bake for 30 minutes, or until a wooden toothpick comes out clean.
- Remove cakes from oven and cool for 15–20 minutes.

Strawberry Sauce
- Heat water, sugar, and strawberry liqueur over low heat until sugar dissolves; set aside until needed.

Whipped Cream
- Whip whipping cream, sugar, and strawberry liqueur (optional) on medium-high speed; set aside until needed.

Assembly
- Carefully remove cakes from pans by inverting the pans onto waxed paper on a large cutting board or countertop.
- With a very long, sharp knife, slice each cake in half, horizontally, into two layers.
- Place first cake layer on a serving plate.
- Brush with one-quarter of the strawberry sauce.
- Evenly spread one-quarter of the whipped cream mixture over cake.
- Evenly distribute one-quarter of the sliced strawberries over cake.
- Repeat procedure with two more layers. Place last cake layer on top.
- Top cake with remaining strawberry sauce, whipped cream, and strawberries.
- Place whole strawberries on top and sprinkle a light layer of powdered sugar over the entire surface.

Supermodel Hint
If only Miss Divina's hair could be this tall! Delicate and gorgeous, that's what this is. Who does that remind you of? She's too modest to say, but I can tell you. But you've already guessed, haven't you?

Tipsy Tower of Pisa Chocolate—Crème de Menthe Cheesecake

Makes 8–12 servings.

Makeup:

Crust
12 chocolate wafers, finely crushed
1/2 cup sugar
1/4 cup butter, melted

Filling
1 1/2 cups cream cheese, room temperature
1 cup sugar
1 cup cottage cheese
1/3 cup unsweetened cocoa
1/4 cup all-purpose flour
1/4 cup crème de menthe
1 teaspoon green food coloring
1 teaspoon vanilla extract
1/4 teaspoon salt
1 egg
2 tablespoons semisweet chocolate for chocolate curls or mint wafers, for garnish (optional)

Application:

Crust
- Preheat oven to 350 degrees F.
- In a medium bowl, combine chocolate wafers and sugar.
- Add melted butter and stir.
- Press crumb mixture along the bottom and sides of a 9-inch springform pan.
- Chill for 30 minutes.

Filling
- In a mixing bowl or food processor, combine cream cheese, sugar, cottage cheese, unsweetened cocoa, flour, crème de menthe, food coloring, vanilla, and salt; mix until smooth.
- Add egg and mix until well blended.
- Slowly pour mixture over crumb crust.
- Bake in oven for 45–50 minutes, or until cheesecake is set and a wooden toothpick comes out clean.
- Let cool on a wire rack.
- Cover and chill for at least 8 hours.
- Remove sides of pan, and carefully transfer cheesecake to a serving platter.
- Garnish with chocolate curls or mint wafers if desired.

Supermodel Hint
To make amaretto cheesecake, substitute amaretto for the crème de menthe and omit the green food coloring. Either recipe has been known to make potentials weak at the knees.

Makeup:

3 egg whites
1/4 teaspoon cream of tartar
6 tablespoons sugar
1/2 teaspoon vanilla extract

Application:

- In a medium bowl, beat egg whites and cream of tartar with an electric mixer on high speed until foamy.
- Beat in sugar, 1 tablespoon at a time; continue beating until stiff and glossy. Do not underbeat.
- Beat in vanilla.
- Spoon onto hot pie filling or other dessert you are preparing. Spread over filling or other dessert, carefully sealing meringue to edge of crust to prevent shrinking or weeping.
- Bake 8–12 minutes, or until meringue is light brown.
- Cool away from draft for 2 hours.
- Cover and refrigerate cooled pie or other dessert until serving.

Supermodel Hint

For the best meringue, be sure not to get any egg yolks into the egg whites while separating the eggs.
Any yolk in the whites will prevent them from beating properly.

Chocolate Desserts

Chocolate–Grand Marnier Pecan-atchya Balls (p. 267)

Blonde-Bombshell Brownies

Makes approximately 16 servings, depending on how large or small you cut them.

Makeup:

Brownies
1/2 cup unsalted butter
1 cup white chocolate chips, divided
1 1/2 cups sugar
4 large eggs
2 teaspoons vanilla extract
1 1/2 cups all-purpose flour
1/2 teaspoon salt

Frosting
4 ounces cream cheese, room temperature
1/2 cup unsalted butter, room temperature
1 cup confectioners' sugar
2 ounces white chocolate, melted
1/2 teaspoon vanilla extract

Application:

Brownies
- Preheat oven to 350 degrees F.
- Melt butter and 1/2 cup white chocolate chips in a medium saucepan over medium heat. Mix well.
- Whisk in sugar until completely combined.
- Transfer chocolate/butter mixture to a large mixing bowl.
- Using a hand mixer, add eggs and vanilla and beat until frothy.
- Mix in flour and salt and blend well.
- Mix in remaining 1/2 cup white chocolate chips.
- Batter will be thick.
- When mixture is thoroughly mixed, spread in a well-greased 10 x 12–inch pan with 1/4-inch sides.
- Bake for approximately 35 minutes, covering loosely with aluminum foil halfway through.
- Test the brownies with a wooden toothpick after 30 minutes. If it comes out with wet batter, the brownies are not done. Keep checking every 2 minutes until center is no longer moist.
- When brownies are done, remove from oven and place on a wire rack to cool completely before adding the frosting.

Frosting
- In a large bowl, beat cream cheese and butter with an electric beater until smooth and creamy.
- Add confectioners' sugar, melted white chocolate, and vanilla.
- Beat on low speed for 30 seconds; then switch to high speed and beat for 2 minutes.
- Spread frosting on cooled brownies, slice, and serve.

Supermodel Hint
Everyone loves delicious, moist brownies! Your friends will love these tempting blondes!
Maybe it's true—blondes do have more fun!

Chocolate—Grand Marnier Pecan—atcha Balls

Makes approximately 20–24 pecan balls, depending on size.

Makeup:

1 (12-ounce) package vanilla wafer cookies
1 cup pecans, chopped
1/2 cup dutch cocoa
1/4 cup dark corn syrup
1/2 cup granulated sugar, divided
1/2 cup Grand Marnier
1/2 cup powdered sugar
1/2 cup coconut flakes, finely ground

Photo of individual Pecan Balls shown.

Application:

- In a food processor, combine cookies, pecans, and cocoa. Process until mixture is reduced to fine crumbs.
- Add corn syrup, 1/4 cup granulated sugar, and Grand Marnier.
- Mix until well blended.
- Using your hands, form dough into 1-inch balls.
- Roll each ball in powdered sugar or coconut flakes and place on a serving dish. Vary the coatings based on your preference.
- Form a cone from cardboard for a tree-shaped presentation. Place the cone on a dish and encircle the bottom with balls. Working your way up around the cone, layer the balls on top of each other to complete the tree.
- Caramelize remaining 1/4 cup sugar in a double boiler, and with a spoon, swirl the sugar over the balls. Sugar will harden immediately. However, it is very delicate, so be careful.
- Decorate according to the festivity or event, such as holly leaves during the Christmas season.

Supermodel Hint

These are very sweet, but who doesn't like something or someone sweet to nibble on?
No one can eat just one of these morsels.

Cookies

Ooh-La-La Chocolate-Oatmeal Cookies (p. 274)

Almond Be Enjoying These Cookies

Makes approximately 15–20 cookies, depending on cookie size.

Makeup:

1 (14-ounce) bag sweetened coconut flakes
1 (14-ounce) can sweetened condensed milk
2 cups semisweet chocolate chips
2/3 cup chopped lightly salted almonds
1/4 cup brown sugar

Application:

- Preheat oven to 325 degrees F.
- Grease and flour a large baking sheet and set aside. Make sure to grease the pan well. These cookies will stick to the sheet if you don't
- In a large bowl, combine coconut, sweetened condensed milk, chocolate chips, almonds, and brown sugar.
- Stir until mixed thoroughly.
- Place small drops of dough onto cookie sheet.
- Moisten the tips of your fingers with water and shape dough into disks. Pat the tops flat.
- Bake for approximately 15 minutes, or until tips of coconut are just starting to turn golden brown.
- Remove cookies from oven and let cool completely on baking sheet.
- Transfer to a serving plate when cool.

Note: These cookies are very flimsy once they are done, so make sure to give them 2–4 hours to cool. It's best to make these the day before you plan on serving them.

Supermodel Hint

Miss Divina and her darling niece, Dylan, love to spend a day in the baker's corner making these delicious cookies. Naturally they need to sample the batch to make sure it was baked just right.

269

Jackie Molasses Cookies

Makes approximately 24–30 cookies, depending on cookie size.

Makeup:

1/2 cup molasses
1/2 cup vegetable shortening
1/4 cup sugar, plus additional for garnish
2 large eggs
2 3/4 cups all-purpose flour
1/4 cup dry sugar substitute
2 teaspoons baking soda
1 teaspoon cinnamon
1 teaspoon nutmeg
1 teaspoon ginger
1 teaspoon salt
1/2 cup coffee, hot
1 tablespoon lemon juice

Application:

- Preheat oven to 375 degrees F.
- Mix molasses, shortening, and sugar together at medium speed until light and fluffy.
- Add eggs and mix at medium speed until creamy. Scrape bowl before and after adding eggs.
- In a separate bowl, stir flour, dry sugar substitute, baking soda, cinnamon, nutmeg, ginger, and salt together and blend well.
- Add flour mixture to sugar/molasses mixture and mix well.
- Add coffee and lemon juice and mix well until creamy.
- Place small drops of dough onto lightly greased and floured cookie sheets. You may also line sheets with aluminum foil if you prefer.
- Bake for 12–15 minutes, or until cookies are firm. Do not overcook or burn.
- Remove from oven and sprinkle a bit of granulated sugar on each cookie while they are still hot.
- Let cool to room temperature. Place on a wire rack to cool if you prefer.
- Transfer to a serving plate when cool.

Supermodel Hint

Heads of state always look for these cookies at Jackie's formal affairs! I could just scratch her cat-eyed eyes out!

Lilly Whyte's Chocolate-Peppermint Sugar Cookies

Makes approximately 12–20 cookies, depending on cookie size.

Makeup:

1/2 cup unsalted butter, room temperature
1/2 cup sugar
1/4 cup light brown sugar
1 egg
1/2 teaspoon vanilla extract
1 1/2 cups all-purpose flour
1/2 teaspoon baking soda
1/4 teaspoon salt
1 cup white chocolate chips (about half of a
    12-ounce bag)
1/2 cup crushed candy canes (about 50 small
    candy canes)

Application:

- Preheat oven to 375 degrees F.
- Cream butter until light.
- Gradually add sugars, creaming well until blended.
- Beat in egg and vanilla.
- Stir together flour, baking soda, and salt.
- Add flour mixture to butter mixture, blending well.
- Stir in white chocolate chips and crushed candy canes.
- Place 1-tablespoon drops of dough, 2 inches apart, onto two ungreased large baking sheets.
- Pat each mound into round shape.
- Bake for about 12 minutes, until golden.
- Remove to wire racks to cool.
- Transfer to a serving plate when cool.

Supermodel Hint

Lilly Whyte's reputation for being unapproachable is almost as good as these cookies!
These cookies are a favorite at Miss Divina's Christmas holiday parties!

Love Child Granola Cookies

Makes approximately 12–20 cookies, depending on cookie size.

Makeup:

1 cup all-purpose flour
1 teaspoon baking soda
1 teaspoon salt
1/2 cup salted butter, room temperature
1/2 cup packed light brown sugar
1/2 cup granulated sugar
1 large egg
2 teaspoons vanilla extract
1 cup granola (break down any large clusters)
3/4 cup semisweet chocolate chips (4 1/2 ounces)

Application:

- Preheat oven to 375 degrees F.
- Whisk together flour, baking soda, and salt in a small bowl.
- In a large mixing bowl, beat together butter, sugars, egg, and vanilla with an electric mixer at high speed for about 3–5 minutes.
- Reduce speed to low; then add flour mixture and mix until just combined.
- Stir in granola and chocolate chips.
- Place 1-tablespoon drops of dough, 2 inches apart, onto two ungreased large baking sheets.
- Pat each mound into round shape.
- Bake for about 15 minutes, or until lightly golden, switching position of sheets halfway through baking.
- Remove from oven and let cool for 10 minutes.
- Transfer to a serving plate when cool.

Supermodel Hint

If you want to go crazy, substitute the chocolate chips with butterscotch chips! It makes a delicious alternative.

Mazy's Simple Hazelnut-Lemon Shortbread Cookies

Makes approximately 12–20 cookies, depending on cookie size.

Makeup:

1 1/2 cups unsalted butter, cold and cut into small pieces
1/2 cup white sugar
1/4 cup crushed hazelnuts
juice of 1 lemon
1 teaspoon vanilla extract
1 teaspoon salt
1/2 cup all-purpose flour
powdered sugar, for garnish (optional)

Application:

- Preheat oven to 325 degrees F.
- In a food processor, beat butter at low speed until soft.
- Continue at low speed. Slowly add sugar, nuts, lemon juice, vanilla, and salt.
- Slowly add flour and process until dough forms, scraping the sides of the food processor bowl with spatula if necessary. The dough will be soft.
- On a lightly floured surface, roll dough into 2 logs, each about 1 inch wide.
- Wrap each log in plastic wrap and refrigerate for 1 hour.
- After cookie dough has been in the refrigerator, unwrap plastic and roll out again.
- Shape dough into desired shapes. (See "Supermodel Hint" below.)
- Place cookie slices on an ungreased, parchment-lined baking sheet, spacing about 2 inches apart.
- Bake for about 10–15 minutes. Don't let cookies get too brown.
- When cookies are slightly light golden brown, remove and let cool on baking sheet for 5 minutes.
- Transfer cookies to a wire rack to continue cooling.
- Using a sifter, lightly sprinkle cookies with powdered sugar (optional).
- Transfer to a serving plate.

Supermodel Hint

If you feel energetic, you can shape the shortbread cookie dough into oblong shapes or use cookie cutters you have in the house for other shapes. Miss Divina is partial to stars, being one herself!

Ooh-La-La Chocolate-Oatmeal Cookies

Makes approximately 12–20 cookies, depending on cookie size.

Makeup:

5 cups oatmeal
1 cup unsalted butter, room temperature
2 cups sugar
2 cups brown sugar
4 eggs
2 teaspoons vanilla extract
4 cups flour
2 teaspoons baking soda
2 teaspoons baking powder
1 teaspoon salt
3 cups chopped nuts (walnuts or pecans)
3/4 cup semisweet chocolate chips (4 1/2 ounces)

Application:

- Preheat oven to 375 degrees F.
- Blend oatmeal in a blender to a fine powder. Set aside until later.
- In a large bowl, cream butter and both sugars.
- Add eggs and vanilla.
- Mix together with flour, oatmeal, baking soda, baking powder, and salt.
- Add nuts and chocolate chips.
- Roll dough into 1 1/2-inch balls and place 1 inches apart on a nonstick cookie sheet.
- Bake for 10 minutes.
- Remove when cookies are finished and let cool before removing them to a plate.

Supermodel Hint

To render a man temporarily helpless, apply vanilla ice cream between two of these chocolate-studded dreams. He'll forget his wife and children and follow you anywhere.

Fruit Desserts

Sinfully Simple Homemade Watermelon Sorbet (p. 280)

Baked Sin-a-Man Apples

Makes 4 servings.

Makeup:

4 Granny Smith apples
16 ounces cream cheese, room temperature
1/2 cup raisins
1 teaspoon ground cinnamon
1 teaspoon ground nutmeg
1 teaspoon sugar
1/2 cup honey or maple syrup
1/2 cup raspberry jam or preserves
4 teaspoons confectioners' sugar (1 teaspoon per apple), for garnish
freshly whipped cream, for garnish

Application:

- Preheat oven to 350 degrees F.
- Core apples with small knife so as not to break the fruit.
- Place apples on a nonstick cookie sheet lined with aluminum foil.
- In a small bowl, mix cream cheese, raisins, and cinnamon.
- Sprinkle the inside cores and outsides of the apples with cinnamon, nutmeg, and sugar.
- Spoon even amounts of cream cheese mixture into each apple.
- Dip a spoon into honey or maple syrup and pour over each apple generously.
- Bake in oven for about 15–20 minutes, or until apples achieve desired softness.
- While apples bake, heat raspberry preserves in a small saucepan over medium heat until preserves are liquefied.
- Cover and turn heat to low.
- When apples are cooked to desired consistency, remove from oven and place on individual plates.
- Pour small amount of raspberry sauce around apples or use a tablespoon to drip sauce over plate in desired design.
- Sprinkle confectioners' sugar on each apple for decoration.
- Place mound of whipped cream on top of each apple.

Supermodel Hint
This simple dessert is perfect for that cold fall night by the fire with your significant other or just by yourself.

Dolce Poached Pears with Raspberry Puree

Makes 4 servings.

Makeup:

4 red pears, firm not soft
2 teaspoons lemon juice
5 ounces frozen raspberries in light syrup, thawed
1 1/2 tablespoons brown sugar
1 1/2 teaspoons dark rum
2 tablespoons butter
1/4 teaspoon ground cinnamon
fresh mint leaves, for garnish

Application:

- Wash pears under cool water.
- Slice off small portion of bottom of pears so fruit will stand on its own.
- With a potato peeler, peel in stripes around each entire pear, leaving stripes of peeled and unpeeled areas all around the pear.
- Pour lemon juice over each pear, saving the runoff lemon juice for next step.
- Combine raspberries and remaining lemon juice in a blender or food processor and blend until smooth.
- Strain raspberry puree to remove seeds if desired.
- Heat brown sugar, rum, butter, and cinnamon in a large saucepan until sugar and butter are dissolved.
- Reduce heat and add pears.
- Simmer uncovered until pears are slightly soft but not mushy when pierced with a knife, or about 10–15 minutes.
- Remove from heat and cool pears in the saucepan in the syrup until lukewarm.
- Remove pears to dessert dishes with a slotted spoon, standing pears upright.
- Swirl raspberry puree in a design around each pear and serve.
- Garnish with a few fresh mint leaves.
- Serve warm or chilled.

Supermodel Hint

Miss Divina just adores making this dish during the holidays.
Try substituting cranberry or cherry puree for the
raspberry puree for a change.

I Oughta Grill Her Peaches! with Raspberry Puree

Makes 4 servings.

Makeup:

5 ounces frozen raspberries in light syrup, thawed
1 tablespoon lemon juice
2 medium peaches, peeled, halved, and pitted
1 1/2 tablespoons brown sugar
1 teaspoon ground cinnamon
1 tablespoon rum flavoring
1 tablespoon unsalted butter

Application:

- Depending on which appliance you will be using, either prepare outdoor grill or preheat oven to 350 degrees F.
- Combine raspberries and lemon juice in a blender or food processor and blend until smooth.
- Cover and chill in a bowl.
- Place peaches, cut side up, on foil, with enough foil on sides to later fold over the peaches.
- Combine brown sugar and cinnamon; spoon evenly into center of each peach half.
- Sprinkle with rum flavoring and dot with butter.
- Fold foil over peaches and loosely seal.
- Grill over medium coals for 7–12 minutes or bake in oven on a cookie sheet for 15 minutes.
- If grilling, finish peaches by removing from foil and placing directly on grill, facedown, for 3 minutes.
- Carefully remove peaches from grill or oven and place on serving plates.
- Spoon 2 tablespoons raspberry puree over each peach half and serve.

Perfectly Seductive Chocolate–Covered Strawberries

Makes 24 strawberries.

Makeup:

24 large ripe strawberries
1 cup semisweet chocolate pieces
1 teaspoon vegetable oil
5 tablespoons shredded coconut (optional)

Application:

- Line a large cookie sheet with waxed paper.
- Rinse and dry strawberries on paper towels.
- Melt chocolate in a double boiler until completely melted and creamy, being careful not to burn the chocolate.
- Remove from heat, add oil, and mix thoroughly.
- Dip half of each strawberry in melted chocolate and then coconut (optional) and place on waxed paper.
- Place cookie sheet in refrigerator to cool.

Note: Serve these strawberries with champagne for an especially romantic evening. If you would like variety, roll half of the strawberries in crushed mixed nuts instead of coconut. You can also substitute white chocolate in place of the semisweet chocolate.

Supermodel Hint

Warning! For Miss Divina's sake, don't serve this sensuous dessert with domestic champagne!
Miss Divina has a reputation to uphold!

Sinfully Simple Homemade Watermelon Sorbet

*You will need an ice cream maker for this recipe.

Makeup:

1/2 cup sugar
1/2 cup water
1/4 cup light corn syrup or light agave nectar
1/4 cup freshly squeezed lemon or lime juice
3 pounds watermelon, rind and seeds removed,
   cut into chunks
fresh mint leaves, for garnish

Application:

- In a small saucepan, over medium heat, warm sugar, water, corn syrup, and lemon (or lime) juice together, stirring occasionally, until sugar is dissolved.
- Remove from heat and chill.
- Puree watermelon in a blender or food processor.
- Stir into chilled syrup.
- Freeze in an ice cream maker according to the manufacturer's instructions.
- Pack into an airtight container and store in the freezer.
- Serve cold, garnished with fresh mint leaves.

Note: Try this sorbet recipe with a variety of fresh fruits. Just alter the recipe according to your chosen fruit and its water content.

Supermodel Hint

After a night of unbridled passion, Miss Divina often cools down her man with some variety of this delicious sorbet.

Sister Mary Therese's Peach Cobbler

Makes 8–12 servings.

Makeup:

Filling
1/2 cup unsalted butter
1 cup all-purpose flour
1 cup granulated sugar
4 teaspoons cornstarch
1 teaspoon salt
6 cups fresh peach slices
1/2 cup milk
1 tablespoon lemon juice

Topping
6 tablespoons unsalted butter, room temperature
1/4 cup light-brown sugar
1 cup all-purpose flour
1 teaspoon salt
2 teaspoons ground cinnamon or nutmeg, for garnish (optional)
freshly whipped cream, for garnish

Application:

Filling
- Preheat oven to 375 degrees F.
- Melt butter in a small saucepan.
- Pour melted butter into a 13 x 9–inch baking dish. Spread evenly over entire dish bottom.
- In a medium mixing bowl, combine flour, sugar, cornstarch, and salt, stirring just until dry ingredients are moistened.
- Add peaches, milk, and lemon juice, mixing in well.
- Pour peach mixture evenly over butter in dish (do not stir).

Topping
- In a medium saucepan, heat butter and brown sugar over medium heat, stirring constantly, until butter melts.
- Remove from heat, transfer to a medium mixing bowl, and add flour and salt.
- With your hands, mix until large pieces of dough form. Scatter evenly over peach filling.
- Sprinkle the top of cobbler with cinnamon or nutmeg, if desired.
- Bake for 40–45 minutes, or until the top is golden brown.
- Serve cobbler warm or cold, topped with freshly whipped cream.

Supermodel Hint
Sister Mary Therese taught Miss Divina the gifts of love and generosity. "Pay it forward" was her motto!

Tangy Lemon–Raspberry Bras (Yes, Bras)

Makes about 10–14 bars.

Makeup:

Crust
butter-flavored cooking spray
1 1/2 cups graham cracker crumbs
6 tablespoons salted butter, melted
1/4 cup sugar
zest of 1 lemon

Filling
2 large egg yolks
1 (14-ounce) can fat-free sweetened condensed milk
1 teaspoon lemon zest
1/2 cup freshly squeezed lemon juice
6 ounces fresh raspberries
butter-flavored cooking spray
powdered sugar, for garnish

Application:

Crust
- Preheat oven to 350 degrees F.
- In a medium bowl, combine graham cracker crumbs, melted butter, sugar, and lemon zest.
- Stir until graham cracker crumbs are slightly moist.
- Spray an 8-inch square baking dish with cooking spray.
- Press crumbs into prepared pan, pressing crust mixture 1 inch up the side of the pan.
- Bake for 10 minutes, or until golden in color.

Filling
- While crust cooks, beat egg yolks in a medium mixing bowl.
- Add condensed milk and mix well.
- Stir in lemon zest and juice.
- Stir until mixture begins to slightly thicken.
- Gently fold in raspberries. Fold carefully so you don't break the raspberries.
- Spray the sides of the baking dish with cooking spray.
- Pour lemon-raspberry filling evenly over graham cracker crust.
- Bake in oven for 15 minutes, or until top is light golden brown.
- Remove from oven and let cool.
- When cool, cut into even-sized bars and lightly dust with powdered sugar.

Supermodel Hint
Like a french kiss from Miss Divina, these sweet, tangy, and tart lemon bars will really hit you in the kisser!

Custard, Gelatins, and Mousses

I Vant Bread Pudding (p. 286)

Give Him the Raspberry–Chocolate Mousse

Makes 8 servings.

Makeup:

1 pound bittersweet chocolate, cut into small pieces
6 tablespoons unsalted butter, melted
1/4 cup pureed raspberries, strained of seeds, divided
9 egg whites, room temperature
3/4 cup granulated sugar
mint leaves, for garnish
fresh whole raspberries, for garnish
freshly whipped cream, for garnish (optional)

Application:

- Melt chocolate until smooth in a double boiler over gently simmering water.
- Stir in butter a little at a time, until mixture is blended and smooth.
- Stir in half the pureed raspberries (2 tablespoons); stir until mixture is well blended and smooth.
- Chill remaining raspberry puree for later.
- Remove the top pan from the double boiler; set aside to cool.
- Place egg whites in a medium mixing bowl.
- With an electric mixer, beat egg whites on high speed until foamy.
- Slowly add sugar and beat until stiff peaks form, about 5 minutes.
- Fold one-third of the egg whites into cooled chocolate using a rubber or wooden spatula.
- Fold chocolate mixture into remaining egg whites until well mixed.
- Spoon mousse evenly into eight individual serving bowls and chill for 2–3 hours.
- When ready to serve, place each serving bowl on a plate and swirl remaining raspberry puree around dish for presentation.
- Garnish with fresh whole raspberries and mint leaves and top with freshly whipped cream if desired.

Supermodel Hint

Not ones to have sunny personalities or to like much in the world, Boris and Natasha love this mousse!

Hula-Hula Pineapple-Carrot Gelatin Salad

Makes 8–10 servings.

Makeup:

1 large (6-ounce) package orange gelatin mix
1 (20-ounce) can crushed pineapple, drained,
   with juice reserved
2–3 large carrots, grated or shredded
fresh grated carrots and/or pineapple chunks and
   orange slices, for garnish (optional)
whipped cream, for garnish (optional)

Application:

- Make orange gelatin in a bowl as per package directions but use the reserved pineapple juice for part of the cold water (usually it is 1 cup of cold water per package).
- Pour gelatin into a glass bowl and place in refrigerator for 20 minutes.
- When gelatin has slightly thickened, stir in drained pineapple and carrots.
- Mix well and pour into any design gelatin mold you wish.
- Smooth the top with a rubber spatula.
- Cover and refrigerate until set, at least 4 hours.
- Once gelatin is set, if you are using a mold, place mold in a bowl of warm water for about 10–12 seconds to loosen the sides of the gelatin.
- Place a large serving plate with raised sides on top of the gelatin mold.
- Quickly turn the mold and plate over so the gelatin will be centered on the plate.
- Remove the mold and place the gelatin back in the refrigerator to cool again.
- If you would like, place fresh carrots and/or pineapple and orange slices around the base of the gelatin mold for garnish.
- Serve cold with a dab of whipped cream if you so desire.

Note: Try this recipe with lemon gelatin mix if you want to experiment.

Supermodel Hint

*If you ask Miss Divina which gelatin salad she likes best,
it's a toss-up between this and Mama Yvonne's Cream Cheese
Lemon-Lime Gelatin (see p. 287).*

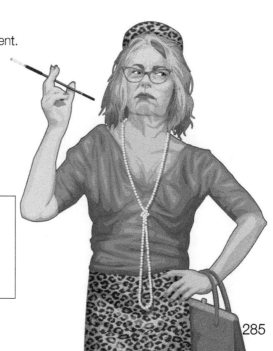

Makes 6 servings.

Makeup:

4 buttermilk bread slices
3 eggs
2/3 cup granulated sugar
1/3 cup packed brown sugar
1/4 teaspoon salt
1/4 teaspoon vanilla extract
2 1/2 cups warm whole milk
2 tablespoons unsalted butter
1/2 cup golden raisins
1/2 finely chopped walnuts
1/2 teaspoon cinnamon

Application:

- Preheat open to 350 degrees F.
- Toast bread lightly and cut into small squares.
- Beat eggs, sugars, salt, and vanilla together.
- Add warm milk and butter; beat until well blended.
- Add bread, raisins, and walnuts.
- Very gently stir to mix all ingredients.
- Place in a 1 1/2-quart casserole dish.
- Sprinkle cinnamon on top.
- Set casserole dish in a shallow pan to depth of 1 inch and pour hot water in pan.
- Set in preheated oven and bake for 60 minutes, or until knife comes out clean in center.
- Remove casserole from hot water; serve warm.

Supermodel Hint

Got lots of leftover bread? Use that for this delicious dessert! I learned that in my bread-and-water days after my school-cafeteria career ended abruptly! Waste not, want not, as I always say!

Mama Yvonne's Cream Cheese—Lemon—Lime Gelatin

Makes 12–16 servings.

Makeup:

Lime Gelatin Layer

1 large (6-ounce) package lime gelatin mix
3/4 cup lemonade
1/4 cup freshly squeezed lime juice
1 large can pear halves
1 small bottle maraschino cherries

Cream Cheese–Lemon Gelatin Layer

1 large (6-ounce) package lemon gelatin mix
1/4 cup freshly squeezed lemon juice
1 (8-ounce) package cream cheese, room temperature
thin lemon slices, for garnish (optional)

Application:

Lime Gelatin Layer

- Prepare lime gelatin mix according to package directions but substitute lemonade for three-quarters of the water and lime juice for the remaining one-quarter of water. Usually it is 1 cup of cold water per package, so that would be 3/4 cup lemonade and 1/4 cup lime juice.
- Refrigerate for 30 minutes.
- Remove gelatin from refrigerator.
- When gelatin starts to harden, place a maraschino cherry in the center of each pear half and evenly place each pear half pitted side down. This will help keep the cherries in place once you add the lemon–cream cheese layer on top.
- Return to refrigerator.

Cream Cheese–Lemon Gelatin Layer

- Prepare lemon gelatin mix according to package directions but substitute one-quarter of the water with lemon juice (most likely 1/4 cup).
- With an electric mixer, thoroughly mix lemon gelatin and cream cheese. Mix until smooth, with no cream cheese chunks.
- Carefully pour over lime gelatin, so as not to upset the pears and cherries, and refrigerate until set, at least 4 hours.
- Once gelatin is set, if you are using a mold, place mold in a bowl of warm water for 10–12 seconds to loosen the sides of the gelatin.
- Place a large serving plate with raised sides on top of the gelatin mold.
- Quickly turn the mold and plate over so the gelatin will be centered on the plate.
- Remove the mold and place the gelatin back in the refrigerator to cool again.
- Serve cold with thin lemon slices as garnish if you so desire.

Supermodel Hint

This dish is a favorite with all of Miss Divina's siblings. It's not a family holiday dinner at her house if this yummy dish isn't sitting on the table ready to be devoured!

Makes 4 servings.

Makeup:

4 large eggs
1/2 cup sugar
1/2 cup dry champagne
2 teaspoons fresh lemon zest, finely grated
3 tablespoons freshly squeezed lemon juice
2 cups heavy whipping cream
1 1/2 ounces raspberries, for garnish
1 fresh peach, thinly sliced, for garnish
fresh mint leaves, for garnish

Application:

- In a medium bowl, beat eggs with an electric mixer at medium speed for 2 minutes.
- Add sugar a little at a time, beating at medium speed for 3–5 minutes.
- Add champagne and lemon juice and beat for 1 minute.
- Transfer mixture to a heavy 2-quart saucepan and cook over low heat, stirring constantly, until mixture is thick (do not boil).
- Stir in lemon zest.
- Transfer to a bowl, cover, and chill for 30 minutes.
- Beat cream in a medium bowl with electric beaters until it just holds stiff peaks.
- Fold cream into lemon mixture and mix thoroughly.
- Spoon mousse into large martini glasses or dessert glasses and chill until cold, about 1 hour.
- Garnish each glass with fresh raspberries or fresh thinly sliced peaches, and 1 fresh mint leaf.

Supermodel Hint

*The villa that Miss Divina grew up in was surrounded by beautiful citrus orchards.
She particularly loves lemons and is always creating recipes that incorporate them.*

Sybil's Upside-Down Custard Caramel Cream

Makes 6–8 servings, depending on the size of your ramekins.

Makeup:

1 1/2 cups granulated sugar
1/2 teaspoon salt
4 whole eggs
8 eggs yolks
4 cups milk
2 teaspoons vanilla extract
1 teaspoon lemon zest (orange zest may be substituted), plus additional for garnish
1 teaspoon lemon juice

Application:

- Preheat oven to 400 degrees F.
- Blend sugar, salt, whole eggs, and egg yolks in a medium mixing bowl with a whisk.
- Warm milk, vanilla, and lemon zest in an ovenproof pan over low heat.
- Gradually add egg mixture to milk mixture; mix well.
- Stir custard constantly until first sign of boiling.
- Pour custard into buttered medium-size ramekins.
- Place ramekins in an ovenproof bain-marie (see "Supermodel Hint" below) filled with a few cups of water.
- Bring water to a boil on the stove top and then place the bain-marie in oven.
- Cook for about 30 minutes.
- Remove and let cool.
- When ready to serve, place ramekins in a bowl of warm water for 10–12 seconds to loosen the sides of each custard.
- Turn over each custard onto a serving plate and garnish with lemon zest.

Supermodel Hint

A bain-marie is a shallow pan filled with water, such as a double-boiler. It protects foods from burning.

Pies

King Alfonso Cinnamon-Apple Pie (p. 293)

All-Buttered-Up Piecrust

Makes 1 piecrust.

Makeup:

1 (9-inch) piecrust, ready-made if possible or
  homemade
1 egg beaten with 1 tablespoon milk (egg wash)

Photo of uncooked pie shell shown.

Application:

Parbaking (or Blind Baking) Your Piecrust

- Chill crust, loosely covered with plastic wrap, for at least 30 minutes.
- Place a baking sheet on a lower oven rack and preheat oven to 425 degrees F.
- Once dough is chilled, place crust in a lightly floured 9-inch glass pie pan.
- Carefully fit crust to the bottom and sides of the pie pan.
- Pierce the bottom and sides of the crust with a fork to prevent air pockets from forming.
- Fill the center of the pie with dried beans, distributed all across the bottom and partly up the sides of the crust.
- Place the pie pan on the preheated baking sheet and reduce oven heat to 400 degrees F. Placing the pie pan on a cookie sheet allows for easy handling when placing and removing piecrust from oven.
- Bake until the edges of the crust are starting to turn golden and the bottom of the crust has lost its translucent "raw" look, about 10–12 minutes.
- Remove piecrust from oven and let cool for 1 minute. Then remove beans and set aside for another use.
- Brush the inside of the crust with egg wash (1 egg beaten with 1 tablespoon milk).
- Return pie and baking sheet to oven and bake for 3 minutes.
- Remove crust and set aside while you prepare or add your pie or quiche filling.

Supermodel Hint

For pies that will go back in the oven, like lemon meringue pies or quiches, the crust can still be warm when you add the filling. Glass pie plates are the best choice for baking your pies, as this type of pie pan conducts heat evenly, which allows the bottom crust of the pie to bake thoroughly.

Apple-of-My-Eye Mincemeat Pie

Makes 6–8 servings.

Makeup:

2 (9-inch) piecrusts, fresh or ready-made
1 pound tart apples, such as Gala or Granny Smith,
   cored, pared, and chopped
1 large orange, seeded and finely chopped
1 small lemon, seeded and finely chopped
1 (15-ounce) box seedless raisins
1 cup firmly packed brown sugar
1/2 cup apple cider
1/2 teaspoon salt
1/2 teaspoon cloves
1/2 teaspoon ground cinnamon
1/2 teaspoon nutmeg
1 egg, beaten (for brushing top of crust)
3 teaspoons granulated sugar
butter (optional; for brushing top of crust)

Application:

- Preheat oven to 425 degrees F.
- Place a rack in the lower half of the oven.
- Place one piecrust in a lightly floured 9-inch glass pie pan and mold to plate.
- Parbake bottom piecrust (see All-Buttered-Up Piecrust, p. 291, for instructions).
- In a large mixing bowl, add apples, orange, lemon, and raisins. Mix well.
- In a small pan, heat apple cider.
- Simmer cider, uncovered, for 15 minutes.
- Add brown sugar, salt, cloves, cinnamon, and nutmeg, and simmer for 20 minutes longer, or until thick.
- Add cider mixture to fruit combination. Stir well.
- Pour fruit mixture into piecrust. Smooth fruit out evenly.
- Cover pie with top crust. Seal and flute edges, or design crust in a lattice pattern.
- Cut slits near center if not designing top crust in a lattice pattern.
- Brush egg over crust.
- Sprinkle sugar over crust.
- Bake 10 minutes.
- Reduce oven heat to 375 degrees F.
- Bake 25 minutes longer, or until crust is golden. Brush crust with egg or butter to keep crust from drying out or burning.
- After pie is cooked, remove from oven and cool on rack before serving. Garnish as desired.

Supermodel Hint
Everyone loves pies and cakes at holiday gatherings. This pie makes a great addition or alternative to pumpkin pie.

King Alfonso Cinnamon-Apple Pie

Makes 6–8 servings.

Makeup:

5 Granny Smith apples
2 (9-inch) piecrusts, fresh or ready-made
1 teaspoon ground cinnamon
1 teaspoon ground nutmeg
1 teaspoon granulated sugar
1 egg, beaten
2 tablespoons butter
extra-aged white cheddar cheese, sliced (optional)

Application:

- Preheat oven to 375 degrees F.
- Peel and slice apples.
- Place one piecrust in a lightly floured 9-inch glass pie pan and mold to plate.
- Parbake bottom piecrust (see All-Buttered-Up Piecrust, p. 291, for instructions).
- Evenly place a layer of apples into parbaked crust and moderately sprinkle some of the cinnamon, nutmeg, and sugar over apples.
- Repeat layers of apple and seasonings until you have a mound pie without the top crust.
- Place top crust carefully over apples. Tuck in and pinch extra crust around edges.
- Cut a few vent holes in the crust for heat to escape.
- If you have extra dough, use cookie cutters to make any sort of design for the top of the pie, such as a leaf design.
- Carefully brush beaten egg over crust with a pastry brush, and sprinkle sugar over the entire crust. This will brown the crust and prevent it from burning.
- Bake in oven for 20 minutes, or until crust is golden. Halfway through bake time, butter crust and shift pie in oven to cook crust evenly and keep from burning.
- If desired, place slices of cheese on top of piecrust for the last 5 minutes of baking.
- After pie is cooked, remove from oven and cool on rack before serving.

Supermodel Hint

Miss Divina's dear Spanish prince, who demands she address him as "Your Majesty," insists she bake this pie whenever she is in Madrid. If she doesn't, it's like the Inquisition! Well, at least it's a free room at the palace!

Patinka's Southern Pecan Pie

Makes two pies, 6–8 servings per pie.

Makeup:

1 1/2 cups chopped pecans
1 1/4 cups light brown sugar
1/2 cup unsalted butter, melted
3 eggs, beaten
3 tablespoons all-purpose flour
2 teaspoons white wine vinegar
2 teaspoons vanilla extract
1 teaspoon salt
2 (9-inch) regular (not deep-dish) pastry piecrust,
  fresh or ready-made
2 cups whole pecans
freshly whipped cream, for garnish (optional)

Application:

- Preheat oven to 325 degrees F.
- Combine chopped pecans, brown sugar, butter, eggs, flour, vinegar, vanilla, and salt in a large mixing bowl.
- Mix thoroughly and set aside.
- Place each piecrust in a lightly floured 9-inch glass pie pan and mold to plate.
- Parbake piecrusts (see All-Buttered-Up Piecrust, p. 291, for instructions).
- Pour filling into pie shells.
- Evenly place whole pecans on top of each pie.
- Bake in oven for 1 hour, or until pies are done.
- After pies are cooked, remove from oven and cool on racks before serving.
- Serve with freshly whipped cream if desired.

Supermodel Hint

If you forgot to buy the whipped cream, look under the bed if you are one of those "adventurous" kind of gals!

Strawberry–Blonde Rhubarb Pie

Makes 6–8 servings.

Makeup:

2 1/2 cups chopped fresh red rhubarb
2 1/2 cups de-stemmed, washed, and cut strawberries
   (in larger pieces)
1 1/2 cups sugar
2 tablespoons minute tapioca
1 tablespoon all-purpose flour
1 teaspoon vanilla extract
1/2 teaspoon lemon zest
1/2 teaspoon lemon juice
1/2 teaspoon ground cinnamon
2 (9-inch) piecrusts, fresh or ready-made
3 tablespoons unsalted butter, in small cubes
1 egg white beaten with 1 teaspoon milk (egg wash)
2 tablespoons large-granule sugar, for sprinkling over crust
vanilla bean ice cream, for serving (optional)

Application:

- Preheat oven to 425 degrees F.
- In a large bowl, combine rhubarb, strawberries, sugar, tapioca, flour, vanilla, lemon zest and juice, and cinnamon.
- Place one piecrust in a lightly floured 9-inch glass pie pan and mold to plate.
- Parbake bottom piecrust (see All-Buttered-Up Piecrust, p. 291, for instructions).
- Pour filling into parbaked piecrust.
- Dot the top of the filling with cubed butter.
- Brush edges of piecrust with egg wash.
- Cover filling with top crust. Seal and flute edges, or design crust in a lattice pattern.
- Cut slits near center if not designing top crust in a lattice pattern.
- Brush top crust with egg wash and garnish with large-granule sugar.
- Cover with foil and bake for 15 minutes.
- Decrease temperature to 375 degrees F, remove foil, and bake for additional 15–20 minutes, or until filling starts bubbling.
- After pie is cooked, remove from oven and cool on rack before serving.
- Serve with your favorite vanilla bean ice cream (optional).

Supermodel Hint

*Caution! Rhubarb leaves contain poisonous substances. Miss Divina urges you to cut off the leaves
and discard them, unless you have a particularly difficult guest that needs to be taught a lesson!*

Makes 6–8 servings.

Makeup:

Crust
1 (9-inch) piecrust, fresh or ready-made

Lemon Filling
1 1/2 cups sugar
1/3 cup plus 1 tablespoon cornstarch
2 tablespoons flour
1 teaspoon salt
3 egg yolks, slightly beaten
2 teaspoons grated lemon peel
1/2 cup lemon juice
3 tablespoons unsalted butter or margarine
3 drops yellow food coloring (optional)

Meringue
See p. 264 for meringue ingredients.

Application:

Crust
- Preheat oven to 350 degrees F.
- Place one piecrust in a lightly floured 9-inch glass pie pan and mold to plate.
- Parbake bottom piecrust (see All-Buttered-Up Piecrust, p. 291, for instructions).
- Remove parbaked crust from oven and cool on a rack. Do not turn oven off.

Lemon Filling
- In a medium mixing bowl, combine sugar, cornstarch, flour, and salt.
- Transfer sugar mixture to a medium saucepan.
- Gradually add 1 1/2 cups cold water, stirring until smooth.
- Over medium heat, bring to boiling, stirring occasionally; boil 1 minute, until shiny and translucent.
- In a mixing bowl, whisk egg yolks and 1/2 cup of hot sugar mixture together.

- Transfer egg mixture to saucepan containing sugar mixture. Cook over low heat for 5 minutes, stirring occasionally.
- Remove from heat; stir in lemon peel, lemon juice, melted butter, and food coloring; mix thoroughly.
- Pour lemon filling into parbaked piecrust.

Meringue
See p. 264 for meringue instructions.

Assembly
- Spread meringue over lemon filling, carefully sealing to edge of the crust and swirling the top decoratively.
- Bake 10 minutes, or until meringue is slightly golden brown.
- Let cool completely on a rack, about 3 hours.
- Cut with warm, wet knife when serving.

Supermodel Hint
As Miss Divina has learned with clarity in dishing and doing in her rivals with sharp gossip, a hot, moistened knife is more effective than unprepared cutlery.

Bodaciously Bountiful Brunches

*Count your blessings,
and you will have a bountiful life.*

Casting Couch Crispy Crab Cakes (p. 312)

There's Got to Be a Morning-After Menu!

Come morning, some guests from the night before may still be lingering at your home. Better an overnight guest than a car crash. Or perhaps you've had a personal guest of a more scandalous nature. Either way, you've still got guests, so you're still on. Just because the sun has risen does not mean you can take off your host cap. This is your chance to use a delicious meal to secure your reputation as a stellar host and to bribe your overnight guests into forgetting the salacious details of last night.

Don't forget the premium refreshments!

Practically anything goes for your spontaneous brunch, a meal invented by Americans who oversleep. Consider setting up a buffet for your guests. The obvious hearty breakfast dishes, such as omelets, bacon, or sausages, are always a hit. Something pretty in fresh fruit or Fashionista Smoked Salmon Pâté in a fish-shaped mold make stunning breakfast centerpieces. For such an occasion, Miss Divina's refrigerator is always filled with things for emergencies, like Smoked-Salmon Eggs Divina over Baked Polenta, Mile-High Quickie Quiche, Hunnie Fay Baker's Ham with Grand Marnier Glaze, and, of course, Paris-Runway Chicken Crepes.

If you want something that makes you look and feel like Betty Crocker, try Miss Divina's recipe for Jane Dough Zucchini Bread. It's especially popular with her more masculine lady friends. You may get so caught up in the zucchini-bread experience that you will forget who you are and that you are a lady or a gentleman.

Always make sure drinks are on hand too, such as Bloody Marys, screwdrivers, or any flavored martinis. Naturally, hot coffee and fresh-squeezed juices must be available too. You know your guests will expect a drink in their condition, in true hair-of-the-doggy style. They may be so hungover that they have no idea what you are putting in front of them, but that's no excuse to slack. In a pinch, you can always order in. An eager delivery boy may be just what you need to start the day!

Paris-Runway Chicken Crepes

Jane Dough Zucchini Bread

Eggs

Smoked-Salmon Eggs Divina over Baked Polenta (p. 307)

Chueca Breakfast Burrito

Makes 3–6 servings.

Makeup:

6 eggs
2 tablespoons half-and-half
1 tablespoon salt
1 tablespoon black pepper
1 teaspoon cayenne pepper
3 small red potatoes
1 medium yellow onion
2 tablespoons extra-virgin olive oil, divided
3/4 cup fully cooked chorizo, diced
6 (8-inch) flour tortillas
1/2 cup salsa (optional)
1 cup shredded manchego cheese
1/4 cup green onions, chopped

Application:

- In a small bowl, whisk eggs with half-and-half, salt, pepper, and cayenne.
- Peel potatoes (or just scrub them clean very thoroughly).
- Slice potatoes into very thin slices.
- Cut onion into small cubes.
- Add 1 tablespoon olive oil to skillet and heat for 2 minutes on medium heat.
- Add potatoes to the skillet and fry very slowly in olive oil.
- When potatoes are halfway cooked, approximately 3 minutes, add onion to skillet. When tender, transfer potatoes and onion to a bowl and set aside until needed.
- In the same skillet, heat remaining 1 tablespoon olive oil over medium heat.
- Add egg mixture; scramble until eggs are completely set.
- Add chorizo, potatoes, and onions and cook over low heat for 2 minutes.
- Warm stacked tortillas in the microwave for 30 seconds with a damp towel over them.
- Remove tortillas and spoon egg mixture down the center, lengthwise, of each tortilla.
- Place a spoonful of salsa (optional) on top of eggs, sprinkle cheese and green onions on top, and roll up each tortilla.
- Serve warm.

Supermodel Hint

Miss Divina's two main squeezes in Madrid, Princes Alfonso and Beny, would roll over and play dead for this yummy morning pick-me-up if Miss Divina asked them to! They are so devoted to her.

Divine Quiche Divina

Makes 6–8 servings.

Makeup:

1 (9-inch) preprepared piecrust
6 eggs
5 slices thick-cut applewood bacon, crisply fried
and chopped
1 1/2 cups half-and-half
1 cup shredded swiss cheese
1/3 cup finely chopped green onions or chives
1/3 cup finely chopped red onion
1 teaspoon salt
1 teaspoon black pepper
1 teaspoon white pepper
1 teaspoon crushed red pepper
1/2 cup shredded parmesan cheese
1 cup crumbled gorgonzola cheese
1 egg beaten with 1 tablespoon milk (egg wash)

Application:

- Preheat oven to 425 degrees F.
- Place piecrust in a lightly floured 9-inch glass pie pan and mold to plate.
- Parbake bottom piecrust (see All-Buttered-Up Piecrust, p. 291, for instructions).
- Remove parbaked crust from oven and cool on a rack.
- Beat eggs slightly in a small mixing bowl.
- In same bowl, mix bacon, half-and-half, swiss cheese, green onions or chives, red onion, salt, black pepper, white pepper, and crushed red pepper.
- Pour egg mixture into parbaked piecrust.
- Cook uncovered for 15 minutes.
- Reduce oven heat to 300 degrees F.
- Sprinkle parmesan cheese and gorgonzola evenly over the top of the quiche.
- Cook uncovered for 20–30 minutes, or until knife inserted halfway between center and edge comes out clean.
- If needed, brush edges of crust with egg wash every 10 minutes to avoid a burnt crust.
- Let stand 10 minutes before serving.

Supermodel Hint
Gorgonzola cheese really gives this a kick and makes your mouth salivate.
It's just like a kiss from Miss Divina. You should be so lucky!

Hurricane Katrina Huevos Rancheros

Makes 8 servings.

Makeup:

5 slices applewood bacon, fried and chopped
 (if desired, reserve bacon grease for sautéing onion)
1 small onion, diced
2 tablespoons butter, extra-virgin olive oil, or bacon
 grease
2 tablespoons fresh garlic, diced
1 (15-ounce) can black or pinto beans
1 (14.5-ounce) can diced tomatoes
1/3 cup chopped zucchini
salt, pepper, cumin, and coriander to taste
hot sauce, such as Tabasco, to taste
2 tablespoons extra-virgin olive oil
8 corn tortillas
shredded cheddar cheese to taste (optional)
8 eggs, fried, over easy
1/2 cup sour cream
1 large avocado, pitted and sliced
1/4 cup chopped green onions

Application:

- In a large skillet, over medium heat, sauté onion in butter, oil, or bacon grease.
- Add garlic to onion.
- Add beans, diced tomatoes, and zucchini.
- Season with salt, pepper, cumin, and coriander.
- Add hot sauce.
- Cook mixture down to remove most of the water.
- In a small skillet, heat oil over medium heat.
- Toast tortillas in skillet.
- Place one tortilla per plate.
- Top each tortilla with bean mix, cheese, and one fried egg.
- Top with sour cream, avocado slices, bacon, and green onions.
- Add more hot sauce as desired.

Supermodel Hint

Miss Divina is always looking out for new family recipes. This one is from one of her favorite nieces.
Miss Divina taught her everything she knows! Well, not everything!

King Louis Lobster Quiche

Makes 10–12 servings.

Makeup:

2 (9-inch) preprepared piecrusts
1 small onion, finely chopped
1 garlic clove, finely chopped
1 tablespoon salted butter
3 medium eggs
1 1⁄2 cups half-and-half
1 1⁄2 cups lobster meat, coarsely chopped
5 slices thick-cut applewood bacon, crisply fried
　and chopped
1 cup grated swiss cheese
1 cup grated extra-sharp white cheddar cheese
1⁄2 teaspoon French tarragon
1⁄4 teaspoon dry mustard
salt and pepper to taste
1 egg beaten with 1 tablespoon milk (egg wash)
fresh caviar, for garnish (optional)

Application:

- Preheat oven to 350 degrees F.
- Cut out pieces of the piecrusts to fit into individual muffin tin spaces.
- Place piecrust pieces in a lightly floured muffin tin and mold to tin.
- Parbake bottom piecrusts (see All-Buttered-Up Piecrust, p. 291, for instructions).
- Remove muffin tin from oven and cool on a rack.
- In a medium skillet, sauté onion and garlic in butter over medium heat until translucent; remove from heat and set aside.
- In a medium bowl, whisk eggs. Add half-and-half and mix thoroughly.
- Stir in lobster meat, bacon, swiss cheese, and cheddar cheese.
- Add onion and garlic, tarragon, dry mustard, salt, and pepper to lobster mixture and combine thoroughly.
- Pour filling into piecrusts in muffin tin.
- Bake for 10–15 minutes, or until quiche is set.
- If needed, brush edges of crusts with egg wash every 10 minutes to avoid burnt crusts.
- Remove from oven and allow to cool for 5 minutes before serving.
- Remove quiches from muffin tin and set on a platter or individual plates.
- Garnish the center of each quiche with a small amount of fresh caviar if desired.

Mile–High Quickie Quiche

Makes 6–8 servings.

Makeup:

1 (9-inch) preprepared piecrust
3 tablespoons butter, divided
10 ounces fresh spinach, cleaned and drained, finely chopped
3/4 cup finely chopped red onion
4 eggs
1 cup ham, chopped
1 cup shredded mozzarella cheese
1/2 cup ricotta cheese
1/2 cup half-and-half
1/2 cup sour cream
1 tablespoon all-purpose flour
1 tablespoon finely chopped fresh basil
1 teaspoon salt
1 teaspoon freshly ground black pepper
1 cup shredded romano cheese
1 egg beaten with 1 tablespoon milk (egg wash)

Application:

- Preheat oven to 350 degrees F.
- Place piecrust in a lightly floured 9-inch glass pie pan and mold to plate.
- Parbake bottom piecrust (see All-Buttered-Up Piecrust, p. 291, for instructions).
- Remove parbaked piecrust from oven and cool on a rack.
- In a medium skillet over medium heat, sauté spinach in 1 teaspoon butter until wilted.
- Add remaining butter and sauté onions until translucent; remove from heat and set aside.
- In a medium bowl, whisk eggs.
- Add ham, mozzarella cheese, ricotta cheese, half-and-half, sour cream, flour, basil, salt, and pepper.
- Mix in spinach and onion.
- Mix ingredients well.
- Pour into parbaked piecrust.
- Sprinkle romano cheese on top.
- Bake for 30 minutes, or until quiche is set and lightly browned around the edges.
- If needed, brush edges of crust with egg wash every 10 minutes to avoid a burnt crust.
- Remove from oven and let stand 5–10 minutes before cutting and serving.

Supermodel Hint

If you don't have beans to weigh down the crust, try using another ovenproof pan if you need to. Pricking the bottom of the piecrust with a fork prevents the dough from popping up while baking. Sometimes all you need is a little prick!

305

Silky Soft-Boiled Eggs

Makeup:

1–4 large fresh eggs, cold from the refrigerator
rice, for serving (optional)
toast, for serving (optional)

Application:

- Fill a medium saucepan with a few inches of water and set it over high heat. Let the water come to a rolling boil.
- Lower the heat and let the water reduce to a rapid simmer.
- Gently lower eggs into the water one at a time.
- Cook eggs for 5–7 minutes.
- Remove eggs with a slotted spoon.
- Run each egg under cold tap water for 30 seconds.
- Set each egg upright in an egg cup or a small ramekin filled with rice (optional). To remove the cap, use an egg cutter or use the edge of a knife to gently tap around the top.
- Eat while the egg is warm! Eat the egg straight from the shell with a small spoon and/or toast (optional) for dipping.

Note: If you are making these eggs for The Great Wall of Chinese Pork Noodle Soup (p. 113), then rinse the eggs under cold water for 1 minute. Then very carefully peel the shell off like you would a hard-boiled egg.

Smoked-Salmon Eggs Divina over Baked Polenta

Makes 2 servings.

Makeup:
Polenta
4 cups chicken stock
1 1/2 cups grated parmesan cheese, divided
1 cup polenta
2 tablespoons butter
1 teaspoon salt
1 teaspoon pepper
1 tablespoon freshly crushed garlic
2 tablespoons butter or butter-flavored cooking spray

Eggs
2 teaspoons white vinegar or rice vinegar
4 fresh eggs
8 ounces smoked salmon
1 cup hollandaise sauce (see p. 310 for recipe)

Application:
Polenta
- Preheat oven to 350 degrees F.
- In a medium saucepan, heat chicken stock to boiling.
- Gradually add 1 cup parmesan cheese, polenta, butter, salt, pepper, and garlic.
- Stir constantly until thickened.
- Butter an 8-inch square baking dish with butter or butter-flavored cooking spray.
- When polenta is thickened, pour polenta mixture into baking dish.
- Smooth out mixture and sprinkle remaining 1/2 cup parmesan cheese on top.
- Bake in oven for 30 minutes, or until fully cooked and golden brown on top.
- Remove and set aside to cool.
- When cooled, cut baked polenta into squares.

Eggs
- Bring a large saucepan two-thirds filled with water to a boil.
- Add vinegar. Bring water to a boil again; then lower heat to a bare simmer.
- Working one egg at a time, crack an egg into a small ramekin and slip ramekin into barely simmering water.
- Once egg begins to solidify, crack another egg into a ramekin and slip it into the water, until you have all 4 eggs cooking.
- Turn off heat, cover pan, and let sit for 2 minutes.
- Remove ramekins from water and gently lift eggs out with a slotted spoon. Take the eggs out in the order you put them in.
- Rinse eggs with lukewarm water to rinse off vinegar.

Assembly
- Place a square of warmed polenta in the center of each serving plate. Refrigerate or freeze any leftover polenta for future use.
- Place smoked salmon on top of polenta.
- Place 2 poached eggs on top of the salmon and spoon hollandaise sauce over the eggs.

Zippy Zucchini Frittata

Makes 6–8 servings.

Makeup:

2 tablespoons butter, room temperature
1 cup shredded zucchini
1/2 cup chopped onion
5 slices bacon, cooked and chopped
4 eggs
1/4 teaspoon salt
1/4 teaspoon garlic powder
1/4 teaspoon cayenne pepper
1 cup shredded swiss cheese

Application:

- Preheat oven to 350 degrees F.
- In a medium skillet, sauté zucchini and onion in butter over medium heat for 2–3 minutes.
- Transfer to a glass dish with sides.
- Add bacon to zucchini and onion.
- Beat eggs and add salt, garlic powder, and cayenne.
- Pour eggs into glass dish with zucchini, onion, and bacon.
- Sprinkle with cheese and bake for about 10–15 minutes, or until eggs are fully cooked and cheese is melted.

Supermodel Hint

Do you have leftover zucchini from last night's dinner? Use it for this wonderful dish to serve a famished overnight guest if the early dinner the night before gave way to other energy-sapping activities.

Main Courses and Essentials

Lovely-You Morning Parfait (p. 313)

Makes 4 servings. Double (or triple) this recipe if you have a larger number of guests or a dish requiring a larger amount of sauce.

Makeup:

5 egg yolks
1 1/2 tablespoons lemon juice
1/2 cup salted butter
1 teaspoon salt
1 teaspoon freshly ground black pepper
1/2 teaspoon cayenne pepper

Application:

- Stir egg yolks and lemon juice together in a small saucepan.
- Add butter over low heat and stir until butter is melted.
- Stir in salt, pepper, and cayenne and stir until mixed well.
- Continue to cook over low heat, whisking continuously, for approximately 10 minutes. Sauce should be the consistency of thick cream when finished.

Supermodel Hint

A metal whisk is vital to making hollandaise sauce. Vigorous whisking protects the eggs from overcooking and incorporates air into the sauce. Be sure to lift the whisk in the saucepan to help accomplish the latter.

Béarnaise Sauce à la Divina

Makes 4 servings. Double (or triple) this recipe if you have a larger number of guests or a dish requiring a larger amount of sauce.

Makeup:

2 egg yolks
2 tablespoons lemon juice
1/2 cup salted butter
2 tablespoons champagne vinegar or white wine vinegar
1 teaspoon salt
1 teaspoon freshly ground white pepper
1 tablespoon finely chopped shallots
1 teaspoon dried tarragon leaves
1 teaspoon french thyme
1 teaspoon chives
1/2 teaspoon cayenne pepper

Application:

- Stir egg yolks and lemon juice together in a small saucepan.
- Add half the butter and heat over low heat. Add remaining butter and stir until butter is melted.
- Stir in remaining ingredients (vinegar, salt, pepper, shallots, tarragon, thyme, chives, and cayenne) and stir until mixed well.
- Continue to cook over low heat, whisking continuously, for approximately 10 minutes. Sauce should be the consistency of thick cream when finished.

Supermodel Hint

Béarnaise sauce is a piquant child of hollandaise,
one of the so-called mother sauces of French cuisine.

Casting Couch Crispy Crab Cakes

Makes 4–6 servings.

Makeup:

10 ounces chilled bay scallops
1 1/2 cups ground saltine crackers or seasoned bread
   crumbs, divided
1 tablespoon whipping cream
1/4 teaspoon salt
1/4 teaspoon pepper
1/4 teaspoon curry powder
1/4 teaspoon ground cumin
32 ounces crab meat
2 tablespoons chopped fresh chives or shallots
11 tablespoons butter
1 cup A Man from Hollandaise Sauce (see p. 310)
   or Béarnaise Sauce à la Divina (see p. 311)

Application:

- Mix bay scallops, 3/4 cup crackers or bread crumbs, cream, salt, pepper, and curry powder in a food processor or blender until chunky.
- Transfer to a large bowl, and stir in crab and chives.
- Divide into four equal patties.
- Place remaining 3/4 cup crackers or bread crumbs in a medium bowl.
- Coat patties with remaining crumbs completely and chill for 1 hour.
- Melt butter in a large pan over medium heat.
- Add crab cakes to pan and cook until fully cooked and golden brown, about 3–5 minutes per side.
- Transfer cooked crab cakes to separate plates.
- Place 2–4 tablespoons of béarnaise or hollandaise sauce over each crab cake, adjusting amount of sauce according to your individual taste.

Serving note: Serve with rice and fresh asparagus or your favorite fresh vegetable.

Supermodel Hint

Crabs are such pinchers! But this dish will turn the tables and have your heartthrob begging for more nibbles from you.

Lovely–You Morning Parfait

Makes 4 parfaits.

Makeup:

1 cup chopped fresh strawberries
1 pint fresh blackberries, raspberries, or blueberries
1/4 cup lemonade
3 cups nonfat vanilla greek yogurt (nonfat variety
    optional)
1 cup fresh granola
1/2 cup fresh honey
4 fresh mint leaves, for garnish (optional)

Application:

- In a medium bowl, combine strawberries, fresh berries, and lemonade.
- Layer 1/4 cup vanilla yogurt into the bottoms of four tall glasses.
- Layer some granola, honey, and then fruit combination in the glasses.
- Repeat layers of yogurt, granola, honey, and fruit until glasses are filled to the top.
- Garnish each glass with a fresh mint leaf.
- Serve immediately to keep granola crunchy.

Supermodel Hint

Being energetic all day requires that you start with a good breakfast.
I know of no better way to enjoy the fruits of life than with this parfait! C'est parfait for a reason!

Paris–Runway Chicken Crepes

Makes 6 servings.

Makeup:

Crepes
1 cup flour
1/4 teaspoon baking powder
1/4 teaspoon salt
1 1/4 cups milk
1 egg
1 tablespoon butter, melted

Chicken Filling
3 tablespoons butter
3 tablespoons flour
1/2 teaspoon salt
1 cup chicken stock
1 1/2 cups finely chopped cooked chicken breast
2/3 cup peeled and finely chopped Granny Smith apples
1/2 cup finely chopped broccoli
1/4 cup finely chopped red onion

Application:

Crepes
- Mix flour, baking powder, and salt in a medium bowl.
- Stir in milk, egg, and melted butter and beat by hand until batter is smooth.
- Lightly butter (1 tablespoon) a 7- or 8-inch nonstick skillet, and heat over medium heat until butter is bubbly.
- For each crepe, pour 1/4 cup of the batter into skillet and immediately rotate skillet until thin film of batter covers bottom.
- Cook until light golden brown, about 1–2 minutes.
- Run wide spatula around the edge of crepe to loosen.
- Flip crepe and cook other side until light golden brown, about 2 minutes.
- Repeat process for the other crepes. Add additional 1 teaspoon butter to pan if needed.
- Stack crepes on a plate, placing waxed paper or paper towel between each. Keep crepes covered and warm to keep them from drying out.

Chicken Filling
- Preheat oven to 350 degrees F.
- In a large saucepan, heat butter over low heat until melted.
- Blend in flour and salt and cook over low heat, stirring constantly, until mixture is smooth and bubbly, about 2–3 minutes. Remove from heat.
- Raise heat to medium. Stir in chicken stock and heat until bubbling, stirring constantly; stock will thicken.
- Boil for about 1 minute.
- In a large mixing bowl, mix together chicken, apple, broccoli, onion, and 1/2 cup of the thickened broth.
- Place small amount of chicken mixture in the center of each crepe lengthwise and roll crepe.
- Place crepes seam side down in an ungreased oblong baking dish.
- Pour remaining broth over crepes.
- Cook uncovered in oven until crepes are hot, or about 15 minutes. Keep an eye on crepes to ensure they don't dry out.

Supermodel Hint
Refrigerate the crepe batter for at least one hour prior to frying. It makes for light, airy crepes. Also, use a heavy-bottomed stainless steel pan. Miss Divina knows that nonstick pans don't brown the crepes evenly. Make sure you coat the pan generously with butter or spray.

Potatoes

Precious and Popular Potato Pancakes (p. 317)

Hashtag Browned Potatoes

Makes 4–6 servings.

Makeup:

5 tablespoons unsalted butter
1 1/2 pound russet potatoes, peeled and diced
1 1/2 cups chopped yellow onion (1 large yellow onion)
1 1/2 cups chopped green bell peppers (2 large bell
  peppers) (red bell peppers may be substituted)
2 teaspoons salt
1 teaspoon freshly ground black pepper
4 large eggs
2 cups ham, fried and chopped
2 tablespoons minced fresh parsley
2 tablespoons chopped scallions
1/4 cup green onions, divided

Application:

- Melt butter in a large skillet over medium-high heat.
- Add potatoes, onion, bell peppers, salt, and pepper and cook for 15–20 minutes, turning potatoes occasionally with a spatula.
- Cook until potatoes are evenly browned and cooked through.
- While potatoes cook, scramble eggs.
- Once potatoes are cooked, add ham to skillet with potatoes and mix.
- Turn off heat and mix in 2 tablespoons green onions, parsley, and scallions.
- Carefully mix in the scrambled eggs.
- Garnish with remaining 2 tablespoons green onions on top.

Serving note: Serve hot with toast, jam, and fresh, hot coffee.

Supermodel Hint

They say a good breakfast is the most important meal of the day. Waking up next to
Miss Divina does wonders for your day as well!

Precious and Popular Potato Pancakes

Makes 6–8 servings.

Makeup:

10 large russet potatoes
2 medium yellow onions
4 eggs
2 tablespoons garlic powder, or to taste
2 tablespoons salt, or to taste
2 tablespoons pepper, or to taste
vegetable oil (for frying)
16 ounces sour cream, for garnish
green onions or chives, chopped, for garnish

Application:

- Preheat oven to 250 degrees F.
- Wash and scrub dirt from potatoes.
- Grate potatoes (peeled or unpeeled) until they are pulp-like.
- Place potato pulp into a large mixing bowl and drain for about 30 minutes, or as long as needed to drain water. (See "Supermodel Hint.")
- Peel and grate onions until pulp-like.
- Add onion pulp and onion juices to potato pulp only after potatoes are well drained.
- Add eggs, garlic powder, salt, and pepper to potato/onion pulp. Adjust seasonings to taste. Salt generously, as potatoes tend to be quite bland.
- Mix well.
- In a large skillet, heat small amount of cooking oil over medium-high heat.
- Using a large serving spoon, place 3–4 spoonfuls of mixture in pan to make 3–4 pancakes at a time.
- Fry each side until crisp (golden brown) so, when using spatula, pancakes will not fall apart. Be careful not to burn.
- Carefully flip pancakes and fry until golden brown on each side.
- Place cooked pancakes in flat glass baking dish and put in preheated oven to keep warm.
- Repeat process until all the mixture is cooked.
- Serve with a dab of sour cream and chopped green onions or chives sprinkled on top of each pancake.

Supermodel Hint

Potatoes have a large amount of water in them. Too much water retention is not a good thing! We girls know how it feels to be bloated!

Sweet Breads

Heroine's Tart Lemon–Poppy Seed Bread (p. 321)

Apple-Peach Cinnamon Dolce Muffins

Makes 12 muffins.

Makeup:

2 cups all-purpose flour
1/2 cup sugar
2 teaspoons baking powder
1 teaspoon cinnamon
1 teaspoon salt
1 1/2 cups buttermilk
1/2 cup unsalted butter, melted
1 egg
1 teaspoon vanilla extract
butter-flavored cooking spray or shortening
1 cup Just-Peachy Applesauce (see p. 234), divided
pinch each of sugar and cinnamon for each muffin top

Application:

- Preheat oven to 375 degrees F.
- In a large mixing bowl, add flour, sugar, baking powder, cinnamon, and salt. Mix well.
- In a separate medium bowl, add buttermilk, butter, egg, and vanilla. Whisk until combined.
- Add wet ingredients to dry ingredients and mix well until combined.
- Spray or lightly grease a muffin tin with butter or shortening. (Omit this step if you are using a nonstick tin.)
- Divide half the muffin batter between the twelve muffin cups, filling each muffin cup halfway.
- Place 1 tablespoon Just-Peachy Applesauce in the center of each muffin cup.
- Spoon remaining batter over each muffin, covering the Just-Peachy Applesauce.
- Bake in oven for 25 minutes, or until muffin centers firm up and tops are golden brown.
- Sprinkle pinch each of sugar and cinnamon over each muffin top.
- Let cool for 5 minutes before serving.

Note: Remove the muffins carefully from the muffin tin. Some of the tops of the muffins may separate from the filling.

Supermodel Hint

These apple-peach cinnamon muffins are a wonderful addition to any breakfast menu.
If you are not using a nonstick muffin tin, make sure to either grease the tin with butter or shortening.
You'll want your muffins to come out of the tin effortlessly!

Don't Scone Me, I'm Innocent!

Makes 12–18 scones.

Makeup:

6 3/4 cups self-rising flour
1/2 cup sugar
2 cups cold butter, cut into pieces
1 cup half-and-half
1 egg
English clotted cream, for serving
strawberry jam, for serving

Application:

- Preheat oven to 400 degrees F.
- Whisk flour and sugar together in a large mixing bowl.
- Using your fingers or a pastry cutter, work butter into the flour mixture until it resembles coarse meal.
- Whisk half-and-half and egg together in a separate small bowl.
- Add 1 cup of the half-and-half mixture to the flour/butter mixture and gently mix together with your hands until a soft (not tacky) dough forms.
- Add more half-and-half mixture, 1 tablespoon at a time, if dough is too dry. Reserve remaining half-and-half mixture.
- Transfer dough to a lightly floured surface.
- Pat dough out to a 1-inch thickness.
- Using a 3-inch round cookie cutter, cut out scones, gently rounding off edges with your hands.
- Gather dough scraps together and repeat process until all dough is used.
- Put scones on a lightly floured baking sheet about 1/2 inch apart.
- Brush tops with remaining half-and-half mixture.
- Bake scones until golden brown, or about 20 minutes.
- Tent foil over scones if tops brown too quickly.
- Transfer scones to a wire rack to let cool briefly.
- Serve scones warm or room temperature with English clotted cream and strawberry jam.

Supermodel Hint

Well, Miss Divina knows that, unfortunately, the best clotted cream is only available in Devon County, England.
Try substituting freshly homemade whipped cream if you can't get a hold of the real thing.

Heroine's Tart Lemon–Poppy Seed Bread

Makes 6–8 servings.

Makeup:

3 1/3 cups all-purpose flour
2 teaspoons baking soda
1 1/2 teaspoons salt
1/2 teaspoon baking powder
2 2/3 cups sugar
2/3 cup buttermilk
1/3 cup sour cream
1/3 cup vegetable oil
peel of 1 lemon, grated
1/4 cup lemon juice
4 eggs
2 tablespoons poppy seeds
1/2 teaspoon vanilla extract
1/2 teaspoon cinnamon
whipped cream, for garnish

Application:

- Preheat oven to 350 degrees F.
- Generously grease and flour two or three loaf pans.
- In a medium bowl, sift flour, baking soda, salt, and baking powder; set aside.
- In a large mixing bowl, combine sugar, buttermilk, sour cream, oil, lemon peel, lemon juice, eggs, poppy seeds, vanilla, and cinnamon.
- Beat at medium speed until well blended.
- Reduce speed to low and gradually blend in flour mixture.
- Transfer batter to prepared pans, smoothing tops.
- Bake until a wooden toothpick inserted into the loaves comes out clean, about 60 minutes.
- Let cool in pans on a rack for 10–15 minutes.
- Remove loaves from pans and let cool completely on rack.
- Slice into 1/2-inch-thick pieces and serve on individual plates with whipped cream on top.

Supermodel Hint

A warm, dry knife inserted around the baking pan will help loosen any side that refuses to let go. Like with paparazzi, the right knife does wonders.

Jane Dough Zucchini Bread

Makes 6–8 servings.

Makeup:

3 1/3 cups all-purpose flour
2 teaspoons baking soda
1 1/2 teaspoons salt
1/2 teaspoon baking powder
2 2/3 cups sugar
2/3 cup water
1/3 cup sour cream
1/3 cup vegetable oil
4 eggs
1 teaspoon cinnamon
1/2 teaspoon ground ginger
1/2 teaspoon nutmeg
3 cups shredded fresh zucchini
2/3 cup chopped walnuts
whipped cream, for garnish (optional)

Application:

- Preheat oven to 350 degrees F.
- Generously grease and flour two or three loaf pans.
- In a medium bowl, sift flour, baking soda, salt, and baking powder; set aside.
- In a large mixing bowl, combine sugar, water, sour cream, oil, eggs, cinnamon, ginger, and nutmeg.
- Beat at medium speed until well blended.
- Reduce speed to low and gradually blend in flour mixture.
- Stir in zucchini and nuts.
- Transfer batter to prepared pans, smoothing tops.
- Bake until a wooden toothpick inserted into the loaves comes out clean, or about 60 minutes.
- Let cool in pans on a rack for 10–15 minutes.
- Remove loaves from pans and let cool completely on rack.
- Slice into 1/2-inch-thick pieces and serve on individual plates with whipped cream (optional) on top.

Supermodel Hint

Miss Divina has wowed princes and PTA presidents with breads in which she substituted plain yogurt for the sour cream called for in this recipe.

Ohio Corn-Fed Hunk-of-a-Man Bread

Makes 10–12 servings.

Makeup:

2 tablespoons butter
1 1/2 cups medium-grind cornmeal
1/2 cup all-purpose flour
1 tablespoon sugar, plus more if you like sweet corn
  bread
2 teaspoons baking powder
1 teaspoon salt
1 1/4 cups buttermilk, plus additional 1–2 tablespoons
  if needed
1 egg
1 cup creamed corn

Application:

- Preheat oven to 375 degrees F.
- Heat butter in a medium ovenproof skillet or an 8-inch square baking pan over medium heat; heat until good and hot, about 2 minutes. Then turn off heat.
- Combine cornmeal, flour, sugar baking powder, and salt in a medium bowl.
- Mix buttermilk and egg together in a separate small bowl.
- Add creamed corn to egg/buttermilk mixture.
- Stir liquid mixture into dry ingredients, stirring just enough to combine; if mixture seems too dry, add another 1–2 tablespoons buttermilk if needed.
- Pour batter into prepared skillet or pan, smooth out the top if necessary, and put in oven.
- Bake about 30 minutes, until the top is lightly browned, the sides have pulled away from the pan, and a wooden toothpick inserted into the center comes out clean.
- Carefully remove skillet from oven.
- Serve hot or warm.

Note: You can make muffins with this recipe also. Just use a muffin tin to bake and reduce cooking time to account for the smaller size of the muffins.

Supermodel Hint

Miss Divina often prefers buttermilk in some recipes that call for milk or creams. The buttermilk in this recipe gives it a little more high-heel kick than just milk! When someone yells, "Got Milk?" she replies, "Buttermilk!"

That's One Big Banana Bread in Your Pocket!

Makes 6–8 servings.

Makeup:

butter-flavored cooking spray
5 tablespoons butter, room temperature
1/2 cup firmly packed light brown sugar
1/2 cup granulated sugar
1 whole egg
2 egg whites
1 teaspoon vanilla extract
1 1/2 cups mashed ripe bananas
1 3/4 cups all-purpose flour
1 teaspoon baking soda
1/2 teaspoon salt
1/4 teaspoon baking powder
1/2 cup heavy cream
1/3 cup chopped walnuts

Photo of individual banana bread loaves shown.

Application:

- Preheat oven to 375 degrees F.
- Spray bottom and sides of a 9 x 5 x 3–inch loaf pan with cooking spray.
- In a medium mixing bowl, add butter, brown sugar, and granulated sugar; mix with hand mixer.
- Add egg, egg whites, and vanilla. Beat until well blended.
- Add banana and beat on high speed for 2 minutes, or until bananas are thoroughly mixed in.
- In a separate small mixing bowl, combine flour, baking soda, salt, and baking powder.
- Add flour mixture to butter mixture.
- Add cream and walnuts to batter; mix well.
- Pour batter evenly into prepared loaf pan.
- Bake for 1 hour and 15 minutes, or until browned.
- Check state of bread with a wooden toothpick; if it comes out clean, bread is done.
- Cool bread on a wire rack for 10 minutes.
- Remove bread from pan, slice, and eat warm with butter generously slathered on top.

Note: Reduce baking time if you are baking this bread in smaller individual-size pans.

West Virginian Bumpkin Pumpkin Loaf

Makes 6–8 servings.

Makeup:

1 3/4 cups all-purpose flour
1 teaspoon baking powder
1 teaspoon baking soda
1/2 teaspoon salt
1 cup canned pumpkin
2/3 cup sugar
1/3 cup sour cream
1/3 vegetable oil
1 egg
3 tablespoons orange marmalade
1 teaspoon cinnamon
1/2 teaspoon ground ginger
1/2 teaspoon nutmeg
2/3 cup chopped walnuts
pumpkin seeds, shelled, for garnish (optional)
1 apple, your choice, sliced, for garnish (optional)
whipped cream, for garnish (optional)

Application:

- Preheat oven to 350 degrees F.
- Generously grease an 8 1/2 x 4 1/2-inch loaf pan.
- In a medium bowl, sift flour, baking powder, baking soda, and salt; set aside.
- In a large mixing bowl, combine pumpkin, sugar, sour cream, oil, egg, marmalade, cinnamon, ginger, and nutmeg.
- Beat at medium speed until well blended.
- Reduce speed to low and gradually blend in flour mixture.
- Stir in walnuts.
- Transfer batter to prepared pan, smoothing top.
- Sprinkle a handful of pumpkin seeds on top for garnish (optional).
- Bake until a wooden toothpick inserted into the loaf comes out clean, or about 60 minutes.
- Let cool in pan on a rack for 10–15 minutes.
- Remove from pan and let cool completely on rack.
- Slice into 1-inch-thick pieces and serve on individual plates with whipped cream (optional) on top and apple slices (optional).

Supermodel Hint

Try baking this bread in a round Bundt cake pan to create your own "bumpkin pumpkin" for the kiddies!

All about the Girl

By Blanche Itche

It is an absolute joy to tell you about the world's most beautiful chef. Some people are born divine; others achieve divinity. Most do neither. Miss Divina did both. The days of Twiggy are gone! Miss Divina is the "it" girl of today! Believe it or not, there are some people in remote parts of this crazy world that still have not heard of my idol. I imagine their lives must be so empty! For those poor souls, here is a brief biography, by me, of that delicious dish lovingly known as Miss Divina Noxema Vasilina, the Italian supermodel.

Miss Divina was born at her family's beloved—and paid for!—Tuscan villa in Italy. The day was January 8, 19— Well, we'll just leave it at that. She's timeless. Besides, when it comes to Divina time, most of us think about when she came to us, not to the whole damn world. Have you ever been asked, "Where were you when Miss Divina first hit the scene?" It seems like yesterday that she popped onto this earth and graced us with her exotic beauty.

The most delightful and innocent Miss Divina having a quiet moment backstage at the tender age of five.

When Divina was just six months old, her father, an international banker, took the whole family to New York to visit poor relations—her family has always been devoted to less-fortunate unfortunates, unfortunately. It was there that she was discovered. As her mama and nanny pushed her stroller down Fifth Avenue, a talent scout for the world-famous Chevrolet modeling agency saw a large crowd huddled around something on the sidewalk. She thought it was a game of sidewalk craps. Curiosity got the best of that old gambling-addict agent. But instead of dice, she found herself gasping at the most incredible sight—that lovely little doll, baby Divina. Those precious cheeks! Those little brunette locks! That Chanel jumper! Who could resist? That scout bet ten to one she could make that little bundle a star (and that little star could make her a bundle)! That's how it all started.

Soon Miss Divina was crawling down the catwalks, strutting her stuff for all the world to see. Well, not all her stuff. She was a baby after all, ya pigs! Miss Divina was headed straight to the top! Luckily, she was teething at the time. The pain left my darling girl with a cranky disposition, which in turn helped develop a ruthless streak good for clawing her way up the ladder. At the same time, her nanny tried to ease the pain with brandy on the gums, leaving her with a taste for the good stuff. Before you could say "strained peas," she was *the* Gerber baby.

Miss Divina was an ambitious child, so it's no surprise she went on to be the most celebrated baby in the history of the modeling world. She had so much more to offer than any of those one-dimensional babies that came before her. And I'm including the famous and multitalented supermodel/actress Rivers Barrier. Before anybody knew what was happening, modeling offers poured in. "We must have Baby Divina! We must have Baby Divina!" People were throwing ridiculous amounts of money at little Miss Divina. And rightly so—she was worth it all. Even when Miss Divina was burping up strained peas, she was a star. Before long, my girl was pulling in more dollars than a Honolulu whore on V-J Day!

Miss Divina has an itch for vintage automobiles. And she doesn't mind a handsome chauffeur to help her with that itch!

By sweet sixteen, when girls blossom into young ladies, Miss Divina had seen and done it all. She didn't want a car for her birthday; she was already riding her third chauffeur! By the time she was eighteen, leaders from around the world were asking her to become the new United Nations secretary general. If anyone could bring men together in peace, it was her! Well, what could she do? All those powerful men from all over the globe … She could have had them all wrapped around her finger (and her legs, if you ask me!). Sultans, kings, princes, and billionaires were all at her beck and call. That's how she became an expert at the honeymoon handshake!

But politics wasn't Miss Divina's bag, baby! She loved the world, but she preferred the men. And what man did not want to be a part of Miss Divina's life? Suitors were never scarce. American royalty Don-Don was just one of the young men that vied for her attention. For a very little while, she was even engaged to a prince—don't ask me who! But "Princess Divina"? That was small potatoes compared to the places she was going. Why buy the cow if you can get the principality for free? She was having too much fun being a temptress. Some say "Temptation" is her middle name. I say it's "SlimFast," but I don't have as big a heart as my dear Miss Divina. Still, who am I to say? That girl brings men to their knees. It's a gift, a powerful gift. So many women wish they had powers like that.

No doubt you have heard that my girl is infamous for her candlelight suppers. The lengths that diva will go to just to let you know that you are welcome in her home will shock you! The incredible energy and thought she puts into her menus is astounding. If I didn't make those required secret trips to the powder room, just to keep my figure, well, I tell you, I would be three hundred pounds heavier! Her dishes are addictive.

And oh my, the people you will meet at Miss Divina's! All the top celebrities and important world figures are there. Everyone who is anyone is there. An invitation to Miss Divina's table means you have arrived. And if you do get an invitation, your life will never be the same again. She is one of the world's greatest hostesses. Many of her friends—and fans, obviously—look up to her and idolize her. If I didn't idolize her as much as I do, I could just scratch her eyes out! She has it all, dammit.

It was only a matter of time before Hollywood knocked at her door. Some of the films weren't so popular, but a nice boy at Netflix tells me they're "cult films" and people still watch 'em. Well, I don't know about any cults, but I know what I like. A few of her movies are *I Was a Supermodel on an All-Male Flight*, *Candy?—Cigars?—Cigarettes?*, *Without Shame*, *Maid in Heaven*, *Will Girls Be Girls?*, and *Driving over Miss Dizzy*, costarring her friend and top model Dizzy Dazie. I still can't get enough! And this year she is making the docudrama *Some Like It Haute!* And then there was the TV pilot for a remake of *The Flying Nun*,

A smashing hit from day one, Miss Divina's album *Unforgivable*.

but it didn't take—she was just too top-heavy! Still, give me Miss Divina over Sally Field any day! Over Sally's dead body, even better. *Smokey and the Bandit* this, silly girl! But Hollywood does have its rewards. This year, the nice people there finally gave Miss Divina her star on the Hollywood Walk of Fame. "You love me! You really love me!" was all she could say. (Eat that, Sally!)

Today, things are still golden for my girl. She's making a TV miniseries called *Two Steps from the Gutter*. It's a tearjerker about a supermodel who runs out to buy some caviar and gets involved in a jewel heist. The story is very close to Miss Divina's heart. And my oh my! She has an angel's voice too, and she's started a singing career. Look for her new hit single, "I'm So Vain," on her album, *Unforgivable*, at your local Big Lots! Vamp, vixen, or victim, Miss Divina is your gal!

Behind the scenes, Miss Divina has always had her secret passion—cooking. When she wasn't strolling down a runway or opening a new supermarket, she was in the kitchen experimenting. It took some time, but after a while she could whip up better meals than the buffets I used to crank out for the schoolkids in Topeka, may they rest in peace. She was a foodie and fantastic at cooking, so why not do something more with it? After all, she had two great mentors, her mama, Yvonne, and her old granny, Nana. And let's face it—Miss Divina is not one to hide her flame. So she stepped out and added another feather to her cap—most beautiful gourmet chef. Ever the creative one, it seemed she was always turning out something new in that kitchen of hers. She turned out quite a few delivery boys in there too! Who's in the kitchen with Miss Divina? You better ask ICE if you want the correct spelling! But these fantastic recipes of hers were such hits that she just had to make them a gift to the world. And that's where this book comes from.

I recall one evening after a simply horrid dinner at one of those snooty Park Avenue restaurants, my dear friends Jackie O'Nasty and Lucid Perverti were at each other's throats over which chef's cooking was the best. Jackie went on about her French chef while Lucid, rather vocally, insisted that his Italian chef was unsurpassed. Well, not being one to hold my tongue (or liquor), I chimed in stating that Miss Divina's cooking was *the* most delicious. No one knows how to toot Miss Divina's horn better than me. Not to mention it helps keep a roof over my head!

When Miss Divina steps out to picnic, it's in style! The family villa in the hills of Tuscany is in the background. That's where the boys are, and someone is always waiting for her!

Undoubtedly, everyone wants to be connected with Miss Divina. I even heard through the grapevine that a handsome millionaire in Madrid named his restaurant in honor of her! Furthermore, I hear that his menu is just like being at Miss Divina's. I suspect that's because he "borrows" her recipes from time to time.

It wasn't too long after Miss Divina decided to put pen to paper that her agent, Michele Dees-Moss, announced that she was writing a book. Everybody was so excited, wondering what Miss Divina was writing about. That's because Missy Moss was keeping a tighter lid on what my Miss Divina was writing about than a jar of strawberry preserves. Well, inadvertently, I spilled the beans. Katie Couric trapped me during happy hour—that bitch! Suddenly everyone wanted to know what was under this Tuscan's sink! It was just a skip and a hop until the world realized there was more talent in Miss Divina's pretty little pinky than in a whole body of some of those so-called cooking gurus you see on cable TV. Before you could say "ripped bodice," she was on every morning TV talk show around the world! One more time, my Miss Divina reinvented herself. You'd think she'd get tired of all the attention!

It seems Miss Divina is always looking for a new avenue for her energy. So when a top toy manufacturer approached her about creating a Barbie rival, she jumped at the chance. Like she told *Vague* magazine, "I always loved my dolls when I was a little girl. The thought of returning that kind of joy to the world's little girls, and boys if that's the case, fills my heart to the brim!" Isn't *she* the doll? And talking about new ways to entertain people, Miss Divina is in negotiations to open an Airbnb rightly named Bedside Manor. She knows all the angles when it comes to delighting guests at the dinner table (and under the table too, if you ask me).

Beyond the haute cuisine, Miss Divina keeps wowing 'em with her gorgeous looks and that angelic voice. She has style and grace—that's why she's Miss Divina! She's still at home on a catwalk, on a concert stage, or on a TV screen. My darling Miss Divina is also one of this world's great humanitarians. Not one to forget the world outside the gates of her sprawling Italian villa, Miss Divina created a charity organization to benefit those less fortunate than she. As founder and president of her charity, **U**nited to **G**ive **L**adies **Y**outh (**UGLY**), she oversees and comforts the many poor souls that can't ever dream of being as stunningly gorgeous as she. At a recent fundraiser Miss Divina said, "It does wonders for one's soul to bring a little sunshine into those lives by providing face-lifts to the unfortunate women in our society." And when the lifts don't take, she still pays for them to get a little youth on the side as a sort of consolation. Ain't she full of it? Heart, that is.

Through it all, she has never lost her head. She doesn't mind being the center of attention. It's a good thing, since she always is! But Miss Divina enjoys the quiet times at home also. I remember her empathizing with Eva Gabor once in a sensational TV interview, stating, "I just adore my penthouse view, so, darling, give me Park Avenue! I adore relaxing on my terrace with my two delightful dogs, Stoli and Abby, at my feet and Blanche hovering somewhere in the background with a drink in her hand, no doubt!"

Don't you worry, honey! Blanche will always be here for you—just keep my tab open!

From crib to catwalk to kitchen, she learned that the world has much to offer. From life's rich bounty, she learned to make the world bend to her wishes. Lucky for you, plenty of what she wished for is edible. I know you'll enjoy recreating the delicious recipes that have whetted many appetites. Good lord, all this appetite talk is getting me whet right now!

It's in those quiet times at home that I can really appreciate the real Miss Divina. She opens up when she's engaging in her favorite hobbies at home, like modeling, eating chocolates, looking at pictures of herself, checking her social media, singing, looking at some more pictures of herself, tweeting, cooking, checking out some more Miss Divina snaps, tempting rich men, and, of course, there's that damned bunch of photos. With only twenty-three years (a number she's sticking with) on God's sweet earth, the world can rest assured that Miss Divina Noxema Vasilina will be around a long time to come. She is here to guarantee that our lives will be beautiful as long as she's a part of them. To many, she is the living, breathing definition of perfection. I agree, but you be the judge. Thank you! You have good taste! Bon appétit!

Most affectionately! B. Itche

That's a Wrap!

Congratulations, my dear ones! You've made it through the entire cookbook. Did you have an exhilarating experience? Were your taste buds exploding? I have no doubt you did and they were! I have unfailing faith in you. After all, you did have the uncanny sense to purchase this book! I hope you found the experience rewarding. Hopefully, the recipes within your grasp have made you a better cook and host.

Now, I know that Blanche can be a bit much to handle at times. But I do hope that her "Supermodel Hints" sprinkled throughout the recipe pages helped you along the way. Yes, she does have a warped sense of humor at times, but go easy on her. It hasn't been an easy life for her. She crawled up from the gutter from cafeteria cook to be by my side and witness to the glittering glories that are part of my world! Her gritty persona only enhances her uniqueness.

I'm too young for a midlife crisis, so that's why I decided to write this "tell-all" recipe book. I hope you enjoyed the journey, had a few laughs along the way, and put some color into your dreary, drab life. If you did your job well, you might have even experienced a few rounds of applause after a particularly successful dinner featuring my recipes.

No doubt your life can't hold a candle to the fabulous life I lead, but I know that you must have glimpsed some hope within these pages to get you through another day. Even if you're not beautiful on the outside, in my opinion, you're gorgeous on the inside. There's always one more recipe you can make to give your friends and family the impression that you are a star of the highest magnitude.

Thank you so much for the opportunity to share my beloved recipes with you. I am sure you tried many recipes. And like potato chips, with my recipes, you can't stop at only one. I truly am grateful. Even gorgeous supermodels like myself have some level of humbleness, however small!

Hugs and kisses,

Divina Noxema Vasilina

Divina Noxema Vasilina

Art and Photo Credits

Cover, Art illustration, Jean Philippe Laplagne, www.dodgerdesign.com
Cover, Art illustration, Rae Crosson, www.greetingsfromcrazyville.com
p. i, Art illustration, Rae Crosson, www.greetingsfromcrazyville.com
p. i, Image ID #21827197, filo, www.istockphoto.com

Dedication
p. iii, Art illustration, Rae Crosson, www.greetingsfromcrazyville.com
p. iii, Art illustration, Jean Philippe Laplagne, www.dodgerdesign.com

Contents
p. v, Art illustration, Rae Crosson, www.greetingsfromcrazyville.com
p. v, Image ID #8893969, heather_mcgrath, www.istockphoto.com

Preface
p. xv, Art illustration, Jean Philippe Laplagne, www.dodgerdesign.com
p. xv, Photo, Jean Philippe Laplagne, www.dodgerdesign.com.com

Acknowledgments
p. xv, Art illustration, Jean Philippe Laplagne, www.dodgerdesign.com
p. xv, Photo, Jean Philippe Laplagne, www.dodgerdesign.com

Introducing Miss Divina
p. 1, Art illustration, Rae Crosson, www.greetingsfromcrazyville.com
p. 1, Art illustration, Jean Philippe Laplagne, www.dodgerdesign.com
p. 3-24, Art illustrations, Rae Crosson, www.greetingsfromcrazyville.com
p. 3-24, Art illustrations, Jean Philippe Laplagne, www.dodgerdesign.com

Cool Cocktails
p. 25, Art illustration, Rae Crosson, www.greetingsfromcrazyville.com
p. 25, Art illustration, Jean Philippe Laplagne, www.dodgerdesign.com
p. 26, Image ID #40037199, Dmitry Lobanov, www.123rf.com
p. 27-53, Art illustrations, Rae Crosson, www.greetingsfromcrazyville.com
p. 27-53, Art illustrations, Jean Philippe Laplagne, www.dodgerdesign.com
p. 28, Image ID #148779904, bluebearry, www.istockphoto.com
p. 28, Image ID #125787412, bluebearry, www.istockphoto.com
p. 34, Image ID #11276742, Anna Khomulo, www.123rf.com
p. 40, Image ID #57947684, Brent Hofacker, www.123rf.com
p. 46, Image ID #13729443, Svetlana Kolpakova, www.123rf.com
p. 52, Image ID #44182244, Joshua Resnick, www.123rf.com
p. 54, Image ID #40924431, Elena Shashkina, www.123rf.com

The Lady and the Ladle
p. 55, Art illustrations, Rae Crosson, www.greetingsfromcrazyville.com
p. 55, Art illustrations, Jean Philippe Laplagne, www.dodgerdesign.com

Tasty Hors d'oeuvres
p. 57-89, Art illustrations, Rae Crosson, www.greetingsfromcrazyville.com
p. 57-89, Art illustrations, Jean Philippe Laplagne, www.dodgerdesign.com
p. 58, Image ID #35151840, yhh5807531, www.123rf.com
p. 59, Image ID #31075618, Sergii Koval, www.123rf.com
p. 59, Image ID #12417787, Inga Nielsen, www.123rf.com
p. 60, Image ID #47337964, Anna Pustynnikova, www.123rf.com
p. 61, Image ID #10764344, Eugene Bochkarev, www.123rf.com
p. 62, Image ID #35151840, yhh5807531, www.123rf.com

p. 63, Jean Philippe Laplagne, www.dodgerdesign.com
p. 64, Image ID #21068686, wiktory, www.123rf.com
p. 65, Image ID #18253950, Denis Tabler, www.123rf.com
p. 66, Image ID #40380729, Natanya Sanders, www.123rf.com
p. 67, Image ID #47337964, Anna Pustynnikova, www.123rf.com
p. 68, Image ID #38641230, czarnybez, www.123rf.com
p. 69, Image ID #18920383, Alexandr Mychko, www.123rf.com
p. 70, Image ID #45677150, Grzegorz Krysmalski, www.123rf.com
p. 71, Jean Philippe Laplagne, www.dodgerdesign.com
p. 72, Image ID #55755067, Ali Safarov, www.123rf.com
p. 73, Image ID #18437995, alein, www.123rf.com
p. 74, Jean Philippe Laplagne, www.dodgerdesign.com
p. 75, Image ID #3432092, Cathy Yeulet, www.123rf.com
p. 76, Image ID #15286400, Paul Cowan, www.123rf.com
p. 77, Image ID #184626153, LauriPatterson, www.istockphoto.com
p. 78, Image ID #15152821, Svetlana Kolpakova, www.123rf.com
p. 79, Image ID #49523596, PaylessImages, www.123rf.com
p. 80, Image ID #28333622, Brent Hofacker, www.123rf.com
p. 81, Image ID #31075618, Sergii Koval, www.123rf.com
p. 82, Image ID #46223129, PaylessImages, www.123rf.com
p. 83, Jean Philippe Laplagne, www.dodgerdesign.com
p. 84, Image ID #48465757, Joshua Rainey, www.123rf.com
p. 85, Image ID #17088712, Krzysztof Slusarczyk, www.123rf.com
p. 86, Image ID #64507343, Brian Rogers, www.123rf.com
p. 87, Image ID #58716368, Stephanie Frey, www.123rf.com
p. 88, Image ID #60508776, Eva Ziat'ková, www.123rf.com
p. 89, Image ID #12417787, Inga Nielsen, www.123rf.com

Sinful Soups
p. 91-116, Art illustrations, Rae Crosson, www.greetingsfromcrazyville.com
p. 91-116, Art illustrations, Jean Philippe Laplagne, www.dodgerdesign.com
p. 91, Image ID #4191236, Talshiar, www.iStock.com
p. 92, Image ID #13283506, Svetlana Kolpakova, www.123rf.com
p. 93, Art illustration, Rae Crosson, www.greetingsfromcrazyville.com
p. 93, Image ID #19423046, Corinna Gissemann, www.123rf.com
p. 93, Image ID #22280031, Olga Miltsova, www.123rf.com
p. 93, Image ID #15285605, Svetlana Kolpakova, www.123rf.com
p. 94, Image ID #44573184, Kriengkrai Choochote, www.123rf.com
p. 95, Image ID #64612807, David Kadlec, www.123rf.com
p. 96, Image ID #19555237, markstout, www.123rf.com
p. 97, Image ID #12405766, Marn Wischnewski, www.123rf.com
p. 98, Image ID #37084489, Jaroslaw Pawlak, www.123rf.com
p. 99, Image ID #62215523, ziashusha, www.123rf.com
p. 100, Image ID #10574506, Marco Mayer, www.123rf.com
p. 101, Image ID #50676513, kabvisio, www.123rf.com
p. 102, Image ID #23670200, Brent Hofacker, www.123rf.com
p. 103, Image ID #19423046, Corinna Gissemann, www.123rf.com
p. 104, Image ID #24970561, margouillat, www.123rf.com
p. 105, Image ID #13283514, Svetlana Kolpakova, www.123rf.com
p. 106, Image ID #39844787, Svetlana Kolpakova, www.123rf.com
p. 107, Image ID #16114150, Maryna Riazanska, www.123rf.com
p. 108, Image ID #19943337, tashka2000, www.123rf.com
p. 109, Image ID #18968789, Eugene Bochkarev, www.123rf.com
p. 110, Image ID #25276926, Elena Shashkin, www.123rf.com

p. 111, Image ID #22280031, Olga Miltsova, www.123rf.com
p. 111, Image ID #15285605, Svetlana Kolpakova, www.123rf.com
p. 112, Image ID #15328055, Simone Voigt, www.123rf.com
p. 113, Image ID #44573184, Kriengkrai Choochote, www.123rf.com
p. 114, Image ID #33728272, Brent Hofacker, www.123rf.com
p. 115, Image ID #43625255, rafalstachura, www.123rf.com
p. 116, Image ID #36930999, Brent Hofacker, www.123rf.com

Superb Salads

p. 117-139, Art illustrations, Rae Crosson, www.greetingsfromcrazyville.com
p. 117-139, Art illustrations, Jean Philippe Laplagne, www.dodgerdesign.com
p. 117, Image ID # 10519065, Rosanna Cunico, www.123rf.com
p. 118, Image ID #57752348, Brent Hofacker, www.123rf.com
p. 119, Image ID #11464880, nitr, www.123rf.com
p. 119, Jean Philippe Laplagne, www.dodgerdesign.com
p. 119, Art illustration, Rae Crosson, www.greetingsfromcrazyville.com
p. 120, Image ID #39570124, Junghee Choi, www.123rf.com
p. 121, Jean Philippe Laplagne, www.dodgerdesign.com
p. 122, Image ID #36184899, Yulia Grogoryeva, www.123rf.com
p. 123, Jean Philippe Laplagne, www.dodgerdesign.com
p. 124, Image ID #12619416, Svetlana Kolpakova, www.123rf.com
p. 125, Image ID #63937707, Wong Yu Liang, www.123rf.com
p. 126, Jean Philippe Laplagne, www.dodgerdesign.com
p. 127, Image ID #57751886, Brent Hofacker, www.123rf.com
p. 128, Jean Philippe Laplagne, www.dodgerdesign.com
p. 129, Image ID #11464880, nitr, www.123rf.com
p. 130, Image ID #41091568, Olga Miltsova, www.123rf.com
p. 131, Image ID #32051071, mackoflower, www.123rf.com
p. 132, Jean Philippe Laplagne, www.dodgerdesign.com
p. 133, Jean Philippe Laplagne, www.dodgerdesign.com
p. 134, Image ID #21364620, vanillaechoes, www.123rf.com
p. 135, Jean Philippe Laplagne, www.dodgerdesign.com
p. 136, Image ID #39570124, Junghee Choi, www.123rf.com
p. 137, Jean Philippe Laplagne, www.dodgerdesign.com
p. 138, Image ID #18417975, vanillaechoes, www.123rf.com
p. 139, Jean Philippe Laplagne, www.dodgerdesign.com

Entertaining Entrées

p. 141-222, Art illustrations, Rae Crosson, www.greetingsfromcrazyville.com
p. 141-222, Art illustrations, Jean Philippe Laplagne, www.dodgerdesign.com
p. 142, Image ID #13195033, Eugene Bochkarev, www.123rf.com
p. 143, Image ID #52431170, Heinz Leitner, www.123rf.com
p. 143, Image ID #15982580, Tatuyoshi Toriu, www.123rf.com
p. 143, Art illustration, Rae Crosson, www.greetingsfromcrazyville.com

Poultry Dishes

p. 144, Image ID #21613561, nitr, www.123rf.com
p. 145, Image ID #14867897, Heinz Leitner, www.123rf.com
p. 146, Image ID #13220883, pitrs, www.123rf.com
p. 147, Image ID #32754422, Joshua Resnick, www.123rf.com
p. 148, Image ID #18935979, David Kadlec, www.123rf.com
p. 149, Image ID #18267584, Maksim Shebeko, www.123rf.com
p. 150, Image ID #30252716, Sergii Koval, www.123rf.com
p. 151, Image ID #48299885, Tatiana Vorona, www.123rf.com
p. 152, Image ID #63569092, Elena Shashkina, www.123rf.com
p. 153, Image ID #21613561, nitr, www.123rf.com
p. 154, Image ID #22577776, Teresa Kasprzycka, www.123rf.com
p. 155, Image ID #11798482, Heinz Leitner, www.123rf.com
p. 156, Image ID #17176806, Elena Shashkina, www.123rf.com
p. 157, Image ID #40233795, vaivirga, www.123rf.com
p. 158, Image ID #58117109, lsvslv, www.123rf.com
p. 159, Image ID #66682267, Zoia Lukianova, www.123rf.com
p. 160, Image ID #62706601, Sergii Koval, www.123rf.com
p. 161, Image ID #45166537, Georgii Dolgykh, www.123rf.com

p. 162, Image ID #34589809, markstout, www.123rf.com
p. 163, Image ID #65575647, Oksana Zhupanova, www.123rf.com
p. 164, Image ID #26673915, Boris Ryzhkov, www.123rf.com
p. 165, Image ID #28248417, Maitree Laipitaksin, www.123rf.com
p. 166, Image ID #36290325, Brent Hofacker, www.123rf.com
p. 167, Image ID #10280588, Rod Wonglikitpanya, www.123rf.com

Fish and Seafood Dishes

p. 168, Image ID #43825576, Heinz Leitner, www.123rf.com
p. 169, Image ID #27864469, Daniel Vincek, www.123rf.com
p. 170, Image ID #34215784, clickandphoto, www.123rf.com
p. 171, Image ID #36222564, Ingrid Balabanova, www.123rf.com
p. 172, Image ID #14609471, laperlafoto, www.123rf.com
p. 173, Image ID #36501970 Sergii Koval, www.123rf.com
p. 174, Image ID #38846095, Fabio Balbi, www.123rf.com
p. 175, Image ID #43825576, Heinz Leitner, www.123rf.com
p. 177, Jean Philippe Laplagne, www.dodgerdesign.com
p. 178, Image ID #14461331, wiktory, www.123rf.com
p. 179, Image ID #21720038, Svetlana Foote, www.123rf.com
p. 180, Image ID #19625130, Jane Rix, www.123rf.com
p. 181, Image ID #54713326, foodandmore, www.123rf.com

Meat Dishes

p. 182, Image ID # 31660515, Joshua Resnick, www.123rf.com
p. 183, Image ID #53876988, Brent Hofacker, www.123rf.com
p. 184, Image ID #24927672, Brent Hofacker, www.123rf.com
p. 185, Image ID #27442986, iodrakon, www.123rf.com
p. 186, Jean Philippe Laplagne, www.dodgerdesign.com
p. 187, Image ID #21909170, foodandmore, www.123rf.com
p. 188, Image ID #24513357, Brent Hofacker, www.123rf.com
p. 189, Image ID #15490647, Ron Sumners, www.123rf.com
p. 190, Image ID #53746996, Tatatiana Bralnina, www.123rf.com
p. 191, Image ID #56677148, Jaroslaw Pawlak, www.123rf.com
p. 192, Image ID #10300923, Raul Taborda, www.123rf.com
p. 193, Image ID #39266582, Lilyana Vynogradova, www.123rf.com
p. 194, Image ID #10856981, Maksim Toome, www.123rf.com
p. 195, Image ID #17634297, Boris Ryzhkov, www.123rf.com
p. 196, Image ID #40697860, Scott Mangham, www.123rf.com
p. 197, Image ID #37708218, zoeytoja, www.123rf.com
p. 198, Image ID #36049206, Joshua Resnick, www.123rf.com
p. 199, Image ID #13603642, markstout, www.123rf.com
p. 200, Image ID #23977995, markstout, www.123rf.com
p. 201, Image ID # 31660515, Joshua Resnick, www.123rf.com
p. 202, Image ID #52431170, Heinz Leitner, www.123rf.com
p. 203, Image ID #20859221, Paul Cowan, www.123rf.com

Pasta Dishes

p. 204, Image ID #7252729, teamcrucillo, www.123rf.com
p. 205, Image ID #13195033, Eugene Bochkarev, www.123rf.com
p. 206, Image ID #30406758, Olga Miltsova, www.123rf.com
p. 207, Image ID #21736877, Nemanja Tomic, www.123rf.com
p. 208, Image ID #57667021, Ivan Mateev, www.123rf.com
p. 209, Image ID # 22963454, Ramon Grosso Dolarea, www.123rf.com
p. 210, Image ID #68106281, Terry Davis, www.123rf.com
p. 211, Image ID #69399675, foodandmore, www.123rf.com
p. 212, Image ID #15982580, Tatuyoshi Toriu, www.123rf.com
p. 213, Image ID #7252729, teamcrucillo, www.123rf.com

Pizza Dishes

p. 214, Image ID #17341217, bombaert, www.123rf.com
p. 215, Image ID #15145653, foodandmore, www.123rf.com
p. 216, Jean Philippe Laplagne, www.dodgerdesign.com
p. 217, Jean Philippe Laplagne, www.dodgerdesign.com
p. 218, Image ID # 71490187, dashu83, www.123rf.com

p. 219, Image ID #13179611, Bogdan Bratu, www.123rf.com
p. 220, Jean Philippe Laplagne, www.dodgerdesign.com
p. 221, Image ID #17341217, bombaert, www.123rf.com
p. 222, Image ID #17474635, Jakub Gojda, www.123rf.com

Sensational Sides

p. 223-247, Art illustrations, Rae Crosson, www.greetingsfromcrazyville.com
p. 223-247, Art illustrations, Jean Philippe Laplagne, www.dodgerdesign.com
p. 223, Image ID #20433857, bluebearry, www.istockphoto.com
p. 224, Image ID #36191616, Ivan Mateev, www.123rf.com
p. 225, Image ID #21997528, Elena Shashkina, www.123rf.com
p. 225, Jean Philippe Laplagne, www.dodgerdesign.com
p. 225, Art illustration, Rae Crosson, www.greetingsfromcrazyville.com
p. 226, Image ID #12072412, kabvisio, www.123rf.com
p. 227, Image ID #35621582, Brent Hofacker, www.123rf.com
p. 228, Image ID #43949035, Rosemary Buffoni, www.123rf.com
p. 229, Image ID #30681295, Nataliia Peredniankina, www.123rf.com
p. 230, Image ID #11926945, Stephanie Frey, www.123rf.com
p. 231, Image ID #39559035, David Kadlec, www.123rf.com
p. 232, Image ID #21997528, Elena Shashkina, www.123rf.com
p. 233, Jean Philippe Laplagne, www.dodgerdesign.com
p. 234, Image ID #37287546, margouillat, www.123rf.com
p. 235, Image ID #12072412, kabvisio, www.123rf.com
p. 236, Image ID #36463457, nitr, www.123rf.com
p. 237, Image ID #41013421, Brent Hofacker, www.123rf.com
p. 238, Jean Philippe Laplagne, www.dodgerdesign.com
p. 239, Image ID #13278176, Desislava Vasileva, www.123rf.com
p. 240, Jean Philippe Laplagne, www.dodgerdesign.com
p. 241, Image ID #12923985, Brian Rogers, www.123rf.com
p. 242, Image ID #13040406, Joshua Resnick, www.123rf.com
p. 243, Image ID # 39766878, arinahabich, www.123rf.com
p. 244, Jean Philippe Laplagne, www.dodgerdesign.com
p. 245, Image ID #20620126, szefei, www.123rf.com
p. 246, Image ID #21977143, Elena Shashkina, www.123rf.com
p. 247, Image ID #36155188, Ivan Mateev, www.123rf.com

Decadent Desserts

p. 249-296, Art illustration, Rae Crosson, www.greetingsfromcrazyville.com
p. 249-296, Art illustrations, Jean Philippe Laplagne, www.dodgerdesign.com
p. 250, Image ID #66970301, Hanna Shapulava, www.123rf.com
p. 251, Art illustrations, Rae Crosson, www.greetingsfromcrazyville.com
p. 251, Image ID #13040388, Joshua Resnick, www.123rf.com
p. 251, Image ID #498462466, alphotographie123, www.istockphoto.com

Cakes

p. 252, Image ID #41730024, Sergejs Rahunoks, www.123rf.com
p. 253, Jean Philippe Laplagne, www.dodgerdesign.com
p. 254, Image ID #10893265, Boris Ryzhkov, www.123rf.com
p. 255, Image ID #66970301, Hanna Shapulava, www.123rf.com
p. 256, Randall R. Reade, www.dodgerdesign.com
p. 257, Image ID #12350204, Ruth Black, www.123rf.com
p. 258, Image ID #498462466, alphotographie123, www.iStock.com
p. 259, Image ID #50034036, milla74, www.123rf.com
p. 260, Image ID #39391399, Elena Schweitzer, www.123rf.com
p. 261, Jean Philippe Laplagne, www.dodgerdesign.com
p. 262, Image ID #41730024, Sergejs Rahunoks, www.123rf.com
p. 263, Image ID #5691658, Ruth Black, www.123rf.com
p. 264, Image ID #50875835, littleny, www.123rf.com

Chocolate Desserts

p. 265, Image ID #13991429, V. J. Matthew, www.123rf.com
p. 266, Jean Philippe Laplagne, www.dodgerdesign.com
p. 267, Image ID #13991429, V. J. Matthew, www.123rf.com

Cookies

p. 268, Image ID #48702720, Steven Cukrov, www.123rf.com
p. 269, Jean Philippe Laplagne, www.dodgerdesign.com
p. 270, Image ID #129591370, arkstout, www.123rf.com
p. 271, Jean Philippe Laplagne, www.dodgerdesign.com
p. 272, Image ID #23875933, Natalia Zakharova, www.123rf.com
p. 273, Image ID #52903735, shopartgallerycom, www.123rf.com
p. 274, Image ID #48702720, Steven Cukrov, www.123rf.com

Fruit Desserts

p. 275, Image ID #42309235, Dusan Zidar, www.123rf.com
p. 276, Image ID #37627452, Elena Shashkina, www.123rf.com
p. 277, Image ID #66145994, Robert Latawiec, www.123rf.com
p. 278, Image ID #1491049, David Smith, www.123rf.com
p. 279, Image ID #36908409, larryhw, www.123rf.com
p. 280, Image ID #42309235, Dusan Zidar, www.123rf.com
p. 281, Image ID #13509241, Svetlana Kolpakova, www.123rf.com
p. 282, Jean Philippe Laplagne, www.dodgerdesign.com

Custard, Gelatins, and Mousses

p. 283, Image ID #34675225, Brent Hofacker, www.123rf.com
p. 284, Image ID #44083341, Oksana Bratanova, www.123rf.com
p. 285, Jean Philippe Laplagne, www.dodgerdesign.com
p. 286, Image ID #34675225, Brent Hofacker, www.123rf.com
p. 287, Jean Philippe Laplagne, www.dodgerdesign.com
p. 288, Image ID #10103380, regenbogen, www.123rf.com
p. 289, Image ID #17956313, Svetlana Kolpakova, www.123rf.com

Pies

p. 290, Image ID #13040388, Joshua Resnick, www.123rf.com
p. 291, Image ID #17700875, Laura Ballard, www.123rf.com
p. 292, Jean Philippe Laplagne, www.dodgerdesign.com
p. 293, Image ID #13040388, Joshua Resnick, www.123rf.com
p. 294, Image ID #22801938, markstout, www.123rf.com
p. 295, Image ID #57170203, Julianna Funk, www.123rf.com
p. 296, Image ID #25369459, Olga Vasileva, www.123rf.com

Bodaciously Bountiful Brunches

p. 297-325, Art illustrations, Rae Crosson, www.greetingsfromcrazyville.com
p. 297-325, Art illustrations, Jean Philippe Laplagne, www.dodgerdesign.com
p. 298, Image ID #25522726, Brent Hofacker, www.123rf.com
p. 299, Image ID #53864948, Brent Hofacker, www.www.123rf.com
p. 299, Image ID #38357667, Boris Ryzhkov, www.123rf.com chicken crepes
p. 299, Image ID #43455597, Elena Shashkina, www.123rf.com

Egg Dishes

p. 300, Jean Philippe Laplagne, www.dodgerdesign.com
p. 301, Image ID #467739089, bhofack2, www.gettyimages.com
p. 302, Image ID #25714351, Kamil Macniak, www.123rf.com
p. 303, Image ID #35434593, Brent Hofacker, www.123rf.com
p. 304, Image ID #23668934, markstout, www.123rf.com
p. 305, Image ID #27658776, tashka2000, www.123rf.com
p. 306, Image ID # 43139884, Georgii Dolgykh, www.123rf.com
p. 307, Jean Philippe Laplagne, www.dodgerdesign.com
p. 308, Image ID #8204578, Steve Woods, www.123rf.com

Main Courses and Essentials

p. 309, Image ID #43567109, peteers, www.123rf.com
p. 310, Image ID #19048662, Corinna Gissemann, www.123rf.com
p. 311, Image ID #29391313, Andreas Berheide, www.123rf.com
p. 312, Image ID #25522726, Brent Hofacker, www.123rf.com Crab cakes
p. 313, Image ID #43567109, peteers, www.123rf.com
p. 314, Image ID #38357667, Boris Ryzhkov, www.123rf.com

Potatoes

p. 315, Image ID #52935776, magone, www.123rf.com

p. 316, Image ID # 27911603, Steven Cukrov, www.123rf.com

p. 317, Image ID #52935776, magone, www.123rf.com

Sweet Breads

p. 318, Image ID #2735839, Rosemary Buffoni, www.123rf.com

p. 319, Jean Philippe Laplagne, www.dodgerdesign.com

p. 320, Image ID #13230513, James Clarke, www.123rf.com

p. 321, Image ID #2735839, Rosemary Buffoni, www.123rf.com

p. 322, Image ID #43455597, Elena Shashkina, www.123rf.com

p. 323, Image ID #28075291, Robert Hainer, www.123rf.com

p. 324, Image ID #13703219, Monika Adamczyk, www.123rf.com

p. 325, Image ID #22711131, Brent Hofacker, www.123rf.com

All About the Girl

p. 326-331, Art illustrations, Rae Crosson, www.greetingsfromcrazyville.com

p. 326-331, Art illustrations, Jean Philippe Laplagne, www.dodgerdesign.com

That's a Wrap!

p. 333, Art illustration, Rae Crosson, www.greetingsfromcrazyville.com

p. 333, Art illustrations, Jean Philippe Laplagne, www.dodgerdesign.com

The End

p. 334, Art illustration, Rae Crosson, www.greetingsfromcrazyville.com

p. 334, Image ID #15820575, pixxart, www.123rf.com

p. 334, Art illustration, Jean Philippe Laplagne, www.dodgerdesign.com

Index

CPSIA information can be obtained
at www.ICGtesting.com
Printed in the USA
BVHW02s2203120818
524318BV00011B/54/P

9 781532 046353